LEADERSHIP IN ADMINISTRATION OF VOCATIONAL AND TECHNICAL EDUCATION

RALPH C. WENRICH
Professor, The University of Michigan

J. WILLIAM WENRICH
Vice President for Administrative Affairs,
Ferris State College

CHARLES E. MERRILL PUBLISHING COMPANY
A Bell & Howell Company
Columbus, Ohio

THE MERRILL SERIES
IN CAREER PROGRAMS

The authors and publisher gratefully acknowledge the following for permission to reprint:

Teachers College Press for an adaptation from Danial E. Griffiths, "Administrative Theory and Change in Organization," in Matthew B. Miles, editor, *Innovation in Education* (New York: Teachers College Press, copyright 1964 by Teachers College, Columbia University), p. 430.

The University of Chicago Press for figure #429 from J. W. Getzels and E. G. Guba, "Social Behavior and the Administrative Process," *School Review,* © 1957 by the University of Chicago Press.

John Wiley & Sons, Inc. for material from Daniel Katz and Robert L. Kahn, *The Social Psychology of Organizations* (New York: Wiley, 1966). Copyright © 1966 by John Wiley & Sons, Inc.

Published by
Charles E. Merrill Publishing Co.
A Bell & Howell Company
Columbus, Ohio 43216

International Standard Book Number: 0-675-08878-X

Library of Congress Catalog Card Number: 73-86161

2 3 4 5 6—78 77 76 75

Printed in the United States of America

THE
MERRILL SERIES
IN CAREER
PROGRAMS

In recent years our nation has literally rediscovered education. Concurrently, many nations are considering educational programs in revolutionary terms. They now realize that education is the responsible link between social needs and social improvement. While traditionally Americans have been committed to the ideal of the optimal development of each individual, there is increased public appreciation and support of the values and benefits of education in general, and vocational and technical education in particular. With occupational education's demonstrated capacity to contribute to economic growth and national well being, it is only natural that it has been given increased prominence and importance in this educational climate.

With the increased recognition that the true resources of a nation are its human resources, occupational education programs are considered a form of investment in human capital—an investment which provides comparatively high returns to both the individual and society.

The Merrill Series in Career Programs is designed to provide a broad range of educational materials to assist members of the profession in providing effective and efficient programs of occupational education which contribute to an individual's becoming both a contributing economic producer and a responsible member of society.

The series and its sub-series do not have a singular position or philosophy concerning the problems and alternatives in providing the broad range of offerings needed to prepare the nation's work force. Rather, authors are encouraged to develop and support independent positions and alternative strategies. A wide range of educational and occupational experiences and perspectives have been brought to bear through the Merrill Series in Career Programs National Editorial Board. These experiences, coupled with those of the authors, assure useful publications. I believe that this title, along with others in the series, will provide major assistance in further developing and extending viable educational programs to assist youth and adults in preparing for and furthering their careers.

Robert E. Taylor
Editorial Director
Series in Career Programs

PREFACE

Increasing numbers of students in our high schools and community colleges are interested in preparing for careers through vocational and technical education programs. Parents and taxpayers in general are urging boards of education to shift the emphasis from preparation for college and the professions to preparation for employment in skilled and technical occupations which require no more than a high school or community college education. This change in attitude is placing pressure on school administrators to plan occupational programs in which youth are interested and for which there are available employment opportunities.

Related to renewed public interest in vocational education are significant conceptual and procedural changes which have been stimulated and supported by the Federal Vocational Education Act of 1963 and the Amendments of 1968. Educators in general, and administrators in particular, recognize that both the public's attitude toward vocational education and vocational education itself have changed. The specific nature of these changes and the implications for educational planners and managers are not as obvious. This book attempts to analyze and interpret these changes and to suggest ways in which the administrator might use this information in planning and operating programs designed (1) to prepare youth and adults for employment and (2) to help them maintain their employability.

Also, during the past decade the behavioral scientists have been engaged in significant research efforts in the areas of organizational effectiveness and leadership in organizations. We have drawn heavily on concepts and research findings from other disciplines as they apply to the administration of vocational and technical education on the secondary and community college levels.

Educational managers are bombarded with the idea that education must be made more accountable; this has encouraged the use of all kinds of management techniques from program planning and budgeting systems (PPBS) to management by objectives (MBO). We have attempted to incorporate some of the concepts and techniques borrowed from business and industry in our suggestions for designing, operating, and evaluating vocational and technical education programs.

Part I deals with the problems of terminology and definitions, providing a brief historical perspective as well as the philosophic rationale for support of vocational and technical programs in the public education sphere. Particular emphasis is given to the classic relationship issues regarding general education and specialized education, liberal arts and vocational education, practical arts and occupational preparation. The analysis illustrates how these conceptual issues are integrated in the emerging career education model which culminates in vocational education. The concluding chapter in Part I discusses the policy-making process which initiates the implementation of vocational education.

Part II provides an overview of administrative theory, with particular emphasis on recent contributions by behavioral scientists. It deals with the key subjects of organization, leadership, and decision-making, especially as they relate to institutions whose primary role is to provide specialized occupational education.

Part III assesses administrative structures for delivery of vocational education and key aspects of the major functions which any educational administrator must perform. The intent of this section is to examine structure and functions from the point of view of specific problems the vocational education administrator is likely to encounter. Wherever possible, we have attempted to illustrate major points with concrete examples relative to occupational programs.

In Part IV we attempt to outline some of the critical issues in the administration of vocational and technical education which remain to be resolved. Our responses to these questions must necessarily be regarded as speculative. We hope they will stimulate the reader to reflect on his preferences for their resolution.

While the reader may use chapters in Part III as references for ideas about specific functions, we feel the content follows a logical sequence and urge the reader to read each section in sequence.

Many people contributed to the development of the manuscript. We are indebted to several colleagues who gave us valuable reviews and critiques of our ideas: George A. Hartford, Jr., John Johnson, Donald Priebe, Curtis Van Voorhees, Robert Smith, Garry Walz, Daniel Vogler, Chester Rzonca, Jay Fennell, Jean Harvey, and Edward Griffin. Barbara Hall, Linda Kresnye, and Marlene Durst patiently typed and retyped our many drafts. Our wives, Helen and Martha, made fruitful suggestions, but more importantly gave us unfailing moral support. We alone, of course, are responsible for any errors in fact or analysis.

RCW
JWW

CONTENTS

Part I   FOUNDATIONS OF VOCATIONAL AND TECHNICAL EDUCATION

Chapter 1   WHAT IS VOCATIONAL AND TECHNICAL EDUCATION?

Vocational and technical education is for people—youth and adults interested in preparing for and progressing in a career in some type of satisfying and productive work. School administrators and program planners on the secondary and post-secondary levels must be concerned about vocational and technical education, because more people are becoming aware of the value of occupationally oriented programs. This chapter covers the scope and function of vocational education and its place in public education. The purposes of this chapter are to help the reader:

1. to appreciate the wide range of occupations included in vocational-technical education;
2. to understand why vocational and technical education is provided in different kinds of institutions and at several different levels of education;
3. to explain the difference between vocational education and the practical arts and the need for both;
4. to explain the relationship between specialized vocational education and a comprehensive occupational education program;
5. to understand the relationship of vocational education and career education.

3

Vocational and Technical Education and the People It Serves

Yes, vocational education is for people interested in preparing for and/or progressing in a career. The kinds of people and programs involved in vocational education are diverse.

Beginning his senior year in an academic high school, Jim was a better than average student whose attitude and scholarship were highly regarded by his teachers. Recognizing his own particular interests, Jim decided to enroll in a commercial printing course at a newly developed area vocational center. While he progressed well in copy preparation, stripping, plate making, offset press operation, and binding operation, Jim found camera and dark room operations particularly to his liking. On graduating from the program, Jim was immediately employed by his local newspaper to do photography work. Eighteen months later, he decided to continue his education in this occupational area and enrolled in a graphic reproduction program at a state technical college. The newspaper would like him to return when he finishes, but Jim has not decided where he will go since he has found job opportunities abound for graduates of his program.

Jane came from a large Mexican-American family which lacked the financial resources to provide her all the opportunities her peers had. While she had average ability, her achievement in a general high school program was below average due to poor attendance and little participation in school activities. Jane was encouraged to enroll in an area vocational center program, Introduction to Health Occupations. Exposure to the various health fields and the opportunity to practice some bedside skills such as taking temperatures, blood pressures, and pulses awakened her interest. But, it was her cooperative education assignment in a dentist's office that really generated her enthusiasm. Her experience there was so successful, that the dentist offered her full-time employment when she graduated. After 15 months, her employer encouraged her to enter a dental laboratory technician program at a nearby community college, with his guarantee of continued employment and promotion when she finishes.

Ed was 42 years old and an eighteen-year veteran of the fire department, where he had advanced in rank to assistant chief. As he watched new firefighters coming to his department with advanced training, Ed realized that to keep himself abreast and to be competitive for further advancement, he needed to upgrade his knowledge about fire science. He enrolled in an evening course in the fire science program at the local community college. Initially, he had no intention of pursuing a degree, but as he became involved in additional courses on firefighting, basics of management, public relations, and other related subjects, he realized he should obtain an associate degree. Two years after completing his Associate in Applied Science degree, Ed was promoted to chief when his former boss retired. Even so, he plans to continue his part-time studies, working toward a Bachelor's degree in public safety at a four-year technical college.

Margie was 24 years old, black, beautiful, personable, and serving a one-to-three-year prison term for theft. Her husband was serving a similar term in a male prison, while her mother cared for her two small children. When the prison undertook an experimental vocational program in the office skills area with the local community college, Margie was one of fifteen inmates selected to participate. She attended school all day, five days a week, and learned typing, shorthand, bookkeeping, operation of various office machines including keypunch, and other related secretarial skills. By the time she was paroled, she was typing 75 words per minute with a high degree of accuracy and she had mastered shorthand so that she could take dictation at 100 words per minute. Shortly after her release, Margie obtained a job as executive secretary to the managing editor of a well-known publishing firm. Two years later she is still employed in the same job—a happy and successful woman.

Although somewhat shy and introverted, Mary had excellent academic ability. Her early achievements made it clear by her junior year that she would be class valedictorian. At that point her comprehensive high school offered a new vocational program which interested her: distributive education. Mary decided to enroll, against the recommendation of her counselors who urged her to follow a college preparatory track. She was enthusiastic about the new subjects exposed to her: techniques of selling, sales demonstrations, cash register operation, inventory systems, merchandising, and advertising theory and practice. In her senior year she was placed in a cooperative education assignment in an elite clothing store. After graduating she accepted a full-time position with the same employer as a commission saleswoman and is still doing an outstanding job.

Darlene was a member of the second class of a private beauty school which contracted with a vocational education program in which five area high schools agreed to collaborate. In this program, the board of education of Darlene's high school granted her three credits toward high school graduation and paid for all school supplies and the first 600 hours of the 1200 hours required to become a licensed cosmetologist. After a few months of employment at a small beauty shop, Darlene landed a job with the major salon. Because of her outstanding ability and performance there she was selected to attend advanced classes in Chicago with all costs paid by her employer. At present, she is continuing her education in specialized beauty salons in New York City, still under the financial auspices of her employer.

Tom at age 28 was general foreman of a small wood products plant whose owners decided to relocate from the Midwest to the South. Although given the opportunity to move, Tom decided to stay where he was and to seek new occupational opportunities. Following some vocational interest tests and counseling, Tom decided that he really wanted to become a dental hygienist. He enrolled at a nearby technical college as the only male in an entering dental hygiene class. Because he had some previous college work, he did not have to repeat some related courses and was able to explore new areas. As he now completes his vocational program, his current plans are to work as a dental hygienist for awhile and then go back for a degree in education so that he can ultimately become an allied health teacher.

Joe retired from the Navy after 20 years of active service and began to prepare for a second career. Avocationally, Joe had always enjoyed being an amateur chef, so he decided to enroll in a two-year food service program in a community college in the area where he and his family wanted to locate. In addition to nutrition and dietetics, food preparation and display, budgeting and sanitation, Joe was particularly interested in wholesale food purchasing. After graduation, Joe accepted a job with a large university in the area. Because of his ability, maturity, and training, he was rapidly promoted from a food service unit manager to assistant director of the entire food service operation, where he has primary responsibility for purchasing food for some 6000 students who are fed through the university system.

Each of these illustrations describes a person who prepared for meaningful employment through public education programs. The administration of these programs is what this book is all about.

After reading the illustrations of how vocational and technical education helped people prepare for and remain viable in the world of work, we can now make some generalizations.

SPECIALIZED EDUCATION

Vocational education is specialized because courses or programs are elected only by those individuals who have a special interest in preparing for a particular occupation or family of occupations. It is that part of the total process of education aimed at developing the competencies needed to function effectively in an occupation or group of occupations. It may be differentiated from general education or "common learnings."

AS BROAD AS THE WORLD OF WORK

Vocational education includes preparation for employment in any occupation for which specialized education is required, for which there is a societal need, and which can be most appropriately done in schools. (Some special training can be provided more effectively and more efficiently on-the-job, but in this book we will deal only with the public school's responsibility for vocational education.) Vocational education is concerned with the whole hierarchy of occupations from those requiring relatively short periods of specialized preparation, such as clerk-typist, to occupations requiring two or more years of specialized education, such as inhalation therapist; it includes the whole spectrum of the labor force from semi-skilled workers to technicians and paraprofessionals.

OFFERED ON THE SECONDARY AND POST-SECONDARY SCHOOL LEVELS

Because the early federal vocational acts, beginning with the Smith-Hughes Act of 1917, placed the emphasis on vocational education in high schools, the notion still exists in the minds of some educators that occupational preparation done in community colleges and technical institutes is not vocational. The term "technical education" is preferred by some to distinguish post-secondary vocational education from secondary level vocational education. In this book the term "vocational education" is used to include specialized "technical" education regardless of the level on which it is found. In fact, since a vocation is a "calling," the term vocational education is broad enough to include preparation for the professions. It has been pointed out that a large university with its many professional schools —medicine, dentistry, law, engineering, social work, public health, and education—could appropriately be called a vocational school. We have, then, a series of terms used to denote specialized education aimed at preparation for employment—vocational education, technical education, and professional education.

This book does not deal with the problems of administration of professional schools. We are concerned primarily with specialized occupational education which is provided on the secondary level and in two-year post-secondary institutions—community (junior) colleges and technical institutes. We will use the term vocational education to mean any specialized preparation for employment on the high school, or community college and technical institute level.

VOCATIONAL EDUCATION INCLUDES MORE THAN MANIPULATIVE SKILLS

A common misconception is that vocational education is concerned only with manual skills; it includes both the mental and the manual and, in addition, it is concerned with values and attitudes. Vocational education includes the cognitive, the psychomotor, and the affective elements of behavior required of the competent worker. Thinking, acting, and feeling are involved in most occupations, in different proportions.

EFFECTIVENESS

Although the objectives of vocational education go beyond job training, the effectiveness of vocational education programs is determined by the extent to which such programs result in employment which is satisfying to the employee and adequate to the employer.

ONLY PART OF THE TOTAL PROCESS

The process of preparing people for careers starts in the elementary grades and continues throughout the entire school system. On the elementary level children are made aware of the world of work and are helped to understand the meaning and value of work to the individual and to society. On the junior high school level they are given opportunities to explore the world of work and to get a variety of experiences in work-related activities. Later in the secondary school they may participate in specialized vocational education programs through hands-on experiences in a family or cluster of occupations or in a specific occupation. Actual work experience in the community, on a part-time basis, may be a part of either the pre-vocational or the vocational education programs. On the post-secondary level basic specialized vocational education is provided for the beginning student in a particular field and more advanced training for those who started their specialized vocational programs in high school.

The term "career education" is used to refer to the total process of helping children, youth, and adults discover and develop their potential for work. Career education is a broad term which includes virtually everything the schools do, from kindergarten through adult education, to help people understand, prepare for, and succeed in the world of work. This total process can be divided into two phases—career development and career preparation (vocational education). Career development includes awareness of the world of work and the meaning and value of work, exploration of the world of work and the making of tentative choices of fields of work. Career development also includes exploratory experiences which may be provided through the practical arts, discussed later in this chapter. Career preparation is that phase of the process which prepares the learner to function in a specific occupation or family of occupations.

Vocational Education and the Practical Arts

Vocational education and the practical arts are often confused even though they are quite different in purpose; the former is "specialized" education and the latter is "general" education. Both general and specialized education are essential ingredients of education for work. While it is imperative that we avoid a dichotomy between the two, it is equally important that we understand the distinctive purpose of each and the relationship of both to occupational education.

GENERAL AND SPECIALIZED EDUCATION

General and specialized education are two interrelated aspects of education which must be considered if the optimal development of all students is to be taken seriously. First, there are those values, attitudes, understandings, and skills that each citizen should possess if he is to plan, work, and act in concert with others; and second, there are those specific talents, interests, and needs which are unique, or shared only by groups. From the standpoint of the organization of education, it is desirable and necessary to distinguish between these two aspects of development because content and method differ significantly. The terms "general education" and "specialized education" are used to designate these two aspects of education. When specialized education is directed primarily toward developing competence in preparation for employment in a particular occupation it is vocational education.

General education is defined as education growing out of the students' common needs. It is general because it is for everyone and is concerned with the total personality. It seeks to meet the *common* needs of youth for competence as a person and as a citizen.

Specialized education is defined as those educational experiences designed for individuals who have a particular interest in any specific field and wish to pursue study in that field beyond the level of general education. Specialized education grows out of the individual's need to investigate further his cultural or intellectual, his avocational, and his vocational interests.

In practice general education is frequently contrasted with vocational education in that all activities of the school which are not planned specifically to develop vocational competence are regarded as general education. This position overlooks the fact that the high school provides many specialized experiences which make no direct contribution to vocational competence.

The Association for Supervision and Curriculum Development of the NEA (*3*, p. 9), in its report *The High School We Need*, takes the position that:

> The program for each individual must contain general education and specialized education. General education is essential to equip our youth for the common responsibilities of free citizenship. Specialized education is equally essential to promote the development of individual abilities and sensibilities. One distinction between general and specialized education lies in the degree of choice given the student. Content and experience required of all students as basic citizenship preparation should be considered general education. Any courses or experiences that the student elects in terms of his unique purposes or interests should be considered specialized education. All vocational courses fall in the special education category, and all college preparatory courses not needed for all citizens are also specialized and elective.

French, Hull, and Dodds bring the matter into focus and make the point that there are some unique problems associated with the organization and administration of vocational programs.

> The specialized offerings in the secondary schools are roughly of two types: Courses organized into a definite sequence of work in preparation for a vocational field or for entrance into an institution for further study, and more flexible courses that satisfy avocational or personal interests. The college preparatory and the various vocational programs are examples of the former; the elective courses in the fine and practical arts, as well as the free electives in most of the academic fields and most phases of the work in physical education, are typical of the latter. The organization of the curriculum in vocational education is unusual enough to call for a special consideration of its problems. (*4*, pp. 215–16)

Those responsible for planning and operating education programs should keep in mind the basic distinctions between general and specialized education. Failure to do this has often resulted in confusion and misunderstanding. Different methods of organization, different teaching materials and sometimes different standards are applicable to the two areas.

The real difference between general and specialized education is not in the subject matter itself, but rather in what use is made of subject matter. The same subject can be taught and learned *either* as general education *or* as specialized education. For example, science can be taught as a common learning to help children and youth understand and use scientific principles in their daily lives (general education). Science can also be taught as it relates to a particular trade or technical occupation (specialized vocational education). There are no *general* subjects as such, and there are no *voca-*

tional subjects. Educational planners can (and do) design differentiated courses for either of the two purposes—general education or specialized vocational education. The purposes of the teacher and the intent of the learner determine the nature of any particular course offering. A particular course may serve both general and specialized goals, but this should occur by design and not by default.

The discussion of the relationship of general and specialized education is not particularly important in the organization and administration of elementary schools since nearly all experiences planned for children on this level are general education or common learnings. But on the secondary and post-secondary levels the relationship is fundamental. The proportion of time devoted to specialized education varies greatly among individuals but generally increases as a student moves through the educational system. This shift in emphasis from general to specialized education is shown in figure 1–1.

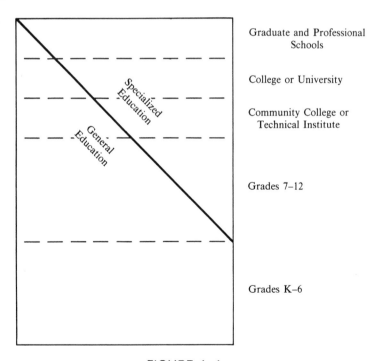

Graduate and Professional Schools

College or University

Community College or Technical Institute

Grades 7–12

Grades K–6

FIGURE 1–1

RATIO OF TIME DEVOTED TO GENERAL AND SPECIALIZED EDUCATION

Figure 1–2 illustrates the kinds of programs and course titles sometimes used to label general and specialized offerings on the high school level.

Most books on secondary school administration deal with the definitions and relationships of general and specialized education on that level. Simi-

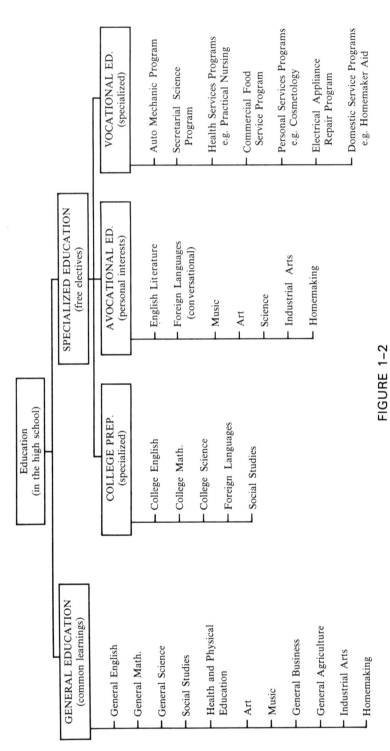

FIGURE 1-2

RELATIONSHIP OF GENERAL EDUCATION AND SPECIALIZED EDUCATION
(WITH EXAMPLES OF PROGRAMS AND COURSES FOUND IN THE HIGH SCHOOL)

12

larly, community college textbooks consider these two aspects of education in such institutions. References at the end of this chapter should be consulted for further information.

The Practical Arts.   We define the practical arts as those phases of general education dealing with the organization, tools, materials, processes, and products of agriculture, business, industry, and the home and with the contributions of workers engaged in these fields. It is a type of functional education with a heavy emphasis on activities and is taught on a nonvocational basis.

Because instruction in the practical arts is in many respects similar to that provided in vocational education, the two are often confused. The practical arts and vocational education both draw their subject matter from the world of work—the practical activities of everyday living. Because the source of content is the same, the subject matter areas are parallel. For example, agriculture can be taught as practical arts or as vocational education; industry can be taught as industrial arts or as vocational industrial education; and business can be taught as general business or as vocational business education. But since the purpose of the practical arts is general education, the content drawn from these areas of life-activity, the organization of this content, and the methods used to present it are geared to the achievement of this purpose.

The practical arts areas most commonly found in the public schools are industrial arts, general agriculture, general business, and general homemaking. The practical arts meet all of the criteria of general education: (1) they are intended for everyone—those planning on going to college as well as those who are not; (2) they are concerned with the total personality—physical and intellectual development, mental and emotional stability, habits and attitudes toward work and workers, as well as skill in the use of tools and materials of our culture and the technical understanding necessary to use our resources most effectively; and (3) they are concerned with the individual's nonspecialized activities—preparation for effective and efficient living no matter what one's vocation.

Industrial arts, the most common practical art, is the study of industrial tools, materials, processes, products, and occupations for general education purposes; the learning activities are usually carried out in shops and laboratories. In industrial arts students receive orientation in production and consumption, through actual experiences in planning, producing, testing, servicing, and evaluating types of consumer and industrial goods. Through these experiences children on the elementary and secondary levels learn how industrial products are made, and how to use and maintain these products intelligently. They develop general skill and resourcefulness in working with technical and mechanical things. They learn about woods, metals, plastics, ceramics, textiles, paper, and other industrial materials. They learn about electricity, motors, engines, structures, and other items of concern to people at home, on the farm, in industry, and in recreation. Above all, they experience critical thinking in solving technical problems, thereby developing an understanding and appreciation of the complex integration of industry into our modern technological society.

The goals of industrial arts are to

1. develop an insight and understanding of industry and its place in our culture;
2. discover and develop talents, aptitudes, interests, and potentials of individuals for the technical pursuits and applied sciences;
3. develop an understanding of industrial processes and the practical applications of scientific principles;
4. develop basic skills in the proper use of common industrial tools, machines, and processes;
5. develop problem-solving and creative abilities involving the materials, processes, and products of industry.

On the elementary school level children work with paper, clay, and other easy-to-form materials in the self-contained classroom; these activities become more involved with the maturity of the children. On the junior high school level industrial arts activities are usually taught in general shops and laboratories. On the senior high school level activities are usually more sophisticated, and are taught in special classrooms, shops or laboratories equipped for these special courses which may be required or elective. Adult industrial arts courses are generally built around avocational interests and "do-it-yourself" home construction and repairs.

The confusion among educators and the general public about the *real* purpose of the practical arts is perhaps most pronounced in relation to industrial arts, especially on the high school level. Laymen and some educators tend to make a one-to-one relationship between industrial arts and vocational education. But industrial arts is a part of general education and is so regarded by most of its teachers. It is true that much of the work in industrial arts may ultimately contribute to the individual's occupational success; but this is no more true of the industrial arts than it is of English, mathematics, and many other subjects taught for general education purposes. Unfortunately the identification of industrial arts and vocational education as one and the same thing continues. Many school administrators, high school teachers other than teachers of industrial arts, and members of the general public tend to think of vocational education as any activity which takes place in a shop. And when they think of industrial arts, they identify it with "teaching boys a trade." Industrial arts is general education, and as such, has a unique purpose and deserves its place in the curriculum.

VOCATIONAL EDUCATION IS SPECIALIZED EDUCATION

The discussion of general and specialized education earlier in this chapter made the point that vocational and technical education is clearly specialized education. In addition, the point was made that professional education is also specialized education; but the organization and administration of professional education is not within the scope of this book.

Vocational education can be defined in terms of the range of occupations with which it is concerned. The first federal vocational education act (Smith-Hughes Act of 1917) limited vocational education to agriculture, home economics, and the trade and industrial occupations. Most of the instruction was provided on the secondary level for high school youth and adults. During the intervening years numerous federal acts were passed expanding the range of occupational areas to be served. The Vocational Education Act of 1963 removed all restrictions as to occupational categories, stating: "The term 'vocational education' means vocational or technical training or retraining which is given in schools or classes under public supervision and control or under contract with a State board or local educational agency and is conducted as a part of a program designed to prepare individuals for gainful employment as semiskilled or skilled workers or technicians or sub-professionals in recognized occupations and in new and emerging occupations or to prepare individuals for enrollment in advanced technical education programs. . . ." The only exclusion stipulated in the act was "any program to prepare individuals for employment in occupations which the Commissioner (of Education) determines and specifies by regulations, to be generally considered professional or which requires a baccalaureate or higher degree." Incidentally, another significant difference between the Vocational Education Act of 1963 and earlier Federal acts is that the purpose of the act is defined, not in terms of occupational categories, but rather in terms of people to be served. The act reads, "so that persons of all ages in all communities of the State—those in high school, those who have completed or discontinued their formal education and are preparing to enter the labor market, those who have already entered the labor market but need to upgrade their skills or learn new ones, those with special educational handicaps, and those in postsecondary schools—will have ready access to vocational training or retraining which is of high quality, which is realistic in light of actual or anticipated opportunity for gainful employment, and which is suited to their needs, interest, and ability to benefit from such training."

The federal legislation makes it clear that vocational education can be provided in *any* occupation, provided there are employment opportunities in the occupation and provided further that it meets the needs, interests, and abilities of the learner. The emphasis is shifted from specified occupational categories to the needs of the economy and the needs, interests, and abilities of people. The legislation also makes it clear that vocational education is to be provided both in high schools and on the post-secondary level.

The above references to the federal vocational education acts are not meant to imply that vocational education should be defined by statute or that for a program to be considered vocational it must meet the provisions of the federal acts. The new legislation does prescribe quite adequately what the authors consider to be valid criteria for vocational education. Obviously, a local school system might operate a program which does not meet all of the federal standards and still be vocational.

Vocational education might be defined as specialized education which is organized to prepare the learner for entrance into a particular occupation or family of occupations or to upgrade employed workers.

COMPARISON OF VOCATIONAL EDUCATION AND PRACTICAL ARTS EDUCATION

Tables 1–1 and 1–2 compare vocational education and practical arts education and identify similarities and differences.

TABLE 1–1
VOCATIONAL EDUCATION AND PRACTICAL ARTS EDUCATION
(SIMILARITIES AND DIFFERENCES)

Vocational Education	*Practical Arts Education*
Specialized education designed to prepare the learner for entrance into a particular vocation, or to upgrade employed workers.	*General education* which deals with the organization, tools, materials, processes, and products of agriculture, business, industry and the home and with the contributions of workers engaged in these fields.
Content drawn from the world of work through analysis of the skills, understandings, values and attitudes of successful workers in a particular field.	*Content drawn* from the world of work in terms of what everyone should know about agriculture, business, industry, and the home in order to appreciate and use the products and services of these areas of activity.
Instruction organized into sequences of courses aimed at preparation for a particular occupation or family of occupations.	*Instruction organized* by subjects, e.g., General Agriculture, General or Basic Business, Industrial Arts and General Homemaking, excepting on the elementary level.
Emphasis on job preparation or advancement in employment.	*Emphasis* on occupational exploration, consumer knowledge, leisure-time interests, manual skills and technical understanding of value to all.

TABLE 1–2

VOCATIONAL EDUCATION AND PRACTICAL ARTS EDUCATION
COMPARED BY GRADE LEVEL

Vocational Education		Practical Arts Education
None on this level.	K–6	Introduction to the world of work through handwork projects and activities integrated with regular classroom activities.
	7–9	
Seldom provided on this level.		Broad exploratory experiences sampling a number of areas within the field of study. Usually required. Time allotted – 2 to 5 periods per week.
	10–12	
Beginning specialized vocational curriculums concurrent with continuation of general education. Elected by students interested in preparing for employment.		Courses aimed at developing competencies needed by all youth regardless of their career plans. May be required or elective. Consumer use emphasized.
	Post-Secondary	
Beginning and advanced specialized curricula aimed at preparing students for employment in skilled, technical, and paraprofessional occupations and up-grading workers in their occupations.		Practical activities related to everyday living. Some creative and experimental activities. Usually elective courses.
	Adult	
Inservice training for those employed and retraining for those seeking employment.		Leisure-time activities. "Do-it-yourself" home mechanics. Usually a part of adult evening school programs.

Both practical arts and vocational education are needed in a comprehensive career education program; neither one is a suitable substitute for the other. The practical arts introduce children and youth to the world of work through exploratory experiences with the tools, materials, and processes of modern technology as a part of their general education for effective living in a technological society. Vocational education, on the other hand, prepares youth and adults for employment in a specific occupation or family of occupations by providing those experiences which will enable them to develop the competencies needed to qualify for such employment. Both the practical arts and vocational education are essential components in a comprehensive program of career education.

The practical arts (general education) should be a part of everyone's education beginning in the elementary grades and continuing throughout life. Specialized vocational education should be elected by each individual at that point in his education—high school, community college, or later—when he is interested in preparing for employment in a particular occupation or family of occupations.

Career Education—A Part of the Total Education Process

Public education in a democratic society is charged with the responsibility for providing to all citizens the opportunity to become and remain occupationally competent. To accomplish this task adequately, career education (including specialized vocational education) should be an integral part of the total education process for everyone. Each level of the educational system has a unique role to play in assisting every student to make wise career choices and to achieve maximum occupational competence. Career education is a developmental process which begins in early childhood and extends from the elementary school through the post-secondary school levels. A brief discussion of the role of each level of education follows.

ELEMENTARY SCHOOL

The elementary school should develop in children an awareness of the world of work and some insights about the need for and value of work, including positive attitudes about it. Children should learn that all citizens in a democracy are producers of services, products, and ideas. Occupationally oriented learning at this level should be integrated into the regular instructional program; reading, social studies, and science are examples of subjects which can be enriched by including occupational concepts. Educational television, field trips, and movies have great potential for providing experiences which can help children understand the world of work. Activities involving the use of some of the basic tools and materials of our culture and the simple processes of our technology should also be included in the experiences of all children.

EARLY SECONDARY SCHOOL

The middle school or junior high school and early senior high school should continue the developmental process by providing experiences through which youth can explore the world of work. Included at this level should be a variety of experiences in the practical arts as well as part-time work experiences through which youth can assess their interests and abilities in relation to occupations, resulting in more intelligent career planning.

HIGH SCHOOL

Throughout high school, youth should be given the opportunity to explore further the world of work and their interests and aptitudes in relation to particular occupations. For those who have made a choice of occupations, even though it may be tentative, specialized vocational education programs should be available. These specialized programs should be varied and flexible enough to serve the needs of several categories of students: (1) those who will seek employment immediately upon leaving high school and therefore should develop sufficient salable skills to enable them to compete successfully for entry type jobs, (2) those who will continue their vocational preparation on the post-secondary level and therefore need to acquire some of the basic knowledge and skills for their chosen occupation.

POST-SECONDARY INSTITUTION

The role of the community college or technical institute is to provide specialized vocational and technical education for (1) those who want to continue their vocational and technical studies started in high school; (2) those who may not have had the opportunity in high school for specialized education in the occupation of their choice; and (3) those adults who are unemployed or employed but need additional training.

A COMPREHENSIVE PROGRAM

A comprehensive career education program attempts to put together all of the components outlined above. Preparation for the world of work should be a part of everyone's education beginning with common experiences (general education) on the elementary and junior high school levels with specialized (vocational) education made available in high schools to youth who are ready for it. Other youth will get their specialized vocational and technical education on the community college or technical institute level and those preparing for the professions will get it in a four-year college or professional school. Throughout this entire process, occupational guidance and career counseling services must be made available to assist the individual in assessing accurately his own career interests and potential. Table 1–3 outlines a comprehensive career education program model.

The comprehensive approach to career education which involves the whole school system, kindergarten through adult education, has been evolving for some time and now the concept appears to be gaining support. The term career education is now being defined as a conceptual model comprised of four separate but integrated phases: (1) career awareness, (2) career exploration, (3) career specialization, and (4) career advancement. These phases are not fixed and uniform periods in the lives of all people,

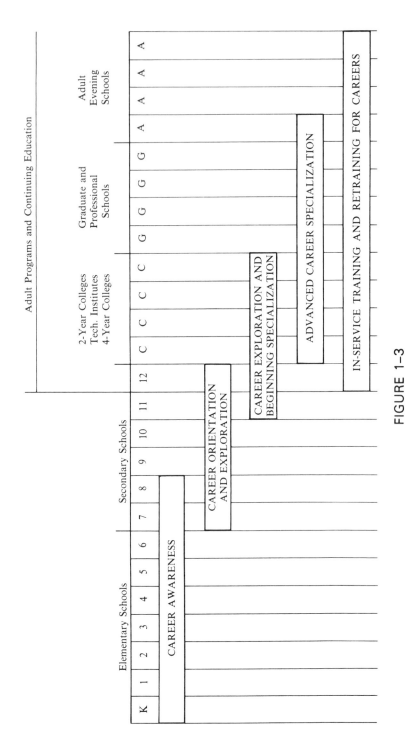

FIGURE 1-3

THE CAREER EDUCATION CONCEPT

22

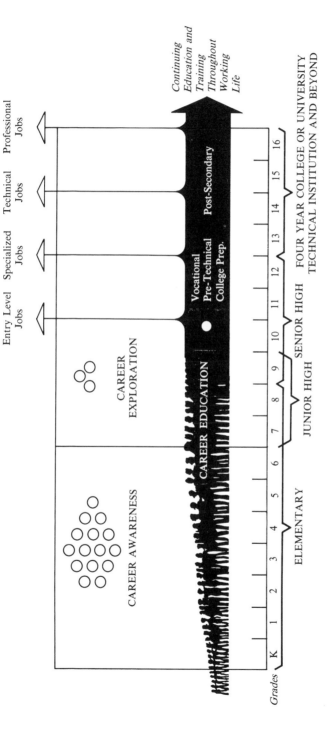

THE WORLD OF WORK

Professional Jobs

Technical Jobs

Specialized Jobs

Entry Level Jobs

CAREER EXPLORATION

CAREER AWARENESS

CAREER EDUCATION

Vocational
Pre-Technical
College Prep.

Post-Secondary

Continuing
Education and
Training
Throughout
Working
Life

Grades   K   1   2   3   4   5   6   7   8   9   10   11   12   13   14   15   16

ELEMENTARY   JUNIOR HIGH   SENIOR HIGH   FOUR YEAR COLLEGE OR UNIVERSITY
TECHNICAL INSTITUTION AND BEYOND

FIGURE 1–4

CAREER EDUCATION. SOURCE: U.S. DEPARTMENT OF HEALTH, EDUCATION AND WELFARE, PUBLICATION NO. (OE) 72–39

23

8. Youth have tentative career plans based upon their understanding of the world of work and their own strengths and weaknesses.
9. Youth acquire specialized vocational education preparing them for an entry occupation prior to terminating their full-time formal education.
10. Youth develop their capacity for continued learning so that they are able to maintain and improve their efficiency as workers.
11. Adults avail themselves of opportunities for additional education and training so as to maintain employment stability.

The comprehensive approach to career education views specialized vocational and technical education in the perspective of the total process of education for the world of work.

The public school's role in preparing people for entry into and adjustment to the world of work is a process which should start in the elementary grades and continue throughout life. One phase of this developmental process is specialized vocational and technical education. School administrators responsible for planning and operating vocational and technical programs need a working knowledge of the terms and concepts used in this area of education.

REFERENCES

1. American Vocational Association. *Vocational Technical Terminology.* Washington, D.C.: 1971.

2. Anderson, Lester W. and Lauren A. VanDyke. *Secondary School Administration.* Boston: Houghton Mifflin, 1972.

3. Association for Supervision and Curriculum Development. *The High School We Need.* Washington, D.C.: National Education Association, 1959.

4. French, Will, J. Dan Hull and B. L. Dodds. *American High School Administration—Policy and Practice.* New York: Rinehart, 1960.

5. Goldhammer, Keith and Robert E. Taylor. *Career Education: Perspective and Promise.* Columbus, Ohio: Charles E. Merrill, 1972.

6. Hoyt, Kenneth B., Rupert N. Evans, Edward F. Mackin and Garth L. Mangum. *Career Education: What It Is and How To Do It.* Salt Lake City, Utah: Olympus, 1972.

7. Linden, Ivan H. and Henry M. Gunn. *Secondary School Administration.* Columbus, Ohio: Charles E. Merrill, 1963.

Chapter 2   A RATIONALE FOR VOCATIONAL AND TECHNICAL EDUCATION

People need to work and they need to be helped to appreciate the value of work and its function in life. The total educational system should be involved in the process of helping children, youth, and adults develop their potential for satisfying and productive work.

This chapter attempts to provide a rational basis for vocational and technical education as a part of public education. The purposes of this chapter are to help the reader:

1. to better appreciate the meaning of work in the lives of people;
2. to appreciate the fact that education for work can be as humanizing as the liberal arts;
3. to explain the role of vocational and technical education;
4. to substantiate the need for vocational and technical education.

Education for Work

Vocational education is one phase of the process of education for work. We need, therefore, to understand the meaning and value of work in the lives of people. There are two reasons why it is

25

important that educational planners understand work. First, through education we can help youth and adults better understand the function of work and its relationship to a full life and thereby motivate them to develop more fully their potential for work. Second, and perhaps more important, as educational decision makers come to realize how important work really is in the lives of people, they will attach more importance to, and become more knowledgeable about, programs of education for work.

WHAT IS WORK?

Each of us has a different perception of work, depending upon our intellectual understanding of what work is and the experiences we have had with it. The divergence of attitudes and opinions about work is striking. Henry Van Dyke recognized the differences in opinion among people when he wrote, "This is my work; my blessing, not my doom." On the one hand, many people view work as good and desirable; others consider it a necessary evil which must be endured in order to provide the material necessities of life. Why this tremendous range—from disgust to elation—in the attitudes of people toward their work? A closer examination of work might be useful.

Work can be defined as physical or mental effort directed toward some end or purpose. When one works at a *job* the "end," or "purpose," may be the paycheck, or it may be the joy and satisfaction derived from turning out a beautiful and/or useful product. When one works as an officer of the local parent-teacher association, the end or purpose may be to improve the school which his children attend, or it may be to satisfy a personal need, such as the need for recognition or a desire to be of service to his community. In any event there is, whether he recognizes it or not, an end or purpose which motivates him to work, both on and off the job. Frequently, the motivation to work is based upon a consideration of several purposes.

We can be helped to understand work by considering play. On the surface work and play may appear to be antithetical. Certainly, the difference is not in the nature of the activity since two people might engage in the same activity, such as dancing, yet one is working while the other is playing. Few work harder physically than professional dancers, yet most of them seem to derive considerable pleasure from their "work." A farmer works in the fields, then relaxes by reading a magazine, while the magazine editor does just the opposite; he works while he is reading the magazine and relaxes by tending his garden. It is obvious then that the difference between work and play is not in the activity, but in the purpose. If the purpose is to extract from the activity all the intrinsic values without considering extrinsic rewards, then it is fun and can be called play.

To the extent that people can get intrinsic or ego satisfactions as well as extrinsic rewards through their work, their work becomes more like play, more pleasurable, more fun. While it is unlikely that we will ever achieve the Utopia in which everyone enjoys his work, and everything about it, we can approach this condition by helping people understand that work is an essential function in our lives, and that the personal satisfactions we derive from it depend in part upon our attitude toward work and the way work is structured.

WORK THROUGH THE AGES

The meaning of work has changed considerably through the ages. A brief review of the dominant meanings which people have attached to work at different times in history is both interesting and enlightening.

Like the Greeks and Romans, the Hebrews thought of work as painful drudgery. Early Christianity followed the Jewish tradition by regarding work as a punishment laid on man by God because of man's original sin; but Christianity added a positive function, that work is necessary not only to earn one's living, but, above all, so that he who wished could share his profits with the poor. With the advent of the Reformation came a new atmosphere and a changed attitude toward work. Once man worked for a livelihood—a means of subsistence. Now he worked for something beyond his daily bread; he worked because it was the right and moral thing to do. This Protestant or Puritan work ethic reached the United States during the middle of the nineteenth century, where it obtained its fullest expression. The impact of this "gospel of work," as it later came to be known, is discussed by DeGrazia.

> Perhaps the linking of work to God is no longer so clear as it once was, yet we can certainly see that the shadows of the great reformers fall over the idea of work in America. Here, all who can must work, and idleness is bad; too many holidays and nothing gets done, and by steady methodical work alone can we build a great and prosperous nation. Here, too, work is good for you, a remedy for pain, loneliness, the death of a dear one, a disappointment in love, or doubts about the purposes of life. (5, p. 45)

WHY MEN WORK

Men work because they *need to work.* The need may be economic, but when this need is satisfied, they still want to work. There are social and psychological needs which may be just as forceful. Brown (4, pp. 187 and 190) in his book, *The Social Psychology of Industry,* states: "Work is an essential part of man's life since it is that aspect of his life which gives him status and binds him to society. . . . That there are often many aspects of work which men do not like, is self-evident, but there are few people who are not more unhappy without work than with it, even when we exclude the financial reward altogether."

Herzberg and others (*14*, p. 137) did a study dealing with the motivation to work. They concluded that the one most significant thing to be done to raise the mental health of the majority of our citizens is to increase the potential for motivation in their work. They recognized that there are large segments of our society which could not apply their prescriptions, but they rejected "the pessimism that views the future as one in which work will become increasingly meaningless to most people and in which pursuits of leisure will become the most important end of our society." They expressed the feeling that the "greatest fulfillment of man is to be found in activities that are meaningfully related to his own needs as well as those of society." To structure the work situation so that the worker can get maximum satisfaction of personal needs and at the same time meet the needs of the work organization or of the larger society is the task of every manager.

In a society oriented toward the material aspects of life, we tend to overemphasize the economic motives of humans. Management incentive systems as well as labor contracts emphasize the economic rewards and tend to ignore the intrinsic satisfactions which workers can and do derive from their work activities. Some people may work solely for financial reward, but to say that this is the only reason people work is to reveal a lack of understanding of the social and psychological needs of people.

Friedman and Havighurst (*12*), in a study of the meaning of work, identified its functions: (1) income, (2) expenditure of time and energy, (3) identification and status, (4) association, and (5) source of meaningful life experiences.

The functions of work can also be translated in terms of the needs of the individual. The following is a list of needs which can be satisfied, in part at least, through work. It is interesting to note that many of these needs can also be satisfied through other kinds of life-activity, including play.

1. *People need income.* The need for money is basic. A man works when he is hungry, but continues to work when he is well-fed, well-clothed, and well-housed. In a study done a number of years ago, Morse and Weiss (*15*) asked a national sample of employed men whether or not they would continue to work if they inherited enough money to live comfortably. Eighty percent said they would.

2. *People need activity.* The activity can be mental or physical, but usually it is a combination of both. People have time and energy to spend and need something to do to "fill the day." Most people prefer to have a routine which they can follow; even retired people work out a routine of activity for themselves.

3. *People need self-respect and the respect of others.* Most people need recognition—some more than others. People need to maintain or improve their social status.

4. *People need social contacts and participation.* They need to be associated with other people and they need to have friendly relations with people.

5. *People need to express themselves creatively.* They need to find ways in which they can express their personalities in activities which have meaning for them. People need to have a purpose in life and most people need to feel useful and of service to others.

Work has been studied in terms of its satisfactions and dissatisfactions. It is important to make a distinction between internal or ego satisfactions and extrinsic satisfactions. Ego satisfactions reflect the extent to which the job is an expression of some aspect of self and come from the *kind* of work one does, its interest, value, variety, and the skills involved; the opportunities that the job offers for the expression of responsibility, independence, and confidence and the potential that the job offers for the gratification of interpersonal and friendship needs. Extrinsic satisfactions are those which are concerned with such things as money, job security, and working conditions. Professional persons and technicians are more likely to report ego satisfactions than are clerical workers, semi-skilled workers, and unskilled workers. It is interesting to note that while persons in high status jobs— professional, paraprofessional, and technical personnel—have relatively high levels of ego satisfaction, these groups are also among the highest in ego dissatisfactions or frustrations. It appears that people in high status jobs not only get more ego satisfaction in their work, but seek this gratification more, with a consequent greater frustration experience when these needs are felt to be unsatisfied.

WORK AND LEISURE

As our country shifts from a work-centered society to an economy of abundance, people will have time for more work activities outside of employment. These work activities during leisure time can have all of the intrinsic satisfactions or ego gratifications which people get from work on the job. In fact, it is possible that the noneconomic values of work can nearly all be discovered and realized more fully in leisure time activities than they are in employment.

It was pointed out earlier in this chapter that work and play have many common characteristics. As technology advances, more and more of the drudgery is taken out of work on the job and the old dichotomy of work and play may become meaningless. Whereas play was considered a rest from the burden of work, as work becomes less burdensome the distinction between work and play will become less and less. Friedmann and Havighurst (*12,* p. 192) have stated a principle of "equivalence of work and play": "in our economy of abundance, where work is reduced in quantity and burdensomeness to a level where it is not physically unpleasant, many of the values of play can be achieved through work and of work through play."

Work, including the work we do in our daily employment, is the activity around which each of us organizes much of his daily experiences and through which each of us hopes to establish a meaningful and rewarding life routine. One has but to witness the lives of men without work, or of men who lack edifying work, to realize the validity of the point of view that work is indeed a way of life.

Experiences must be provided in the elementary and secondary schools which will help children and youth understand and appreciate the value of work and its functions in life and help them develop their potential for satisfying work. Also, planners and managers of educational programs should structure their work organizations in such a way that all participants —students, teachers, counselors, and supervisors—can get maximum ego satisfaction through their work. We will come back to this application of work in subsequent chapters dealing with organization and administration.

Peter Drucker (*7,* p. 300) sums up this point of view about work and at the same time points up the need for education for work: "The old assumption that people do not want to work is not true. Man not only lives under the spiritual and psychological necessity of work, but he also wants to work at something—usually quite a few things. Our experience indicates that what a man is good at is usually the thing he wants to work at; ability to perform is the foundation of willingness to work."

DEFINITION

Public education in a democratic society is dominated by the idea or the ideal that all children and youth be provided with equal educational opportunities so that each individual might develop his potential as far as possible. All too frequently the phrase "equal educational opportunities" is taken to mean the *same* opportunities for all. But children and youth, like adults, are unique; no single curriculum or set of learning experiences can be expected to discover and develop the talents of all; diversity of educational programs is needed. *Education for work can be defined as the total process of discovering and developing the individual's potential for work.* Specialized vocational and technical education on the high school and post-secondary levels is an important part of the process of developing the individual's potential for work.

RELATIONSHIP OF WORK AND EDUCATION

Primitive man did not need much formal education in order to work. Even in the early history of the United States most men and women learned to work by association with experienced workers. The skills and abilities needed both to earn a livelihood and to make a life were generally learned in the home or on the farm, the father teaching the sons, the mother teaching the daughters. Apprentice training was sometimes provided for other than sons—orphans and poor children—but even this form of education for work was frequently carried on in the craftsman's shop which was part of his home. The family was a production unit as well as a social unit. Work and education were combined.

With the shift to industrialization and specialization, work and education became separated. In fact, it was not uncommon for youth to be encouraged to stay in school and get an education so that they would not need to work as hard as their parents. Education was seen as a means to more leisure. There was danger of developing a labor class and a leisure class in our democratic society.

Over a hundred years ago Abraham Lincoln, in an address before the Wisconsin State Argicultural Society (September 30, 1859), said, "henceforth educated people must labor. Otherwise education itself would become a positive and intolerable evil . . . the great majority must labor at something productive. From these premises the problem springs. 'How can labor and education be the most satisfactorily combined?' "

The opportunity to work, especially in a technological society, is dependent upon one's education and training. Whereas education has long been recognized as essential for those who are preparing to work in the professions, it is now also necessary for those who want to work in paraprofessional, technical, skilled and semi-skilled occupations.

Vocational Education and Liberal Education

The traditional conflict between vocational education and liberal education is no longer valid. It is based upon misconceptions of both; it is not based upon the way these two purposes of education are currently conceived. Vocational education has been misinterpreted by some as being too narrow and too specialized, concerned only with manual skills, aimed at preparing for employment those youth who cannot succeed in academic pursuits. On the other hand, liberal education has been misunderstood by those who think it is too broad and too general, has no practical value, and is appropriate only for the intellectually gifted students. These and other misconceptions about both vocational and liberal education do have some basis in fact when examined from an historical point of view.

The authors take the position (which has been credited to John Dewey) that liberal education is any education which "liberates" humans as determined by the quality of their total life experiences, rather than by the supposition that certain subjects of study possess more power of liberation than others. Liberal education, then, must be defined in terms of life's problems as men face them; it must have human orientation and social direction; and the content must be relevant to the demands of modern society. All men should have the benefit of an education that liberates; that is, liberal education with its content and methods shifted from its original aristocratic intent to the service of democracy. Defined in this way, liberal education is not the exclusive right of any segment of our society.

DEFINITION

Good's *Dictionary of Education* (1945 edition, p. 240) defines liberal education in both the historical and modern sense: "(1) historically, the education suitable for a freeman as distinguished from that suitable for a slave; originally identified with the seven liberal arts of antiquity, namely, grammar, logic, rhetoric, arithmetic, geometry, astronomy and music, and hence education for leisure as contrasted with education for work or *vocational education:* (2) in the modern sense, a broad, academic education, as opposed to a strictly vocational education, especially that type of education given in the academic high school and the liberal arts college." This definition is followed by an interesting note which states, "In preparation for certain professions, as, for example, that of professor of English, a *liberal education* may be regarded, strictly speaking, as a form of *vocational education.* The term, however, generally implies that the emphasis is on general culture."

In the 1959 edition of the *Dictionary of Education,* the definition is stated as "any education accepted as relatively broad and general, rather than narrow and specialized, and as preparation for living, rather than for earning a living . . ." (p. 318).

VOCATIONAL EDUCATION IS BROAD

Although vocational education is specialized education, it need not be narrow or restrictive. The scope of vocational offerings in the small high school is a limiting factor, but area vocational centers serving youth from a number of high schools in the area greatly enlarge the range of offerings. (Other ways of expanding the range of available vocational offerings on the secondary and post-secondary levels are discussed in chapters 7 and 15.)

The individual enrolled in a vocational education curriculum has the opportunity to broaden his program through elective courses. He is engaged in studies dealing directly with his area of specialization for only part of the time; the remaining time can be used to explore subjects outside the prescribed program or to pursue cultural or avocational interests.

Vocational education is concerned not only with the manual skills involved in an occupation. It is concerned with all of the competencies needed to function effectively in employment. This includes the cognitive and the psycho-motor skills required in the particular occupation. Obviously, the proportions of each vary greatly from one occupation to another. But vocational education goes beyond the mental and the manual skills needed; it is also concerned about the attitudes and values of the worker—the affective domain.

Vocational education has a broadening effect in that it can motivate the learner who becomes interested in preparing for a particular occupation and then discovers that subjects which he may have previously rejected are essential to his performance in that field. The relevance of mathematics, science, the communication arts, and almost any other subject may not become evident for some learners until they face real problems requiring a knowledge of these subjects for their solution.

Vocational education, if properly organized, should encourage and promote upward mobility; it is not terminal education. That is, it is broad enough to prepare for a range of occupations within each family or cluster of occupations so that a student may "spin off" after a short period of preparation into a relatively low-skilled job in that occupational field or he may continue his education in the same institution or in higher institutions and prepare for employment requiring a higher level of preparation; this is the "ladder concept" in vocational education. Community colleges generally have an open door policy so that youth who graduate from high school in a vocational curriculum may continue their education in the same area of specialization. Four-year colleges are also interested in high school vocational graduates, if they have the ability to succeed in college.

VOCATIONAL EDUCATION IS HUMANISTIC

In the early history of vocational education the emphasis was on meeting the manpower needs of society. While this is still an important function, the emphasis has shifted so that vocational educators are now more concerned about what vocational education can do to enrich the lives of the people it serves. The federal Vocational Education Act of 1963 and subsequent amendments reflect this change in emphasis. Some critics of vocational education claim that it has been used to exploit youth by providing cheap labor for employers by limiting training programs to those occupations for which there are job opportunities in the local community. As we have seen, vocational education can and should *increase* the options available to youth. This is one of the recognized objectives of vocational education. This goal, however, cannot be achieved in small high schools offering only one or two specialized vocational curricula. In the report of the Association for Supervision and Curriculum Development, *Humanizing the Secondary School,* Saylor states: "A humane secondary school is one that provides a broad and comprehensive curriculum in which ample opportunity exists for the optimum exploration and development at the adolescent level of talents and capabilities of all youth of the community, and one in which teaching and instruction are primarily designed to foster such development" (*3* p. 124). This book is devoted to the development of specialized vocational and technical education programs which must be a part of such "broad and comprehensive" programs in secondary and post-secondary institutions. Making a wide range of vocational programs available to youth will help them realize their capabilities and potential for success in the world of work and thereby serve to liberate them from the boredom of an educational program which lacks relevance for them.

Vocational education is frequently thought of as materialistic and concerned only with the economics of earning a living. If properly conceived, it can and should be as humanistic as any other education. Furthermore, any subject which carries a vocational label can be as liberal (or cultural) as any so-called liberal arts subject. It isn't the subject matter, but rather what educators do with subject matter, that determines the values in education.

VOCATIONAL EDUCATION CAN LIBERATE

Friedenberg refers to liberal education as "decorative adjustment" and claims that it includes vocational education. He writes:

> This trivial conception of liberal education (decorative adjustment) is also the source of the false notion that liberal education and vocational education are in conflict. Since what a man is in our society is so largely defined both by himself and others in terms of what he does for a living, vocational education is in fact an indispensable part of liberal education—the part on which everything rests, its hindquarter. Whether vocational education strengthens liberal education or cripples it depends on the spirit in which it is undertaken. If it induces a rigorous analysis of what the job for which the student is preparing means to its holder and to society, it is liberalizing; if it merely trains the student in the techniques he will be expected to know and indoctrinates him in the ideology that will make him acceptable to his colleagues, it is like much teacher education, slavish. (*11*, p. 224)

> Liberal education, then, includes vocational education; it must, because it must take full account of any factor so central to the lives of its students. (*11*, p. 225)

Greene sees liberal education and vocational education as different but complementary components of education. He says:

> What is obviously needed is a truly liberal academic community in which the study of art and typewriting, of philosophy and accounting, of theology and medicine, of pure and applied science are, though admittedly very different, judged to be equally honorable and valuable in their several ways. In such a community the so-called liberal disciplines would indeed be liberal because they would be studied and taught with an eye to the total enrichment of the life of responsible members of a free society; and in such a community the acquisition of the vocational skills, from the simplest to the most complex, would be equally liberal because they would be taught, not in a spirit of predatory egoism, but in the spirit of deep social concern for the needs of others and for the common good. (*13*, p. 119)

The problem of integrating vocational and technical studies with the liberal arts may be most keenly felt at the college and university level; but since high schools and community colleges are engaged in the preparation of youth for further education, the problem is imposed on these institutions as well. The problem is not limited to institutions in the United States. British educator Sir Eric Ashby suggests that the study of technology could "become the cement between science and humanism." He believes that this could be accomplished by "making specialist studies the core around which are grouped liberal studies which are relevant to these specialist studies. But they must be relevant; the path to culture should be through a man's specialism, not by by-passing it." He then uses the following example to illustrate how this scheme might work.

> Suppose a student decides to take up the study of brewing; his way to acquire general culture is not by diluting his brewing courses with popular lectures on architecture, social history, and ethics, but by making brewing the core of his studies. The *sine qua non* for a man who desires to be cultured is a deep and enduring enthusiasm to do one thing excellently. So there must first of all be assurance that the student genuinely wants to make beer. From this it is a natural step to the study of biology, microbiology, and chemistry: all subjects which can be studied not as techniques to be practiced but as ideas to be understood. As his studies gain momentum the student could, by skillful teaching, be made interested in the economics of marketing beer, in public-houses, in their design, in architecture; or in the history of beer-drinking from the time of the early Egyptian inscriptions, and so in social history; or, in the unhappy moral effects of

drinking too much beer, and so in religion and ethics. A student who can weave his technology into the fabric of society can claim to have a liberal education; a student who cannot weave his technology into the fabric of society cannot claim even to be a good technologist. (2, p. 81)

Occupations as the Basis of Education

John Dewey, while on the faculty of the University of Michigan (1884–1894), became interested in education and recognized the need for educational reform. He developed the idea of making occupations the vehicle for elementary and secondary education.

Dewey's philosophy was based upon the idea of a total organism interacting with its environment and he conceived of the mind as the process by which organisms and environment become integrated. He believed that human intellectual life developed in relation to needs and opportunities for action and that the problem of education was to create a program that would not only include initial school experiences appropriate for children beginning their school work, but also serve as a basis for a unified progression of studies at more advanced levels. Occupations seemed to supply the answer.

The use of occupations, such as gardening, cooking, textile work, and carpentry, provided, in the words of Dewey in a lecture on pedagogy, (Wirth, 18, p. 131) "activities which are genuine and timeless. Their reality excites the interest of the child and enlists his efforts, for they are what his elders do, have done, and must continue to do." The occupations as the basis for structuring an educational program conformed with Dewey's psychological theory which was that there are four natural instincts or impulses of children: (1) the constructive, (2) the investigative and experimental, (3) the social, and (4) the expressive. "The fundamental point in the psychology of an occupation," said Dewey, "is that it maintains a balance between the intellectual and practical phases of experience. As an occupation it is active or motor; it finds expression through the physical organs, the eyes, the hands, etc. But it also involves continual observation of materials, and continued planning and reflection in order that the practical or executive side may be successfully carried on. . . ."

Dewey was concerned about having a conceptual unity and coherence in the whole educational effort from the preprimary level through to the university. But he recognized a problem at the high school level since it had then, as now, a dual role—the traditional and long-standing college preparation function and a major responsibility as a "people's college" for those who would not continue their education beyond high school. He recognized, according to Wirth, "that the high school is characterized by more specialization as the child's interest and society's needs demand it. Specialization wrongly pursued, however, can lead to narrowness and monotony. Therefore, the task is to emphasize the benefits of specialized work and avoid its negative aspects. Specialized study must never lose sight of the connectedness and interaction with the whole experience of which the subject at hand is a mere fragment" (*18*, p. 224).

In a day when most of the occupations, other than the professions, involved little more than manual skill and the repeated applications of a few rules-of-thumb, the idea of vocational education as illiberal may have had some validity. But technology has brought the sciences and the arts to vocations, so that study in preparation for a vocation is a means of providing a broad and liberating education. Dewey was opposed to vocational education that would be limited to the mere acquisition of job skills; he felt that the underlying principles of the work processes and the social significance of work must be included. He further felt that through vocational studies culture might be made truly vital for many students.

Just as it is important for the employment-bound student to be exposed to science, history, and literature, it is equally important that the college-bound student become acquainted with the tools, materials, and reality of the world of work. The trend is definitely toward a lowering of the educational wall between vocations and culture and between vocational education and liberal education. The traditional dichotomy should be eliminated.

In 1944 Dewey said: "a truly liberal and liberating education would refuse today to isolate vocational training on any of its levels from a continuous education in the social, moral and scientific contexts within which wisely administered callings . . . must perform" (*6*, p. 156). The concept of occupational education and career education finds a great deal of support in the Dewey philosophy. It is also made valid through the research efforts of the social scientists, including some curriculum specialists. One recognized authority in the field of curriculum and instruction, would have us change child labor laws and compulsory school attendance laws so as to give children and youth more opportunity for interaction with the real world of work. Foshay states:

> One aspect of the confrontation of the school with external reality is often overlooked: the relationship of school to real work—real, productive work. If the school is to deal more thoroughly with reality than it has in the past, then the reality of work must be allowed to enter into schooling from the beginning. The child labor laws and compulsory attendance, those twin enactments of the 19th century viewpoint, are probably dysfunctional now. There is very good reason for young children to begin the process of being productive in the world as early as they are capable of

doing so. There is no reason to suppose that because they are being productive, they are therefore being exploited. Work experience for young children, which is clearly mandated by these times, could be kept under control of the educational authorities in such a way as to ensure its educative value. But to deny children the opportunity to take part in the real world is to portray to them an irreal version of childhood. A direct relationship between the world of work and the world of education needs to be established early in the game and continued throughout its duration. If we are to respond to Dewey's old injunction that education be life, not preparation for life, we should take at least this one small step, making the necessary changes in the law. (*10,* pp. 33–34)

Objectives of Vocational Education

Vocational and technical education was defined earlier as a program of specialized studies designed to prepare the learner for employment in a particular occupation or family of occupations. It is a phase of the total process of discovering and developing the individual's potential for work. Vocational and technical education is found in many different kinds of institutions—both public and private—and takes many different forms, but we are concerned only with vocational programs in public secondary and post-secondary schools.

The specific content for any particular vocational curriculum is determined by the requirements of that occupation. Consequently, the content (or subject matter) can be just as broad as the world of work. Instruction in a foreign language might be included in a vocational curriculum, if competence in another language is required for successful participation in a particular occupation. The primary objective of vocational education is to prepare the learner for entry into employment, and advancement in his chosen career.

Evans has identified three basic objectives of any public school vocational education curriculum. They are: "(1) meeting the manpower needs of society, (2) increasing the options available to each student, and (3) serving as a motivation force to enhance all types of learning" (*8,* p. 2). He points out the fact that these are listed in chronological order of their acceptance as goals.

Need for Vocational Education

Vocational education, as a responsibility of the public school system, can be justified only if it is planned and organized so as to achieve, to the maximum degree possible, the three objectives listed above. A brief discussion of each of these objectives with some implications for administrators of vocational programs might be helpful.

MANPOWER NEEDS

Evans (*8*) makes the point that the earliest and most widely accepted objective of vocational education was to supply the manpower needs of the local community; but today the needs of the nation or society as a whole must also be considered. Educational planners must be most knowledgeable about the manpower needs within the service area of their schools, but they must also be informed about the migratory patterns of people in the area. To the extent that students are likely to leave the community for employment, programs must be designed with the wider manpower needs in mind. However, vocational programs cannot be justified on the basis of some vaguely defined national manpower needs; nor can they be justified on the basis of national or regional needs which would not result in direct employment. "The name of the game is jobs" and only programs which result in employment which is satisfying to both the employee and the employer can be justified.

The educational planner responsible for vocational programs should be aware of manpower trends. The most significant trend is the sharp reduction in the number of unskilled workers in the labor force. The shift from goods-producing occupations to service-producing occupations is another trend with implications for vocational educators as is the increase of women in the labor force. To understand these national trends is important, but the local administrator of a vocational-technical program must be equally aware of local trends and conditions. Techniques for assessing local manpower needs will be discussed in chapter 8.

INDIVIDUAL OPTIONS

The opportunity to choose from a number of alternatives is an important concept in a democratic society and in education. Education should serve to increase the number of alternatives available to the individual and should also help him to make wise choices from among these alternatives. These options might include choices from among different occupations, kinds and levels of education, income, employment, and many other areas.

Those opposed to vocational education on the secondary level have frequently used the argument that we reduce the options available to youth when we encourage them to enroll in a specialized vocational curriculum. The solution offered was the "general" curriculum, which has recently been discredited. Project TALENT, a study of students in United States' high schools in 1961 by Flanagan and others (9), indicated that the general curriculum enrolls 25 percent of the students, yet it produces 76 percent of the high school dropouts. Furthermore, the study showed that the graduates of the general curriculum ranked behind both the college preparatory and the vocational graduates on nearly every measure of success, including (1) proportion who go on to college, (2) annual earnings, (3) job satisfaction, and (4) length and frequency of unemployment. Evans (8, p. 29) uses these and other data to show that the options of students in vocational curricula are markedly increased over those in the general curriculum. Vocational educators (and especially educational planners and administrators) who accept increasing individual options as an objective of vocational education can take steps to increase them even further.

Individual options are increased (1) when a larger variety of specialized vocational programs are available from which the individual can choose; (2) when vocational programs are offered by the public schools, as opposed to the vocational training provided by employers; (3) when high school programs are broadened so that youth are prepared for families of occupations, thereby giving them greater flexibility in the labor market; (4) when adult programs are readily available for the upgrading and retraining of employed persons; and (5) when job placement services are provided by the schools to assist youth in finding suitable employment.

LEARNING

Vocational education can serve as a motivating force to enhance all types of learning. Just as college-bound students are motivated by the fact that the occupation (profession) of their choice requires a college education and colleges have certain admission requirements, so employment-bound youth in high school can be challenged by the occupation of their choice and the job-entry requirements.

Perhaps more important than these delayed gratifications is the current interest of the learner; if a young man with a deep and enduring enthusiasm about electronics or auto mechanics is given the opportunity to specialize in his area of interest, he soon comes to recognize the importance of mathematics and science or even the ability to read (instruction manuals, if nothing else). These subjects now take on new meaning and value for the learner because they are relevant. Youth are motivated to engage in activities in which they are interested and which satisfy their needs. Learning experiences related to a purposeful activity and essential to the completion of tasks associated with such activity are intrinsically more satisfying and more enduring than learning experiences for which the learner has no perceived need. Vocational and technical education has always served this purpose for some youth; it could enhance the learning of all youth who go directly from our high schools and community colleges into employment.

REFERENCES

1. American Vocational Association. *American Vocational Journal* 49, No. 1 (1973). January issue featuring the American work ethic.

2. Ashby, Sir Eric. *Technology and the Academics: An Essay on Universities and the Scientific Revolution.* London: Macmillan, 1958.

3. Association for Supervision and Curriculum Development. *Humanizing the Secondary School,* chapter by J. Galen Saylor, "Some Characteristics of a Humane Secondary School." Washington, D.C.: Association for Supervision and Curriculum Development, National Education Association, 1969.

4. Brown, J. A. C. *The Social Psychology of Industry.* Baltimore, Md.: Penguin, 1958.

5. DeGrazia, Sebastian. *Of Time, Work, and Leisure.* New York: Twentieth Century Fund, 1962.

6. Dewey, John. "Challenge to Liberal Thought," *Fortune* 30, No. 2 (August 1944).

7. Drucker, Peter. *The Practice of Management.* New York: Harper, 1954.

8. Evans, Rupert N. *Foundations of Vocational Education.* Columbus, Ohio: Charles E. Merrill, 1971.

9. Flanagan, John C. and others. *Project TALENT—The American High-School Student.* Pittsburgh: University of Pittsburgh, 1964.

10. Foshay, Arthur W. *Curriculum for the 70's: An Agenda for Invention.* Washington, D.C.: National Education Association, 1970.

11. Friedenberg, Edgar. *Coming of Age in America.* New York: Random House, 1963.

12. Friedmann, Eugene A. and Robert J. Havighurst. *The Meaning of Work and Retirement.* Chicago: University of Chicago Press, 1954.

13. Greene, Theodore M. "A Liberal Christian Idealist's Philosophy of Education" in *Modern Philosophies and Education.* Chicago: National Society for the Study of Education, 1955.

14. Herzberg, Frederick, Bernard Mausner, and Barbara Block Snyderman. *The Motivation to Work.* New York: John Wiley, 1959.

15. Morse, Nancy C. and Robert S. Weiss. "The Function and Meaning of Work and the Job," *American Sociological Review* 20 (April 1955): 191–98.

16. Schaefer, Carl J. and Jacob J. Kaufman, eds. *Vocational-Technical Education: A Prospectus for Change.* Boston, Mass.: Advisory Council on Education, 1967.

17. Venn, Grant. *Men, Education and Manpower.* Washington, D.C.: American Association of School Administrators, 1970.

18. Wirth, Arthur G. *John Dewey as Educator—His Design for Work in Education.* New York: John Wiley, 1966.

19. Wirth, Arthur G. *Education in the Technological Society—The Vocational-Liberal Studies Controversy in the Early Twentiety Century.* Scranton: Intext Educational Publishers, 1972.

Chapter 3 POLICY AND POLICY MAKING

Schools exist in a complex, intricate, and changing social environment. Educational policy has its origin in this milieu. Effective educational leadership requires a thorough understanding of these social, economic, and political forces and how to work with them. The problem for the vocational and technical education administrator is further complicated by the fact that, in addition to the social, economic, and political forces which concern all education, he must be concerned about technological changes, manpower trends, current and projected labor force demands, unemployment, and a host of related problems and conditions which may influence policy regarding vocational education programs.

The purposes of this chapter are to help the reader:

1. to understand what is meant by policy and how the policy-making process works;
2. to understand the role of the federal government in the development of policy regarding vocational education;
3. to understand the role and responsibility of the state in policy making in vocational education;
4. to understand the role and responsibilities of the intermediate and local school districts in policy making in vocational education;
5. to use some recommended approaches and techniques available to

local vocational education administrators through which they can have an impact on policy.

The Policy-Making Process

Policy may evolve from practices and procedures followed in any organization or institution over a period of time, but it must also undergird and give direction to what we do on a day-to-day basis. Policy is used here to mean those formulations of broad goals or purposes usually developed outside the schools, often by laymen, but hopefully, with information provided by professional educators. Hamlin (*11*, p. 63) takes the position that professional educators in this country cannot legally make policy; it must be made by citizens or their representatives.

Policy should not be confused with philosophy, although philosophy should undergird it. It should not be confused with the rules or procedures for operating school systems. The operating policies which are used to carry out the administrative functions of the school will be considered in later chapters dealing with such functions.

On the local level educational policy is generally developed by the entire community including the board of education and the chief administrator. Any school personnel who will be affected by the policy, including students and teachers, should have the opportunity to participate in the formulation process. Obviously, final enactment of a policy can only be done by action of an officially designated body, such as a board of education or city council.

Not all policy regarding education is made at the local level. In some states intermediate units of administration have the authority to make some policies. The several states and the federal government are heavily involved in making educational policy which has its impact on local schools. The federal and state involvement is an especially significant factor in relation to vocational and technical education because of the federal vocational education subventions since 1917. Most educational policies are the result of formulation activity on all levels—federal, state, and local; this is especially true of vocational education, again because of the federal government's special interest in this area. Policy formulation at the state and federal levels is even more complex than it is at the local level. It is important, therefore, that anyone interested in giving leadership to the development and operation of vocational and technical education programs understand the policy-making process on all levels.

Campbell, et al. (*4*) devote a chapter of their book to educational policy formation. They believe that policy has its inception in the social, economic, political, and technological developments in our society, and that these basic forces are national or worldwide in scope. As a result of these forces, movements get started, some of which are nonofficial, such as the National

Merit Scholarship program and the civil rights movement; and some official, such as the White House Conference on Education and President Kennedy's Panel of Consultants on Vocational Education. Foundations and the media frequently provide assistance for such movements or reinforce their national impact. The next step is one of political activity resulting in organizations and government taking action. For example, after the report of President Kennedy's Panel of Consultants for Vocational Education, the American Vocational Association organized their forces to get legislative action. The last step in the process is formal enactment which, to continue the example used above, was the passage of the Vocational Education Act of 1963. The Campbell (*4,* p. 315) analysis of the policy-making process is described in Table 3–1. This is an excellent description of the process of policy formation. Our experience, however, would suggest that while the basic forces (step I in the process) are usually national in scope, they grow out of local and state problems and issues, and very often form the basis for action (steps II, III, and IV) on the local or state level as well.

TABLE 3–1

I	II	III	IV
Basic Forces	*Antecedent Movements*	*Political Action*	*Formal Enactment*
Social, economic, political, and technological forces, usually national and worldwide in scope	Usually national in scope such as the Rockefeller Bros. studies, Conant studies, National Assessment, etc.	By organizations usually interrelated at local, state, and national levels such as U.S. Chamber of Commerce, AFL-CIO, and NEA	May be at local, state, and national levels; and through legislative, judicial, and executive agencies

Federal Government Involvement

For more than a century the federal government has been promoting occupational education. The first federal legislation of this kind, the Morrill Act of 1862, was aimed at preparing people for the "agricultural and mechanical arts" through land grant colleges. Early in the twentieth century the need for occupational education for high school youth was recognized and a number of states started such programs. One of the first and most influential states was Massachusetts, where in 1905 a law was passed authorizing the appointment by the governor (Douglas) of a commission to study the need for "education in the different grades of skill and responsibility in the various industries of the Commonwealth." It is suggested by some that vocational education in the United States had its beginning in Massachusetts with the report of the Douglas Commission. Other states were involved in similar activities, and in 1906 vocational education became a national movement; the National Society for the Promotion of Industrial Education was organized.

In 1914 Congress was persuaded to enact a resolution creating the Commission on National Aid to Vocational Education. Although the Commission recognized the need for vocational education for many different kinds of occupations, attention was centered on that kind of vocational education that would prepare workers for the common occupations which employed the greatest number of workers. The Commission report defines the needs:

> There is a great and crying need of providing vocational education of this character for every part of the United States—to conserve and develop our resources; to promote a more productive and prosperous agriculture; to prevent the waste of human labor; to supplement apprenticeship; to increase the wage-earning power of our productive workers; to increase the demand for trained workmen; to offset the increased cost of living. Vocational education is therefore needed as a wise business investment for this Nation, because our national prosperity and happiness are at stake and our position in the markets of the world cannot otherwise be maintained. (15, p. 12)

In 1917 Congress passed the Smith-Hughes Act which provided a grant in perpetuity to aid the states in the promotion of agriculture, trade, industrial, and home economics education. This was the first of a series of federal acts which established a cooperative relationship or partnership with the states for the purpose of ensuring "the economic well-being of the nation and the democratizing of the American public school system."

The Smith-Hughes Act required the creation of a Federal Board for Vocational Education made up of the Secretary of Agriculture, the Secretary of Commerce, the Secretary of Labor, and the U.S. Commissioner of Education and three citizens to be appointed by the President—one to represent manufacturing and commercial interests, one to represent agricultural interests, and one to represent labor. The Federal Board was a policy-making body in that it was authorized to make studies, investigations, and reports. The history of the early development of vocational education in the United States is interesting and illustrates how social, economic, and political forces operate to achieve national goals. This history is well-documented by Hawkins, Prosser and Wright (12), Swanson (16), and Barlow (2).

For more than forty years following the passage of the Smith-Hughes Act, the policy of the federal government in vocational education changed little. One exception was during the period of World War II; because of a critical shortage of skilled workers to produce the materials needed to mount the war effort, the federal government appropriated large sums of money for a War Production Training Program. The vocational education facilities of the public schools across the nation were used to train the manpower needed to meet this crisis.

This long-established federal-state program of cooperation for the development of vocational education is based upon three principles:

1. the development of vocational education is in the national interest because it is essential to the national economy, defense, and welfare;
2. that federal funds are necessary to stimulate and assist the states in making adequate provision for vocational education;
3. that the local schools and the states exercise control of the program through State Boards for vocational education and state plans.

Federal policy, as reflected in Vocational Education Acts beginning with the Smith-Hughes Act, through numerous acts including the George-Barden Act of 1946, placed the emphasis on the economic functions of vocational education. But President Kennedy recognized the need for changes in the federal policy, and shortly after taking office, in his message to Congress on American Education (February 20, 1961), he said:

> The National Vocational Education Acts, first enacted by Congress in 1917 and subsequently amended, have provided a program of training for industry, agriculture and other occupational areas. The basic purpose of our vocational education effort is sound and sufficiently broad to provide a basis for meeting future needs. However, the technological changes which have occurred in all occupations call for a review and re-evaluation of these acts, with a view toward their modernization. To that end, I am requesting the Secretary of Health, Education and Welfare to convene an advisory body drawn from the educational profession, labor, industry, and agriculture, as well as the lay public, together with representatives from the Departments of Agriculture and Labor, to be charged with the responsibility of reviewing and evaluating the current National Vocational Education Acts, and make recommendation for improving and redirecting the program.

On October 5, 1961, the Panel of Consultants for Vocational Education, headed by Benjamin C. Willis, then Superintendent of Schools in Chicago, was appointed. The report of the Panel titled, *Education for a Changing World of Work* (*19*), published early in 1963, had quite an impact on the general public and particularly on Congress. The new directions given vocational education as a result of the Vocational Education Act of 1963 were a direct consequence of the work of the Panel and their recommendations for the improvement of vocational and technical education.

Contributing to the work of the Panel of Consultants on Vocational Education were a number of special reports commissioned by the Panel. For example, Clark (*6*) did a study of the economic and social background of vocational education in the United States, and concluded that laws and regulations should require that vocational education and training be available for all persons and in all occupations, but that the formal school system should not attempt to offer all of this training. He further recommended that a voluntary occupational training council be organized in each community to decide which agency or institution should do what part of the comprehensive occupational educational program. Brookover and Nosow (*3*) did a sociological analysis of vocational education in the United States for the Panel; they concluded that it is not only job skills which are involved in vocational education, but attitudes, values, and life styles. Since vocational education reflects the needs of the community and the needs of the individual, and since individual self-esteem, personal adjustment, and status in the larger community are directly related in contemporary American society to the occupational structures, these crucial personal variables cannot be neglected in an analysis of the meanings of work and preparation for occupational status. Emerson (*10*) did a study for the Panel of Consultants on Vocational Education regarding technical training and emphasized the need for technicians. He saw the technical institute as the best type of institution for such training, but thought the community college was the most promising agency for large-scale expansion of technical training.

The Panel of Consultants for Vocational Education concluded that "the vocational education programs of the American educational system must be expanded and accelerated *both* to train more skilled workers and to offer young people greater opportunity to develop their talents and abilities" (*19*, p. 16). The report then went on to state

> The goals of vocational education in the United States derive from the central tenets of democracy and from a common, deep appreciation of the value and dignity of work. Vocational education aspires to aid the development of individual worth and dignity in all people regardless of their differing degrees of educability by
>
> 1. Helping them enter and find a rewarding place in the world of work;
> 2. Enabling them to advance economically and socially by virtue of their capabilities; and
> 3. Enhancing their sense of individual adequacy through release and exercise of the creative impulses latent within them.
>
> Vocational education also strives to contribute to the stability and growth of the local, state, and national economies that sustain it. Moreover, vocational education stands to serve the needs of the United States as a major world power in a time of unprecedented peril and change, strengthening its bargaining power in world markets through increased individual productivity and strengthening its system of national defense through the optimum deployment of manpower resources.

The work of the Panel of Consultants and the deliberations which followed in Congress resulted in the Vocational Education Act of 1963. For the first time since 1917 Congress had given fundamental and philosophical attention to vocational education.

Although the immediate motivation was high unemployment among untrained youth, a more far-reaching impetus was provided by the growing importance of formal preparation for employment in an increasingly technical and sophisticated economy. The Vocational Education Act of 1963 not only addressed itself to changing manpower requirements but endorsed a profound shift in the interpretation of principles of federal support for vocational education. The 1917 Act had grown out of the demands of an economy just reaching industrial maturity; its primary objective was to meet the needs of the labor market. The 1963 Act was the product of a growing sensitivity to human welfare, and its emphasis was upon the people who needed skills rather than upon the occupations which needed skilled people. In place of the previous focus on seven occupational categories as the boundaries of federally supported vocational education, the dimensions of the new Act were the employment-oriented educational needs of various population groups. Federal policy was markedly changed by the 1963 Act. The emphasis was now on people and their needs as distinguished from the earlier emphasis on occupations and manpower needs.

The authors of the Vocational Education Act of 1963, recognizing the need for flexibility in a rapidly changing society and the difficulties of reorienting institutions to keep pace with new demands, built into the act an evaluation system. One part of that evaluation process was the requirement that the Secretary of Health, Education, and Welfare appoint in 1966 an Advisory Council on Vocational Education to appraise the results of the Act and recommend administrative and legislative improvements. The Advisory Council appointed in November of 1966 was charged with the responsibility to report their findings and recommendations no later than January 1, 1968. The report of the Advisory Council (17) published under the title, *Vocational Education—The Bridge Between Man and His Work,* served as the basis for the 1968 Amendments to the Vocational Education Act of 1963. The 1968 Amendments call for a continuing National Advisory Council on Vocational Education (as well as state advisory councils).

The National Advisory Council meets at least four times a year and advises the United States Commissioner of Education on the administration and effectiveness of the broad vocational education programs mandated by the Act. The Council is also required to submit to the Secretary of Health, Education, and Welfare annual reports on its findings and recommendations for transmittal to the Congress. The Act requires that the twenty-one members of the Council be broadly representative, to include labor, management, education, and the general public (no less than one-third). Among the education specialists must be persons who are knowledgeable about administration, the problems of the handicapped and disadvantaged, and post-secondary and adult vocational programs.

Policy was made by Congress with the passage of the Education Amendments of 1972, which created a "Bureau of Occupational and Adult Education" in the United States Office of Education headed by a person in the rank of Deputy Commissioner; it also created a Community College unit as a part of this Bureau.

The Department of Labor also has considerable influence on federal policy as it relates to vocational education and manpower development. In fact, the responsibility for administering manpower training programs is shared jointly by the Secretary of Health, Education, and Welfare and the Secretary of Labor. While both of these departments are in the executive arm of government, they have a substantial impact on policy through studies and reports made to the public and to Congress. An example is the *Manpower Report of the President and a Report on Manpower Requirements, Resources, Utilization and Training,* which is an annual report to Congress prepared by the Department of Labor, as required by the Manpower Development and Training Act of 1962. The Department of Labor also contracts for studies to be done by outside agencies; for example, the Lecht study (*13*) which projects the manpower needs of the seventies in order to meet the national objectives identified by the President's Commission on National Goals.

Another significant factor in policy making on the national level is the Center for Vocational and Technical Education, financed by the U.S. Office of Education and located on the campus of The Ohio State University in Columbus. The Center's mission is "to strengthen the capacity of state education systems to provide effective occupational education programs consistent with individual needs and manpower requirements." The Center conducts research and program development activities, provides state leadership training programs, and operates an information storage, retrieval, and dissemination system for vocational and technical education through an affiliated ERIC Clearinghouse. The Center, in operation since 1965, has produced over two hundred publications on relevant problems in vocational and technical education. The research efforts of the Center have a major impact on federal policy.

National Educational Associations

Of the many educational associations which have an impact on policy relating to vocational education, the following are the most influential:

American Vocational Association (including numerous affiliates)
American Association of Community and Junior Colleges

National Education Association (including ASCD and other affiliates)
American Association of School Administrators
National Association of Secondary School Principals
American Council on Education
National Society for the Study of Education
The Council of Chief State School Officers.

The American Vocational Association (AVA), with a membership of over 50,000, has offices in Washington, D.C. Through the work of the AVA staff, with the assistance of leaders from the states, the Association has had considerable influence on federal legislation. Also, the annual AVA convention, the monthly *American Vocational Journal,* and other publications of the Association serve to constantly examine and revise policy. The Association also has, within its structure, a number of affiliates, each interested in a particular aspect of vocational education. An affiliate of special interest to administrators is the National Council of Local Administrators of Vocational Education.

The American Association of Community and Junior Colleges (AACJC) has a particular interest in post-secondary (including adult) vocational and technical education. The AACJC is an association of two-year junior and community colleges and has had considerable influence on the rapid rate of growth of such institutions and the development of occupational education programs in community colleges. The Association has a monthly *Junior College Journal* and also publishes reports which influence policy.

The National Education Association (NEA) has, until recently, shown relatively little interest in vocational education. But the Representative Assembly of the NEA in 1971 adopted the report of a task force on vocational education and passed the following resolution:

> The National Education Association believes that preparation of children for careers, vocations, and productive jobs should be a basic policy of education. Educational programs should be developed for all children which will assure equal opportunity for career and occupational development. A continuing program for training, retraining, advancement, and promotion should be provided to out-of-school youth and adults. The Association will seek legislation to provide a comprehensive national manpower development policy as the basic foundation for vocational and career education. It will also assist its affiliates in implementing similar programs and legislation.

Among the NEA affiliates which have had a significant impact on vocational education policy is the Association for Supervision and Curriculum Development.

The National Association of Secondary School Principals (NASSP) has made its position known in regard to vocational education through its meetings and publications, including *The Bulletin* of the Association's periodical. Several years ago an issue of *The Bulletin* was devoted to vocational education (May 1965, "Vocational Education—Time for Decision"). Also, in 1967 Draper *(9)* completed a study for the National Committee on Secondary Education of the NASSP in which the Committee said: "The public educational system has a basic obligation to aid the preparation of all young people for effectiveness in the world of work. The obligation is accentuated today because the transition from school to job is more difficult than it was, and vocational success is more dependent upon schooling. The nature of work is changing, and a growing proportion of jobs require a new order of competence. Since, for the foreseeable future, a high proportion of youth will enter the labor market at or before high school graduation, the secondary schools have a major responsibility."

The American Association of School Administrators (AASA) have been interested and active in vocational education policy making through discussions at their annual meetings and through publications. In 1970 they published a book by Venn *(23)* titled *Man, Education and Manpower,* a copy of which was furnished each member superintendent.

The American Council on Education published a report in 1964 titled *Man, Education and Work,* also written by Grant Venn, which had considerable impact, especially on post-secondary vocational and technical education.

The National Society for the Study of Education annually publishes a yearbook. It is interesting to note that the Fourth Yearbook (1905 Part II) dealt with *The Place of Vocational Subjects in the High School Curriculum* and the Sixth Yearbook (1907 Part I) was titled *Vocational Studies for College Entrance.* The most recent yearbook of the Society dealing with vocational education was edited by Barlow *(1)* and published in 1965.

Public school educational policy in general has been determined largely by educators. Perhaps the most powerful policy-making body in the history of public education in the United States was the Educational Policies Commission, a creature of the National Education Association and the American Association of School Administrators. The numerous reports of this Commission reflected the thinking of the "educational establishment" as it was called by Conant and others. Conant *(8,* p. 7), who served on the Commission for more than twenty years, says: "In retrospect I think it is clear that the educational establishment was not as responsive as it should have been to the changing attitudes of the public toward education." Conant recommended an interstate agency which would be responsible for planning a nationwide educational policy. Such an interstate education planning commission or "compact for education" was formed in 1965 and all but a few states participate in the Education Commission of the States (ECS).

The Education Commission of the States serves as a clearing house of legislative information but in addition does surveys and studies of interest to the states. It is concerned with elementary and secondary education and has special projects including National Assessment of Educational Progress, handicapped children's education, early childhood education, and educational technology. ECS also has a Task Force on Occupational Education in Post-Secondary Education which produced a report in 1971 titled *Vocation as "Calling."*

While traditionally educators may have dominated the policy-making function of education in general, this is not the case in regard to vocational education; noneducational groups have had considerable influence on federal vocational education policy from the beginning.

Other National Agencies

Since vocational education is closely related to the economy of our nation, it is a matter of major concern to both management and labor, as well as to education.

Representatives of labor and management have been involved from the beginning; they were members of the National Society for the Promotion of Industrial Education which influenced passage of the Smith-Hughes Act. Labor and management are represented on all national and state advisory councils. Because of this close working relationship over a long period of time, the vocational education movement in the United States has had considerable support from both labor and management. The AFL-CIO in their policy resolution passed at the 1963 convention, states: "The labor movement is in full accord that all young people must have access to job training under vocational education and under the apprenticeship programs. . . . Those young people who do not look forward to higher education must be given the opportunity to learn in their schools vocational skills which are realistically related to the needs of modern industry. Schools must treat skilled workmanship as something as worthy of our best young people as is pre-professional training." At least one national management group, the United States Chamber of Commerce, has been especially supportive of vocational and technical education as expressed in their formal policy statements and in certain specific programs which that group has undertaken.

There are a number of special interest groups which have from time to time shown interest in and concern for the problems of youth and adults as related to employment. They include the National Committee for Children and Youth, the National Committee on Employment of Youth, the National Urban League, the National Committee for the Support of Public

Schools, the National Conference of Parents and Teachers, the National School Public Relations Association, the National School Boards Association, and the Association of State Boards of Education.

There are a number of national independent, nonprofit organizations devoted to research, education, and publication on major and emerging issues of national importance. For example, in 1966 the Brookings Institution prepared and published a paper on the critical issues in the development of vocational education. The National Planning Association is another example; the Center for Priority Analysis of the National Planning Association has done studies aimed at identifying priority areas for planning vocational and technical education programs. The W. E. Upjohn Institute for Employment Research has done many studies and has published numerous reports on problems relating to the further development of vocational education and manpower training.

There are several foundations which have had an impact on policy relating to vocational education. The Ford Foundation has allocated funds for innovative programs in vocational and technical education and for research, including the Center for Studies in Vocational and Technical Education at the University of Wisconsin. The Foundation has been especially interested in the improvement of vocational-technical teacher training. The Carnegie Corporation of New York has supported a number of vocational education projects, including the University of Michigan Leadership Development Program for the training of local administrators of vocational and technical education. The Kellogg Foundation of Battle Creek has been especially interested in vocational education for the health occupations.

Federal Legislation

A review of policy and policy making in regard to vocational and technical education in the United States clearly indicates the significant influence of the federal government. Even though the Constitution of the United States makes no provision for federal support or control of education, Congress has for more than a hundred years considered it in the national interest to give support to vocational education. Beginning with the Morrill Act in 1862, which established land grant colleges aimed at preparing people for the "agricultural and mechanical arts," the federal government has had an enduring interest in vocational and technical education. The most significant federal legislation during this century can be summarized as follows:

1917 *The Smith-Hughes Act* provided a continuing appropriation for vocational education in agriculture, in trades and industry, in homemaking, and for teacher training in each of these fields.

1929 *The George-Reed Act* authorized additional funds for vocational home economics and vocational agricultural education.

1934 *The George-Ellzey Act* extended the provisions of the Smith-Hughes and George-Reed Acts.

1937 *The George-Deen Act* extended the earlier acts to include distributive education.

1946 *The George-Barden Act* authorized increased appropriations for programs specified in earlier acts and provided more flexibility in the use of these funds.

1963 *The Vocational Education Act of 1963* was enacted (1) to extend programs previously authorized and to develop new programs, (2) to encourage research and experimentation, and (3) to provide work-study programs to encourage youth to continue in vocational programs. The act also authorized funds for the construction of area vocational facilities.

1968 *The Vocational Education Amendments of 1968* authorized federal grants to the states to assist them to maintain, extend, and improve existing programs of vocational education, to develop new programs of vocational education, and to provide part-time employment for youths who need the earnings from such employment to continue their vocational training on a full-time basis, so that persons of all ages in all communities of the State—those in high school, those who have completed or discontinued their formal education and are preparing to enter the labor market, those who have already entered the labor market but need to upgrade their skills or learn new ones, those with special educational handicaps, and those in post-secondary schools—will have ready access to vocational training or retraining which is of high quality, which is realistic in the light of actual or anticipated opportunities for gainful employment, and which is suited to their needs, interests, and ability to benefit from such training.

1972 *The Education Amendments of 1972* created a Bureau of Occupational and Adult Education in the U.S. Office of Education, which includes a community college unit.

The Vocational Education Act of 1963 was significantly different from earlier vocational education legislation in that it shifted the earlier emphasis on occupations and manpower needs to a new emphasis on people and their needs. Furthermore, the Vocational Education Amendments of 1968 gave special attention and priority to certain categories of people with special needs—the disadvantaged and the handicapped. The 1968 Amendments also specified that a minimum of 15 percent of the funds allotted to a state

shall be used only "for vocational education for persons who have completed or left high school and are available for study in preparation for
entering the labor market." This provision assures a significant role for
technical institutes, community colleges, and four-year technical colleges.

Federal Control

There is evidence to suggest that the federal
government, through legislative subventions, has had a significant influence
on educational policy, especially as it relates to vocational and technical
education. But there is also some evidence to suggest that there has been
a shift of power. The Act of 1963 and the Amendments of 1968 have given
the states considerably more flexibility in program planning and, in addition, these acts have given policy-making power to the states through the
requirement that each state establish a state advisory council for vocational
education, which is separate and independent from the state board of education, with membership broadly representative of business, industry, labor,
and education in the state.

The states have assumed a more dynamic role in policy making for
reasons other than those provided in federal legislation. State and local
funding of vocational education has increased to a point where these units
of government are not as dependent upon the federal government as they
once were. Also, states and local communities have developed professional
personnel who are qualified to give the kind of leadership needed to exercise
a significant role in policy making.

It is our position that there needs to be a balance of power in policy
making as it affects vocational and technical education, but that the major
responsibility should rest with the local units of government; these local
units, however, should be large enough to serve most of the educational
needs of the community. The role of the states should be to ensure a
coordinated state-wide program of vocational and technical education services related to the total needs of the state and to give leadership in the
development of new and innovative programs to meet these needs.

Relationship of Federal
Government and the States in
Policy Making

The federal government publishes regulations
for the administration of vocational education programs under the provisions of the Federal Vocational Education Acts. Every vocational adminis-

trator knows about *Vocational Education Bulletin No. 1, Administration of Vocational Education—Rules and Regulations (18)*. Regulations more recent than the last edition of this bulletin are published in the *Federal Register*. (For regulations resulting from the 1968 Amendments, see *Federal Register* 35, No. 91 (May 9, 1970), Part II, Dept. of HEW, Office of Education, "State Vocational Education Programs.")

These documents include the regulations which govern programs operating under the Vocational Education Act of 1963 and Amendments of 1968 for youth and adults leading to useful employment in any occupation which is not generally considered to be professional and which does not require a baccalaureate or higher degree. Regulations regarding the administration of other federal laws pertaining to vocational education, such as the Manpower Development and Training Act and the National Vocational Student Loan Insurance Act of 1965 appear in other publications. The documents referred to include only the federal laws and regulations relating to the administration of vocational education programs in states and territories operated by a state board for vocational education under a state plan for vocational education. Grant Venn's foreword to *Vocational Education Bulletin No. 1* states:

> Although regulations are necessary in administering a program of vocational education, effective planning requires that persons responsible for vocational education consider factors other than these regulations. Some factors significant in operating an effective program of vocational education are: (1) employing highly qualified and efficient personnel; (2) relating the program directly to employment opportunities and needs of youth and adults for opportunities in vocational education; (3) analyzing occupations as to the bases of specific course content; (4) providing needed facilities and equipment; (5) allowing sufficient time for instruction to develop skills and judgment for the accepted levels of performance in the student's chosen occupation; and (6) evaluating and continual revising of the program; as well as (7) engaging in needed research; and (8) cooperating with interested groups. (*18*, p. vi)

Any state desiring to receive federal funds under these Acts is required to designate or create by state law a state board (of not less than three members) having all necessary power to cooperate with the United States Office of Education in the administration of the state plan.

STATE PLANS

The federal Vocational Education Acts require that any state desiring to receive the amount for which it is eligible under the Acts shall submit a state plan, which is approved by the United States Commissioner of Education if it meets the criteria specified. The state plan must be prepared in consultation with the state advisory council for that state and designate the state board as the sole agency for administration of the state plan. A public hearing of the plan is required and all statements of general policies, rules, regulations, and procedures issued by the state board must be made available to the public. The plan must set forth in detail the policies and procedures to be followed by the state in the distribution of funds to local educational agencies and for the use of such funds. The state plan must include provisions regarding (1) evaluations of local and state programs in light of needs and job opportunities; (2) minimum qualifications for teachers, supervisors, and administrators; and (3) cooperative arrangements with the system of public employment offices of the state and other agencies, organizations, and institutions concerned with manpower needs and job opportunities, such as institutions of higher education, model city, business, labor, and community action organizations. The guidelines are quite specific yet comprehensive. The state plan must give assurance that funds will not be used for any program of vocational education which cannot be demonstrated to prepare students for employment, or be necessary to prepare individuals for successful completion of such a program, or be of significant assistance to individuals enrolled in making an informed and meaningful occupational choice.

The state plan is, in effect, a contract between the state and federal government describing how the state will use the funds allocated to it and giving assurance that funds will be used in conformity with the requirements of the federal acts. Each state has a plan, and no two are alike. Consequently, we have in reality fifty different state programs of vocational education, rather than one federal program. This cooperative arrangement between the federal government and the states has been in existence since 1917 and is sometimes identified as a model for other federally supported programs.

State plans are generally made available to local administrators and to students of administration. In some states, because of the legalistic form, an administrative guide or manual is used to interpret it for local administrators. The student of administration of vocational and technical education will want to become familiar with the federal requirements for state plans and the plan for his state.

FEDERAL-STATE RELATIONSHIPS

The federal Vocational Education Acts make it mandatory that the programs be administered by the states through the state board as presribed in the state plan. Consequently, the federal government since 1917 has been careful to work with and through the states and not become involved with local educational agencies. The one exception to this is in the 1968 Amendments, Part C, where provision is made for "Research and Training in

Vocational Education." Under the provisions of this section, the United States Commissioner of Education may use fifty percent of the funds "to make grants to and contracts with institutions of higher education, public and private agencies and institutions, state boards, and, *with the approval of the appropriate state board,* to local educational agencies in that state. . . ." (italics added). The purpose of this part of the Act is to promote research and development projects and to test research findings through demonstration and pilot programs.

The State's Role in Policy Making

The U.S. Constitution makes no provision for federal support or control of education. But Article X of the Bill of Rights states: "The powers not delegated to the United States by the Constitution, nor prohibited by it to the states, are reserved to the states respectively, or to the people." Education is now generally recognized to be a state responsibility. Most state constitutions have sections devoted to education in which the legislature is charged with the responsibility of establishing and maintaining a system of free public education. School districts are a creation of the state and derive their powers from the state legislature.

While the United States government for more than a hundred years has enormously influenced the development of our educational system through land grants and appropriation of money for the individual states, Congress does not have the power to determine a total national educational policy without a revision of the Constitution. Although Congress and the federal government have had considerable influence on vocational education in the several states, this area of education is no less a state responsibility than any other facet of public education. Through federal subventions a federal-state partnership has been created which permits the states to tailor their vocational and technical programs to fit the state's conditions and needs.

Policy in regard to vocational education is developed and formalized at all three levels of government. As we have seen, the federal government has been very active in vocational education and therefore may have taken some initiative away from the states. But state governments cannot abdicate their responsibility for any one area of education. While vocational education is important to the nation because it contributes to our national security, economic welfare, and social mobility, it is equally important to the states for the same reasons.

THE STATE GOVERNMENT AND VOCATIONAL EDUCATION

In a sense the legislature of each state is the "big school board" responsible for policy in that state. It is at this level that all the forces—social, economic, and political—are brought to bear on educational problems and policy. The legislature has the final decision on basic policy questions regarding the public schools of the state.

Nearly all states have state boards of education and all states wishing to participate in the federal support for vocational education have a state board for vocational education. In many states the state board of education is also designated the state board for vocational education. The state boards for vocational education have full responsibility for the administration of vocational education in the states and for the supervision of its administration by local educational agencies. These boards perform policy making roles by filling in the general directives of federal and state legislation. They also oversee the administrative operations in state departments of education, and in most states the administration of vocational education is an integral part of the total public school program.

The state department of education may exert considerable influence on vocational education policy making, not only through the work of its professional staff, but also through the efforts of lay and professional advisory committees appointed by the department. Other departments in state government may be involved in policy making, including departments of labor, agriculture, commerce, and economic development.

OTHER STATE ORGANIZATIONS

Most of the national educational associations discussed earlier in this chapter have their counterparts on the state level. Educational organizations on the state level frequently play vigorous roles in policy making; for this reason it is important that each state have a strong and unified state vocational association through which all vocational teachers and administrators can have an impact on policy. The vocational administrator should become acquainted with and seek membership in the state council of vocational education administrators, which, in most states, is affiliated with the National Council of Local Administrators of Vocational Education.

The vocational administrator should not overlook the impact of labor and management organizations on vocational education policy in the state; in many states the State Chamber of Commerce and the state AFL-CIO are very much interested in vocational education and have a significant role in policy making. Groups representing parents and taxpayers also can be influential, as well as groups interested in a particular segment of the economy, such as agriculture, tourism, or retail sales. These special interest groups seldom initiate policies but are often instrumental in changing or vetoing suggested policies.

State policy can also be influenced by governmental agencies' studies, state advisory councils, colleges and universities, or by private research firms. Examples of such studies are numerous, but one done by Little (*14*) for the California State Board of Education deserves special mention.

THE ROLE OF THE STATE ADVISORY COUNCIL

The Vocational Education Act of 1963, as amended, requires that each state which desires to receive funds from the Act establish a state advisory council to be appointed by the governor or the state board for vocational education (if the members of such board are elected), and that the advisory council be separate and independent from the state board. It is also mandatory that the state advisory council membership be broadly representative of the various interests, including at least one person representing each of the following: (1) state industrial and economic development agencies; (2) community colleges, area vocational schools, technical institutes, and post-secondary or adult education agencies; (3) local educational agencies; (4) school boards; (5) manpower and vocational education agencies; (6) school systems with large concentrations of disadvantaged students; and (7) the general public. Membership must also include at least one person knowledgeable in each of the following areas: (1) vocational needs and problems of management and labor; (2) administration of state and local vocational education programs; (3) vocational education, but *not* involved in administration; (4) vocational and technical education including programs in comprehensive high schools; (5) special education needs of handicapped persons.

The function of the state advisory council is to advise the state board on the development of the state plan and on policy matters arising in the administration of the state plan, to evaluate programs, services and activities under the state plan, and to publish and distribute reports on their evaluations, including an annual report with recommendations for changes warranted by the evaluation. State advisory councils are required to conduct at least one open meeting each year when the public is given the opportunity to express views concerning vocational education.

Each state advisory council submits its annual budget to Washington and appropriated funds go directly to the councils from the United States Office of Education to be used at the sole discretion of the councils for the employment of staff and for evaluations and studies.

State advisory councils have been organized in all fifty states and range in size from twelve to thirty-five with an average of twenty members. Councils are free to organize as they wish and to determine the particular problems or areas which most need to be studied and evaluated. The state council is free to evaluate any facet of the state's programs, services, or activities. The council reports to the state board which must act upon the council's recommendations by either (1) accepting or (2) rejecting them. If rejected by the state board, the council's recommendations must be returned to them immediately.

It is obvious that a state advisory council for vocational education consisting of influential members, representing diversified educational and economic interests, with a budget to hire staff and to do independent studies and evaluations, can have considerable power in the development of policy regarding vocational education in the state.

An Example of a State Policy

The Michigan State Board of Education adopted a policy statement in 1971 titled *The Common Goals of Michigan Education*. These goals were developed by a Task Force consisting of students, teachers, administrators, local school board members, and other laymen. The tentative policy statement developed by the Task Force was then reviewed at public meetings held at twenty-five locations all over the state before final adoption by the State Board of Education. The statement lists and defines three goal areas:

I. *Citizenship and Morality* which includes goals dealing with (1) morality, (2) citizenship and social responsibility, (3) rights and responsibilities of students.

II. *Democracy and Equal Opportunity* which includes goals on (1) equality of educational opportunity, (2) education of non-English-speaking persons, (3) education of exceptional persons, (4) allocation of financial resources, (5) parental participation, and (6) community participation.

III. *Student Learning* which includes the following goals: (1) basic skills, (2) preparation for a changing society, (3) career preparation, (4) creative, constructive, and critical thinking, (5) sciences, arts, and humanities, (6) physical and mental well-being, (7) self-worth, (8) social skills and understanding, (9) occupational skills, (10) preparation for family life, (11) environmental quality, (12) economic understanding, (13) continuing education.

Goals 3 and 9 from the student learning area are particularly relevant to vocational and technical education; they are defined in the policy statement as follows:

> Goal 3—*Career Preparation.* Michigan education must provide for each individual the opportunity to select and prepare for a career of his choice consistent to the optimum degree with his capabilities, aptitudes, and desires, and the needs of society. Toward this end, he should be afforded, on a progressive basis, the necessary evaluation of his progress and aptitudes, together with the effective counseling regarding alternatives available, the steps necessary to realize each of these alternatives, and the

possible consequences of his choice. In addition, each individual should be exposed, as early and as fully as possible, to the adult working world and to such adult values as will enable more thoughtful and meaningful decisions as to career choice and preparation.

Goal 9—*Occupational Skills.* Michigan education must provide for the development of the individual's marketable skills so that a student is assisted in the achievement of his career goals by adequate preparation in areas which require competence in occupational skills.

Policy Making
on the Local Level

There are at least six classes of individuals involved in formulating vocational education policy at the local level: boards of education, the professionals (teachers and administrators), students, parents and qualified voters, local civic leaders, and business and industrial leaders (both labor and management). Education in general and education for work in particular can no longer be considered a function which can be delegated solely to those who staff our schools; it is a community function and responsibility. Consequently, policy making for schools, and especially for vocational programs, has transcended school government and has been thrust into the arena of general government. To the extent that educational problems become interwoven with other community problems, mayors, councilmen, and other civic and industrial leaders become interested and assume responsibilities. Vocational education, if properly conceived, organized, and administered, is related to many community problems, including school dropouts and delinquency, poverty and unemployment, student unrest and rebellion, and racial relations. The interrelationships between the school and the community are discussed in chapter 13.

For too long education has been thought of as being outside the realm of politics. For this reason it has operated in a completely separate system of local government and efforts have been made to keep it as far from political control as possible. But since education is a public concern, and all policy matters relating to it come within the purview of political bodies representative of the citizens who support the schools, the administrator of vocational education programs cannot remain outside the political arena.

THE BOARD OF EDUCATION

Vocational education policy on the local level must obviously be formalized by the elected representatives of the people—the board of education.

The local board is a creation of the state and is governed by state laws. If a local school board wishes to participate in programs supported by the federal Vocational Education Acts, its actions must also be guided by the state policies governing the administration of the acts. While the board must carry out its policy making function within the framework of federal and state statutes, it must also look to the immediate community for inputs. These will come from other community agencies and organizations and leaders in the community, but the most substantial policy making information should come from the board's professional staff of administrators and teachers.

ADMINISTRATIVE STAFF

In principle the board of education makes policy and the staff executes the policy. According to this theory, policy making and administration are separate functions and the policy maker should not get involved in administration; neither should the administrator make policy. The principle is frequently violated but the problem is to find ways in which the administrator, on the one hand, can contribute to sound policy development for education and, on the other hand, make it possible for the public to review administrative practices and procedures.

The tendency has been for the chief school administrator to recommend to the board policies which he and his staff had developed in response to a recognized community educational problem or need. All too often little opportunity has been given relevant groups to provide inputs. The leader in administration of vocational education programs will seek information not only from reference groups within the schools—teachers, students, supervisors—but he will also seek the results of research. Also he will interact with concerned community groups so that he might better understand the problems or issues and therefore be of greater assistance to his board of education in making policy decisions.

Teachers and students are demanding the opportunity to participate in the governance of schools, which includes the process of policy formulation. Teachers' unions (and now student unions) are evidence of the need for these groups to participate significantly in the important decisions affecting education.

TEACHERS

That teachers are demanding a greater voice in policy making is quite evident. The role of the teacher must be redefined to include participation in the policy making process. The expertise of teachers must be recognized and utilized on the secondary and community college levels as it has been on the college and university levels. It should not be limited to informal arrangements initiated in isolated situations by administrators. Provision for faculty input should be built into the policy making structure of the school and community. This can be achieved, in part at least, by establishing more effective relationships between administrators and teacher organizations in which teachers can participate effectively and responsibly.

STUDENTS

While students are interested in exercising more control over their environment, high school students are more concerned about control of the internal affairs of the schools. This may be caused by a feeling that they have relatively little influence in the power structure outside the schools. Post-secondary students are more likely to feel that they have some control over both the internal and the external environment, especially where the legal age-of-majority is now eighteen. The vocational administrator should be aware of the students' potential for power in the community and should seek inputs from student groups in the development of educational policies. Students should also be invited to serve on committees of faculty and administration where policy matters are being considered.

Traditionally, school administrators have made a pretense at student involvement through various forms of student government. In many high schools, however, students have not been allowed to deal with problems of real concern to them, some of which might serve to alter basic educational policies. In one high school all members of the student council resigned and formed a student union which operates outside the framework of the school government. It is interesting to note that one of the problems identified by the newly formed student union is the need for more relevant programs for employment-bound students. The appointment by the board of education of a student advisory committee is another way of providing student input to the policy making process.

PARENTS AND VOTERS

Next to students and the professional staff, parents are the group most directly involved with education. They generally have a deep interest in the kind and quality of education their own children and grandchildren are receiving, but they may also be asked, from time to time, to vote for millage issues for the support of the schools. While parent and taxpayer groups seldom initiate policy matters relating to education, they do have the power to influence boards of education on issues under consideration.

The school administrator who wishes to exercise educational leadership in his community will encourage the formation of parent and taxpayer groups and will become involved in their activities. Too often parent and taxpayer groups are formed outside the school structure in reaction to a particular situation or issue, and operate without the information which school personnel could supply.

COMMUNITY LEADERS

The community is an interdependent social system with many forces at work influencing social policy, including education. While the board of education is charged with responsibility of taking formal action on school policy matters, the members of the board may be influenced by community leaders in government, business, industry, the professions, and others interested in community affairs.

The literature on the power structure of the community suggests that policy decisions regarding schools are not always made by the members of the board of education. There may be key people in the community who make the decisions and instruct the board members how to vote. In some communities there is a monolithic power structure of a small group of leaders who must legitimize any policy or program before action is taken by official bodies, while in other communities the power is diffused among competing power groups. The school administrator should study the power structure of his community so that he knows who the opinion leaders are and who influences policy decisions. The vocational administrator should establish a working relationship with some of these community leaders, especially those concerned with business and industry and the welfare of those employed in these enterprises.

LOCAL POLICY REGARDING VOCATIONAL EDUCATION

What is the policy of your community school—high school or community college—as to its role and responsibility in the education of youth and adults for employment? Has the policy been formally adopted and when was it last reaffirmed? Should the policy be reexamined and possibly restated in light of present conditions and needs?

The experience of the authors suggests that local policy statements regarding the goals and broad purposes of public education are frequently vague and meaningless. Often they are not the product of thoughtful consideration by school personnel and community groups, but rather they consist of hackneyed phrases often taken from policy statements which were developed by others in a different setting.

REFERENCES

1. Barlow, Melvin L., ed. National Society for the Study of Education. *Vocational Education Sixty-fourth Yearbook Part I.* Chicago: University of Chicago Press, 1965.

2. Barlow, Melvin L. *History of Industrial Education in the United States.* Peoria, Illinois: Chas. A. Bennet, 1967.

3. Brookover, Wilbur and Sigmund Nosow. "A Sociological Analysis of Vocational Education in the United States." *Education for a Changing World of Work—Appendix III.* Washington, D.C.: United States Government Printing Office, 1963.

4. Campbell, Roald F., Edwin M. Bridges, John E. Corbally, Jr., Raphael O. Nystrand, and John A. Ramseyer. *Introduction to Educational Administration.* Boston: Allyn and Bacon, 1971.

5. Campbell, Roald F. and Donald H. Layton. *Policy Making for American Education.* Chicago: Midwest Administration Center, 1969.

6. Clark, Harold F. "The Economic and Social Background of Vocational Education in the United States." *Education for a Changing World of Work—Appendix III.* Washington, D.C.: United States Government Printing Office, 1963.

7. Clary, Joseph Ray. *Review and Synthesis of Research and Developmental Activities Concerning State Advisory Councils on Vocational Education.* Columbus, Ohio: ERIC Clearinghouse on Vocational and Technical Education, 1970.

8. Conant, James B. *Shaping Educational Policy.* New York: McGraw-Hill, 1964.

9. Draper, Dale C. *Educating for Work.* A Report of The National Committee on Secondary Education of the National Association of Secondary School Principals. Washington, D.C.: The Association, 1967.

10. Emerson, Lynn A. "Technical Training in the United States." *Education for a Changing World of Work—Appendix I.* Washington, D.C.: United States Government Printing Office, 1963.

11. Hamlin, Herbert M. *Public School Education in Agriculture—A Guide to Policy and Policy Making.* Danville, Illinois: Interstate, 1962.

12. Hawkins, Layton S., Charles A. Prosser and John C. Wright. *Development of Vocational Education.* Chicago: American Technical Society, 1951.

13. Lecht, Leonard A. *Goals, Priorities, and Dollars—The Next Decade.* New York: Free Press, 1966.

14. Little, Arthur D., Inc. *A Policy and System Study of California Vocational Education.* Sacramento, California: California State Board of Education, 1970.

15. *Report of the Commission on National Aid to Vocational Education.* Washington, D.C.: United States Government Printing Office, 1914. Vol. I.

16. Swanson, J. Chester. *Development of Federal Legislation for Vocational Education.* Prepared for the Panel of Consultants on Vocational Education. Chicago: American Technical Society, 1962.

17. United States Department of Health, Education and Welfare. *Vocational Education—The Bridge Between Man and His Work.* General Report of the Advisory Council on Vocational Education. Washington, D.C.: United States Government Printing Office, 1968.

18. United States Department of Health, Education and Welfare. *Administration of Vocational Education—Rules and Regulations.* Vocational Education Bulletin, No. 1, Revised 1966. Washington, D.C.: United States Government Printing Office, 1966.

19. United States Department of Health, Education and Welfare. *Education for a Changing World of Work.* Washington, D.C.: United States Government Printing Office, 1963.

20. United States Department of Labor. *Occupational Outlook Handbook 1972–73 Edition.* (Published every two years) Washington, D.C.: United States Government Printing Office, 1972.

21. United States Department of Labor. *Manpower Report of the President and a Report on Manpower Requirements, Resources, Utilization, and Training.* Washington, D.C.: United States Government Printing Office. Annual Report, 1973.

22. United States Senate. *Notes and Working Papers Concerning the Administration of Programs Authorized Under the Vocational Education Act of 1963, Public Law 88-210, As Amended.* Prepared for the Subcommittee on Education of the Committee on Labor and Welfare, United States Senate. Washington, D.C., March, 1968.

23. Venn, Grant. *Man, Education and Manpower.* Washington, D.C.: American Association of School Administrators, 1970.

24. Wenrich, Ralph C. *Review and Synthesis of Research on the Administration of Vocational and Technical Education.* Columbus, Ohio: ERIC Clearinghouse on Vocational and Technical Education, 1970.

Part II   **FOUNDATIONS
OF
ADMINISTRATION
AND
SUPERVISION**

Chapter 4 ORGANIZATIONAL CONCEPTS

Public vocational and technical education programs are generally operated in schools or colleges. The successful administrator of vocational programs should understand the characteristics of these organizations and how to improve organizational performance. In this chapter we will define some of the terms and concepts used in organization and describe the results of research efforts in this field. We will also identify some organizational issues which affect vocational and technical education. For this and the next chapter we have drawn heavily upon the work of social scientists who have studied organizational effectiveness and administrative leadership in all types of organizations, including schools.

The purposes of this chapter are to help the reader:

1. to understand organization as an important administrative function;
2. to understand the important characteristics of social organizations and how they function;
3. to see the school as a social organization—a social system within a larger system and with its subsystems;
4. to understand how organizations can be structured to increase their effectiveness;

5. to see how schools might be structured or restructured to enhance the vocational and technical programs offered.

Organization as used here has two meanings: (1) that which is organized (a body of persons united for a special purpose) and (2) the process of organizing. We will discuss organization as a process first so that the reader might see more clearly the relationship to other administrative functions. We will then discuss some characteristics of social organizations, different concepts of organizations, and some emerging practices growing out of these concepts. We will conclude the chapter with the identification of some organizational problems or issues which interfere with the development of vocational and technical education.

Organization as a Function of Administration

Organization and administration are interrelated and interdependent processes or functions. The two terms are often used together (as in the title of a course or textbook) as if they represented quite different and unrelated concepts. The authors consider "organization" to be an important administrative function and therefore the term "administration" encompasses organization. When organization is considered as a process or function it applies to those activities designed to develop a structure or organism through which desired outcomes (purposes) can be achieved. It includes (1) the organization of the work to be accomplished, such as clear definition of purposes and identification of tasks to be performed, and (2) the organization of the people to accomplish the work. These are clearly administrative functions. This process of organizing the activities of people for specific purposes is one meaning of organization.

Organization then is one phase of the process of effectively accomplishing the purposes of a social system; the other phase of this process is administration. The organizational phase deals with the development of a plan or structure through which the purpose can be realized. The administrative phase of purpose achievement is concerned with the conduct, operation, control, and management of the enterprise (as organized) so that the purposes continue to be achieved. Thus the two phases complement each other. The school administrator is responsible for *both* phases and, in practice, he combines the two concepts into "administration."

Organization, according to Griffith, et al., is

> that function of administration which attempts to relate and ultimately
> fuse the purposes of an institution and the people who comprise its work-
> ing parts. It is the continuously developing plan which defines the job, and

shows how it can be efficiently and effectively accomplished by people functioning in a certain social environment. (*7*, p. 10)

Social organizations can be compared to biological organisms; in this context, the study of organization can be compared to the study of anatomy, and administration to physiology. Just as anatomy and physiology are interrelated so are organizational structures and administrative processes.

Too little attention has been given by school administrators to the *structuring* (or restructuring) of the work situation, often resulting in failure to satisfy the purposes of the organization. There is a tendency to work within awkward and obsolete administrative structures rather than to reexamine and redesign these structures. Gardner, in discussing the topic "How to Prevent Organizational Dry Rot," said that organizations seeking continuous renewal must have a fluid internal structure.

> Obviously, no complex modern organization can exist without structural arrangements of divisions, branches, departments, and so forth. I'm not one of those who imagine that the modern world can get away from specialization. Specialization and division of labor are at the heart of modern organization. . . . But jurisdictional boundaries tend to get set in concrete. Pretty soon no solution to a problem is seriously considered if there is any danger that it will threaten jurisdictional lines. But these lines aren't sacred. They were established in some past time to achieve certain objectives. Perhaps the objectives are still valid, perhaps not. Most organizations have a structure that was designed to solve problems that no longer exist. (*4*, pp. 20–22)

The administrative structures used in many schools and colleges were designed years ago, probably when the institutions were first organized; even though the purposes of these schools and the character and needs of the student body may have changed, the structures remain essentially the same. Many years ago, Walter Cocking, then editor of a magazine for general school administrators, said that school administrators tend to accept school organization as "fixed and unchangeable."

Organizational Characteristics

We are a society of organizations, each structured to achieve a specific goal or goals. Bennis has defined organizations as "complex goal-seeking units" (*2*, p. 223). The behavioral scientists have done considerable research on problems relating to organizations; although most of the applied research has been done in organizations other than schools, the generalizations may be equally applicable to educational institutions.

Pfiffner and Sherwood have defined organization as follows:

> Organization is the pattern of ways in which large numbers of people, too many to have face-to-face contact with all others, and engaged in a complexity of tasks, relate themselves to each other in the conscious, systematic establishment and accomplishment of mutually agreed purposes. (*12,* p. 30)

This definition includes the following elements: (1) "large numbers of people"—a small number might be called a group but not an organization; (2) "complexity of tasks," which results in task specialization; (3) "conscious" and "systematic," are words implying rationality, and (4) "purpose."

Organizations have goals or purposes toward which the activities of the people in them are directed. They also have individuals in offices or roles, each responsible for definite tasks. In more permanent types of organizations, such as schools, the roles are more stable than the occupants themselves, resulting in a *structured* social organization. Organizational structures can be defined as those patterns of behavior in the organization that are relatively stable and that change slowly.

We think of organizations as more or less self-contained units (such as high schools or community colleges). But organizations are usually a part of a larger social system and are made up of a number of subsystems. The school, for example, can be considered a social organization which is a part of the local school system, which, in turn, is a part of the state school system. Also, the school is made up of subsystems, such as the student personnel services subsystem, the instructional subsystem, and the managerial subsystem; each of these subsystems might be composed of small work groups or social systems. Every individual in the organization interacts with others in his immediate group or social system, but he may also interact with persons in the larger system of which his unit is a part. Thus, the individual occupies a role (or roles) in a work group, within an organization, within a culture. Griffiths illustrated the levels at which the individual may interact within the organization and with the supporting culture or environment by a series of circles with one point of tangency, indicating the interaction involved. See figure 4–1.

Organizations then are social systems (sometimes called *social* organizations or *human* organizations) made up of people who occupy various positions or offices. These positions are arranged to show the relationship to each other. This hierarchy of superordinate-subordinate relationships serves to facilitate the allocation of roles and resources in order to achieve the goals of the organization. Any given position is the location of one individual or class of individuals within the social system. The way people behave in these positions depends in part on how they think they are expected to behave; but their behavior is also influenced by the expectations of others. These expectations go to make up "roles" in the organization.

Organizational structure is the instrument by which members of an organization together with their *clients outside of the organization* arrive at mutual goals and ways of achieving them. Two aspects of organizational structures—formal and informal—will now be considered.

FORMAL ASPECTS OF ORGANIZATION

The formal organization is the official organization, generally designed by those in authority. It consists of the roles and relationships of the persons in the organization as prescribed by management.

Formal organization theory has its roots in the period of the industrial revolution when work organizations expanded rapidly in both size and complexity. The industrial organizations of that era considered man as a machine. The traditional organizational theory was the "machine model" which views workers as automatons. The basic unit of organization is the position, which is made up of tasks to be performed by a single worker. In studying formal organizations, the position or job is the important element and personalities filling these positions or jobs are to be ignored. People

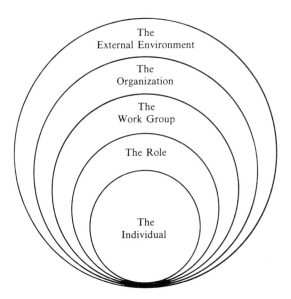

FIGURE 4-1

THE INTERACTION OF THE INDIVIDUAL WITH THE SEVERAL LEVELS
OF THE ORGANIZATION AND THE EXTERNAL ENVIRONMENT

Adapted from Daniel E. Griffiths, "Administrative Theory and Change in Organizations," in *Innovation in Education,* ed. Matthew B. Miles (New York: Bureau of Publications, Teachers College, Columbia University, 1964). Copyright 1964 by Teachers College, Columbia University.

must adapt themselves to organizational needs and those unable to meet the demands of their jobs should be replaced. Under the machine model leaders are chosen on the basis of merit and they are expected to direct and supervise the efforts of production workers. The machine model was derived from autocratic institutions such as the military, the Roman Catholic Church, and industrial firms. The flavor was authoritarian and organizations were characterized by the use of terms such as command, control, authority, direction, and communication through channels.

Any consideration of the formal organization must include the work of Weber (*18*) who was one of the first scholars to examine the relationship of structure to the achievement of the goals of large organizations. Weber considered the bureaucracy model the most efficient form of organization devised by man. It had the following characteristics:

1. *Emphasis on form*—fixed and official jurisdictional areas, governed by rules, regulations and policies
2. *The concept of hierarchy*—levels of authority that insure a system of super- and sub-ordination with each office or position under the control and supervision of a higher one
3. *Specialization of task*—incumbents are chosen on the basis of merit and ability to perform specialized aspects of a total operation
4. *A specified sphere of activity*—clear delineation of the various specializations and relationships to be observed between them
5. *Established norms of conduct*—written documents setting forth policies and procedures to be followed by individual actors in the organization
6. *Records*—administrative acts and decisions are made a matter of record to insure predictability in performance within the bureaucracy.

Weber's Model was a kind of ideal type of bureaucracy which he thought might function rationally to serve some of the complexities of large scale organizational activity. The Weber Model was based on the assumption that man had to be a free agent—free in the sense that the master-slave relationship was definitely inappropriate.

While Weber's concepts have been criticized by many, including social scientists, most organizational research recognizes the fact that organizations traditionally have been designed along the lines of the Weber Model; schools are no exceptions.

The formal structure represents the deliberate intent of management to prescribe the processes that will take place among the members of the organization. In the typical work organization this takes the form of a definition of task specialities, arranged in levels of authority, with clearly defined lines of communication from one level to the next. It is a kind of official administrative blueprint of the intentions of the designers. It is never fully realized in the behavior of its members.

INFORMAL ASPECTS OF ORGANIZATION

The informal or operating structure of an organization refers to the unplanned, informal set of groups, friendships, and attachments that inevitably develop when people are placed in regular proximity to one another. The relationships which grow out of the personal needs of members are not fully accounted for by the formal organization. In fact, these behaviors and attitudes have no place in the formal plan; officially, they do not exist. Yet they have a significant effect on the total organizational effort.

Pfiffner and Sherwood (13) analyzed and synthesized the formal and informal aspects of organizations in "The Concept of Overlays," starting with the typical organization chart or diagram—the job-task pyramid. This is the official version of the organization in which task specialities are defined, arranged in levels of authority, and lines of communication defined. The actual processes of interactions among the individuals represented in this formal plan will vary from the plan because co-existing with the formal structure are other ways individuals interact in the organization. These have been defined and isolated by behavioral scientists, but in reality they never function quite so distinctly; they are intermixed in an organization, which also follows to a large extent its formal structure. Pfiffner and Sherwood suggest that these overlays or modifying processes must be studied one at a time but we must never forget their "togetherness." The overlays are:

1. The sociometric network
2. The system of functional contacts
3. The grid of decision-making centers
4. The pattern of power
5. The channels of communication.

The idea that these five processes are overlays upon the conventional job-task pyramid is not to imply that the formal organization is unimportant or can be ignored, although much of the research might give this impression. The overlay approach recognizes that there is a formal structure of superordinate–subordinate relationships but that organization *also* consists of a wide variety of informal relationships. The actual operating organization may be significantly different from the formal organization.

The *sociometric overlay* recognizes the fact that in any organization there is a set of relationships among people which is purely social in nature. There are desired relations (people's preferences regarding interaction they want with others) and rejected relations (interaction with other people in the organization which are not wanted). These social relationships can be represented graphically on a sociometric chart. When this network of social relationships (or sociogram) is superimposed on the formal organization chart, it will inevitably alter it.

The *functional overlay* consists of a network of functional contacts which are different from the formal authority structure. These relationships are most common where specialized information is needed. Through such functional contacts a staff member or other specialist may exert his influence upon operations even though he has no direct responsibility for the work. It introduces the concept of "multiple supervision" and on some organization charts functional contacts are indicated by the use of dotted lines.

The *decision overlay* recognizes that the structure of an organization is determined to some extent by where the decisions are made and by whom. Normally, it may be assumed that policy-making decisions are made at a higher level in the formal hierarchy and more routine administrative decisions at a lower level, but when the network of the decision-making process is identified, it may be found that the formal organization is not descriptive of the level at which categories of decisions are made.

The *power overlay* is based on the idea that power exists in an organization when someone has the ability to influence the behavior of others in desired directions. Although it is often assumed that the higher one is in the organizational hierarchy the more power one has, a diagram of the actual power centers would seldom follow the formal authority channels. There is a network of personal power which is not institutionalized in that it is identified in organization charts or policy statements. Power may reside in persons relatively low in the job hierarchy.

The *communication overlay* represents the information process of the organization. It affects all the other overlays because communication is central to the relationships in any social system. Patterns of actual communication are generally at variance with the formal organization.

ORGANIZATIONS AS SOCIAL SYSTEMS

Systems theory, as Boulding and others have observed, provides a framework or skeleton for all sciences. Social scientists, recognizing that differences do exist between biological systems and social systems, have adopted the system theory and used it in order to provide a viable model for the study and understanding of social organizations. Katz and Kahn state that

> a social system is a structure of events or happenings rather than of physical parts and it therefore has no structure apart from its functioning. Physical and biological systems such as automobiles or organisms have anatomical structures which can be identified even when they are not functioning. In other words, these systems have both an anatomy and a physiology. There is no anatomy to a social system in this sense. When

the biological organism ceases to function, the physical body is still present and can be examined in a post-mortem analysis. When a social system ceases to function, there is no longer an identifiable structure. (*9*, p. 31)

Systems are either open or closed, the major difference being that closed systems are isolated from, whereas open systems are related to, and exchange matter with, their environments. Katz and Kahn take the position that living systems, whether biological organisms or social organizations, are "acutely dependent upon their external environment and so must be conceived of as open systems."

Katz and Kahn defined an open system as

an energic input-output system in which the energic return from the output reactivates the system. Social organizations are flagrantly open systems in that the input of energies and the conversion of output into further energic input consists of transactions between the organization and its environment. (*9*, pp. 16–17)

The open system model of organizations, according to Schein, holds that "any given organization 'imports' various things from its environment, utilizes these imports in some kind of 'conversion' process, and then 'exports' products, services and 'waste' materials which result from the conversion process" (*15*, p. 90). Thus open systems, such as the schools, depend on outside agencies in the environment for making available required energic inputs (operating funds, teachers, materials) and for absorbing the organization's product (educated and trained students). The significant fact is that open systems must be in intimate contact with the external environment to receive inputs (partly in the form of feedback information) relative to the expectations which are held for the organization.

Most systems have a closed as well as an open dimension: that is, when closed, the focus is on the internal operation (frequently at the neglect of the external environment), the emphasis is on control, and establishing rules, with the ultimate criterion being efficiency. If a system becomes more open, behavior within the organization is less predictable, more difficult to control, and tends to run counter to the inflexible bureaucratic character of the institution. Bennis takes the position that nearly all our institutions are failing today because they are living on the borrowed genius of the industrial revolution, when bureaucracy came into its own.

It was an elegant invention, a creative response to what was then a radically new age. But the passing of that age has left its characteristic form of organization hopelessly out of joint with contemporary reality. (*1*, p. 48)

Schools which operate as open social systems are more likely to adjust the curriculum to meet the changing conditions in the environment supporting the schools. While this relationship between the school and its environment would appear to be desirable for all education, it is obviously essential to the continued operation of dynamic vocational and technical education programs. Vocational teachers and administrators need a constant flow of input from the external environment, including information regarding employment opportunities, feedback from graduates and their employers, and information regarding new developments in business and industry. School personnel—both teachers and administrators—tend to be preoccupied with their concern for efficiency and therefore are reluctant to allow the schools to become truly *open* social systems. If the public schools are to provide effective occupational education programs, they must become more open. The schools must be efficient, but they must also realize the purposes for which they are being supported.

In a study of organizational climate, Halpin and Croft (*8*) studied the behavior of people in six different types of schools ranging from open to closed. They described the climate in schools at both ends of the continuum. At one end:

> *The Open Climate* describes an energetic, lively organization which is moving toward its goals, and which provides satisfaction for the group members' social needs. Leadership acts emerge easily and appropriately from both the group and the leader. The members are preoccupied disproportionately with neither task achievement nor social-needs satisfaction; satisfaction on both counts seems to be obtained easily and almost effortlessly. The main characteristic of this climate is the "authenticity" of the behavior that occurs among all the members. (*8*, p. 2)

At the other end:

> *The Closed Climate* is characterized by a high degree of apathy on the part of all members of the organization. The organization is not "moving." *Esprit* is low because the group members secure neither social-needs satisfaction nor the satisfaction that comes from task achievement. The members' behavior can be construed as "inauthentic"; indeed, the organization seems to be stagnant. (*8*, p. 3)

AUTHORITY SYSTEMS

Organizations attempt to insure orderliness and predictability in several ways, one of which is through a system of authority. For purposes of our discussion, authority is considered to be the right of a person to decide, determine, or influence what others in the organization will do. Authority may be acquired through formal action such as laws and board policies (authority of legitimacy) or conferred by the organization through the position or office which one occupies (authority of position). Authority (or at least influence) may also be acquired through professional or technical competence and/or experience (authority of competence) or by personal characteristics such as seniority, popularity, knowledge of human aspects of administration, rapport with subordinates, persuasive ability, and ability to mediate individual needs (authority of person). Peabody (*12*) classified the first and second categories of authority (legitimacy and position) as formal bases of authority and the latter two (competence and person) as functional authority.

The point in this discussion is that there is a shift in the authority bases for those who administer public schools and colleges. The shift is from formal authority to functional authority bases. As the content and structure of education increases in complexity and diversity, teachers by virtue of competence and person authority have assumed more responsibility for these areas. Managers of vocational and technical programs are especially susceptible to this change since for many years they relied heavily upon the authority derived from federal legislation and subventions and authority conferred upon them by virtue of positions held. But the vocational administrators of the future will need to rely more on competence and person as sources of authority. It should be noted that functional authority shifts from one person to another as function changes. Functional authority is related to successful achievement of given ends; performance is the basis for allocating or removing such authority.

Authority and Power.   Katz and Kahn see organization as "a system of roles" each with a set of prescriptions or behaviors which are to be performed (and typically includes a set of proscriptions or behaviors which are to be avoided). The managerial subsystem of an organization has as one of its functions the process of creating such prescriptions and proscriptions. Some of these prescriptions are broad and apply to every position or role in the organization while others apply to subparts of the system or to a particular position only. Katz and Kahn state:

> If foresight were perfect, if incumbents were flawless organization men or automatons, and if the environment of the organization were unchanging, the problem of management might be at an end once the design had been created and the prescriptions communicated. The organization could be given an initial push, and like a mass in motion in theoretical space, it would continue its cycles undiminished in perpetuity. Nor would there be any need for control and coordination; the parts and their functions would be coordinated in the initial statement of functions and relationships. No more would be necessary. (*9*, p. 201)

Since people with varying kinds and degrees of ability and personality needs are involved and since parts of the organization—both human and nonhuman—wear out and need to be replaced, the organization does not function without controls and coordination. Then, too, organizations function in a changing environment and each change calls for some response from the organization; to make appropriate changes in the organization in response to environmental changes is a function of management. The organization is engaged in a never-ending process of adaptation, replacement, and attempts to insure role performance with the objective of turning out the product which justifies the existence of the organization. To insure role performance the managerial subsystem must have a structure of authority.

Katz and Kahn believe that dependable role performance is a basic organizational requirement and that this, in turn, leads to the requirement that each role be under the close supervision of some other role in order to assure that performance is delivered. But they hold the view that the hierarchical structure of authority may not be the best way to achieve this goal. They propose the hypothesis that the hierarchical system is at its best in terms of survival and efficiency:

1. When individual tasks are minimal in creative requirements, so that compliance with legitimate authority is enough, and identification with organizational goals is not required;

2. When the environmental demands on the organization are clear and their implications obvious, so that information is redundant and can be wasted and the organization need not make use of all the potential receivers and processors of information among its members;

3. When speed in decision-making is a requirement of importance, so that each additional person involved in the process adds significantly to organizational costs and risks;

4. When the organizational circumstances approximate those of closed systems, with minimal change requirements from the environment. (9, p. 214)

They then propose what they call a "democratic" organizational structure which would be maximally efficient when a set of conditions exists which are the opposite of those listed above. The democratic model for the administration of complex social organizations (in contrast to the hierarchical model) consists of essentially the same subsystems as the hierarchical model; the difference is in the administrative or managerial subsystem and in the structure of authority. In the hierarchical organization, authority and power of persons increase with each successive level in the hierarchy. This increase in power is not limited to operational acts; it also includes the power to determine changes which should be made in organizational policy and structure, and the power to hire and fire the individuals who shall fill the various roles in the organization.

One fundamental difference between hierarchical and democratic structures is that in the hierarchical form *both* legislative and executive power is fused in the hierarchy, but in the democratic form legislative power is widely shared among the members, while executive power is still distributed along the lines of the pyramidal structure of authority. Also, under the hierarchical model ultimate organizational power (veto power) is lodged with successively higher levels of authority, while in the democratic forms this power tends to be in the hands of the members of the organization or their representatives. The final criterion which distinguishes democratic from hierarchical forms is the basis on which selection, tenure, and dismissal (especially of officers) are determined. In the hierarchical form each level determines who shall hold the position at the next lower level, but the democratic form implies that each person shall be named to membership and position by the other members. Katz and Kahn claim that all three of these criteria—the separation of legislative from executive, the locus of veto power, and the selection of officers—reflect the principle of government by the active and expressed consent of the governed. They state:

> The appropriateness of democratic and hierarchical structures to different human purposes and conditions is still unsettled. In organizational life, we are inclined to the view that the advantages of hierarchy have been overstated. (*9*, pp. 213–14)

Although the public schools have not fully adopted the hierarchical structure commonly used in big business and the military, they tend toward this form. But if children, youth, and adults are to be educated to function in a democratic society, they should be educated in institutions that are structured on the basis of certain democratic principles. This is not to imply that the structure of a school can or should be totally democratic. The authority for the schools comes from the people who have elected their representatives (to the legislature and boards of education) who have certain authority, some of which they can delegate to executive officers and their staffs. But within this legal structure (see chapter 7) administrators, teachers, and students should be encouraged to create a structure which provides the maximum involvement in the decision-making process of all groups affected by a decision. Students' and teachers' rights must be recognized and respected; personnel problems in the organization must be handled by due process and with integrity.

Katz and Kahn define authority as legitimate power, that is, "power which is vested in a particular person or position, which is recognized as so vested, and which is accepted as appropriate not only by the wielder of the power, but by those over whom it is wielded and by the other members of the system" (*9*, p. 203). They claim that the managerial subsystem and the structure of authority are inseparable.

To understand authority and power we must examine other terms such as influence and control. For our purposes we accept the definitions by Katz and Kahn. The concept of *influence* is a kind of psychological force; it includes virtually any interpersonal transaction in which one person acts in such a way as to change the behavior of another in some intended fashion. *Control* involves the distinction between successful and unsuccessful influence attempts. That is, a person has control over another in some matter if his influence is so strong that the desired behavior will be completed and any resistance or counterinfluences will be overcome in the process. *Power* refers to some potential set of transactions, rather than actions actually occurring; it is the capacity to influence, but it is seldom used to refer to a single act. *Authority* is

> the most restricted of this set of related concepts, as influence is the most general . . . authority is legitimate power; it is power which accrues to a person by virtue of his role, his position in an organized social structure. It is, therefore, power which is lawful and socially acceptable (at least by the people necessary for the maintenance of the structure). (*9*, p. 220)

This discussion of influence, control, power, and authority in organizations is especially significant for anyone concerned about leadership through managerial roles. Katz and Kahn define leadership as "any act of influence on a matter of organizational relevance."

Source of Authority and Power.   The authority for the activity carried on by the members of an organization is derived from three sources: the legal limitations placed upon the organization, the institutional policy, and the agreement on job expectations for each of the members.

According to Katz and Kahn all human organizations have some structure of authority, some criteria for allocating it, and some rules for exercising it. Since the responsibility for education in the United States has been given to the states, the source of legal power which operates in local schools is the state. The form and character of a local school district and its operations are determined, to a large extent, by state laws and regulations; these provide the framework and limits within which the legal power of the school district exists and operates. Within the limits of state law, school boards are agents of the state; as such they exercise and assign the legal authority and power of the state over their respective schools. The board employs a chief administrator (superintendent or president) who serves as executive officer; as the agent of the board he retains some of the legal power vested in his office but assigns certain powers to other members of the organization. This legal power and the legal obligation for insuring the performance of teachers flows from the boards, thence to the chief executive officer, through the several levels of the administrative hierarchy, to the teachers. The set of relationships through which legal power flows forms the legal structure of a school system.

The sources of authority discussed above are derived from the society supporting the institution, the institution itself, the roles, and the role expectations. They constitute the official or formal dimensions of authority.

In the Weberian model the authority structure was limited to this rational-legal type in which the rules and prerogatives of authority are quite separate from the person or personality of the wielder of authority. But authority is also derived from the personal dimensions of organizations—the individual's personality and psychological needs. This is a more informal type of authority structure often exercised through primary groups and combinations of such groups.

Organizational Effectiveness

The success of any organization must be determined by the degree to which it achieves its goals. But this is only one measure of success. There are other problems which the organization must solve if it is to operate effectively. Organizational *effectiveness,* as defined by Georgopoulous and Tannebaum (*5*), is "the extent to which an organization as a social system, given certain resources and means, fulfills its objectives without incapacitating its members." There is a growing acceptance of the idea that organizations must be evaluated on human criteria as well as on goal achievement. Satisfaction and personal growth of people in the organization, as well as productivity, must be considered.

Bennis considers organizations as primarily complex goal-seeking units. He then goes on to say that in order to survive they

> must also accomplish the secondary tasks of (1) maintaining the internal system and coordinating the "human side of enterprise"—a process of mutual compliance here called "reciprocity"—and (2) adapting to and shaping the external environment—here called "adaptability." (*2,* p. 7)

Organizational *effectiveness* should be distinguished from organizational *efficiency.* The former term refers to the degree to which the organization realizes its goals and the latter term refers to the amount of resources used to produce a unit of output.

The literature on organizational effectiveness is extensive; we will attempt to highlight some of the findings. Although social scientists who have studied organizational effectiveness use different terms to describe certain variables, there appears to be rather general agreement that organizations are effective to the extent that they can (1) achieve their goals, (2) maintain internal flexibility, (3) adapt to the external environment, and (4) provide for reduction and management of tensions.

GOAL ACHIEVEMENT

To be effective the organization must pursue its goals or objectives with some degree of success; this is the pay-off. Sufficient resources must be allocated to this function and these resources must be appropriate to the specific tasks to be performed. Members must possess the necessary competencies to pursue the tasks effectively.

The literature on the purposes of secondary education leaves no doubt about the importance of the goal of preparing youth for careers, yet this goal is frequently neglected. One reason is that many individual high school faculties have not accepted this as a legitimate goal and are therefore not really committed to its achievement. A further difficulty lies in our failure to define broad goals in terms of operational objectives. But let us say for the sake of argument, that there is agreement that a major objective of the high school is to provide all students, both graduates and dropouts, with job entry level skills in a career area of the student's choice. To achieve this goal requires special facilities and teachers qualified in the occupational areas for which instruction is to be provided, as well as support personnel such as career counselors. Schools and colleges should be structured so that all members feel that they are contributing to the achievement of the institution's goals. In this way individuals and groups within the school can see *their* goals being satisfied by the achievement of the school's goals.

INTERNAL FLEXIBILITY OR INTEGRATION

To be effective the organization must solve the problem of coordinating its parts and relating them to each other. Members of an organization interact from day to day and activities need to be coordinated, especially as specific tasks and circumstances undergo change. Members of a work group will contribute more to the effectiveness of the organization when their interactions with others are mutually satisfying and reinforcing.

Schools and colleges should be structured so as to increase the potential for members to interact across subject matter lines. For example, teachers of subjects normally thought to be "academic" can come to see the relevance of their subject matter to occupations as they interact with teachers of so-called "vocational" subjects; most school structures do not encourage this kind of interaction.

EXTERNAL FLEXIBILITY OR ADAPTABILITY

To be effective, the organization must cope with its external environment and be able to adapt to it. As a social system it must get its resources from the environment and must therefore be concerned about environmental means.

Schools and colleges, as social organizations, are a part of, and supported by, a larger social system—the community, the state, and the nation. The need to establish a closer working relationship between the school and the community it serves is absolutely essential if it is to have viable vocational and technical programs. This problem is discussed in chapter 13.

TENSION MANAGEMENT

The organization must successfully socialize its members so that they have commitment to the system and its goals. The reduction and management of tensions and strains is extremely important to the effective functioning of the organization. While some tensions may serve a useful purpose, excessive and continued tensions are factors which reduce organizational effectiveness.

LEADERSHIP

Organizations need leadership because (1) the formal designs of organization are neither perfect nor complete; (2) the external conditions under which every organization must operate are constantly changing; (3) the internal conditions of the organization produced by the dynamics of the subsystems are changing; and (4) human beings as occupants of organizational roles have unique characteristics.

REFERENCES

1. Bennis, Warren G. "Organic Populism." In *Psychology Today* 3, February 1970.

2. Bennis, Warren G. *Changing Organizations.* New York: McGraw-Hill, 1966.

3. Carver, Fred D. and Thomas J. Sergiovanni, eds. *Organizations and Human Behavior: Focus on Schools.* New York: McGraw-Hill, 1969.

4. Gardner, John W. "How to Prevent Organizational Dry Rot." *Harpers Magazine,* October 1965, pp. 20–26.

5. Georgopoulos, B. S. and A. S. Tannenbaum, "A Study of Organizational Effectiveness," *American Sociological Review* 22 (1957), 534–40.

6. Griffiths, Daniel E., ed. *Behavioral Science and Educational Administration.* The Sixty-third Yearbook of the National Society for the Study of Education, Part II. Chicago: University of Chicago Press, 1964.

7. Griffiths, Daniel E., David L. Clark, D. Richard Wynn and Laurence Iannacone. *Organizing Schools for Effective Education.* Danville, Illinois: Interstate, 1962.

8. Halpin, Andrew W. and Don B. Croft. "The Organizational Climate of Schools." In *Administrators Notebook* 1, No. 7, March 1963.

9. Katz, Daniel and Robert L. Kahn. *The Social Psychology of Organizations.* New York: John Wiley, 1966.

10. Likert, Rensis. *New Patterns of Management.* New York: McGraw-Hill, 1961.

11. Likert, Rensis. *The Human Organization: Its Management and Value.* New York: McGraw-Hill, 1967.

12. Peabody, Robert L. "Perceptions of Organizational Authority: A Comparative Analysis." *Administrative Science Quarterly* 6, No. 4, March 1962.

13. Pfiffner, John M. and Frank P. Sherwood. *Adminstrative Organization.* Englewood Cliffs, New Jersey: Prentice-Hall, 1960.

14. Saunders, Robert, Ray C. Phillips and Harold T. Johnson. *A Theory of Educational Leadership.* Columbus, Ohio: Charles E. Merrill, 1965.

15. Schein, E. H. *Organizational Psychology.* Englewood Cliffs, New Jersey: Prentice-Hall, 1965.

16. Sergiovanni, Thomas J. and Robert L. Starratt. *Emerging Patterns of Supervision—Human Perspectives.* New York: McGraw-Hill, 1971.

17. Tannebaum, Arnold S. *Social Psychology of the Work Organization.* Belmont, California: Wadsworth, 1967.

18. Weber, Max. *The Theory of Social and Economic Organization.* Translated by A. M. Henderson and T. Parsons, Oxford University Press, 1947. London: Collier-Macmillan, 1964.

Chapter 5 LEADERSHIP IN ADMINISTRATION

We are concerned in this chapter with leadership in public secondary and post-secondary schools and colleges offering vocational and technical education programs particularly as it relates to the role of the administrators of such programs. The vocational administrator should act as leader (at least some of the time), but he should also design and operate the system so that leadership might emerge at all levels. Since we are concerned with organizational leadership, this and the preceding chapter are closely related. The purposes of this chapter are to help the reader:

1. to understand that not all administrators are leaders and that leadership in education can and does come from supervisors, teachers, counselors, and students as well as from administrators;
2. to understand and practice the kinds of leadership behaviors which are most effective in particular situations;
3. to create a work environment in which all members of the organization are encouraged to exercise leadership;
4. to understand the need for dynamic leadership in the administration of vocational and technical education;

5. to understand how to bring about needed changes in order to improve vocational and technical education programs for youth and adults.

Leadership and Administration

According to Little

Leadership may be considered as one of the two primary functions of administration; the other function is management. Leadership is required in the exercise of either function but the two functions make different psychological demands upon the administrator. The *leadership function* requires the capacity to "live ahead" of his institution; to interpret his institution's needs to the public and the public's needs to his institution; and to conceive and implement strategies for effecting changes required for his institution to fulfill its purpose. The *management function* requires the capacity to arrange and operate his institution in a manner which elicits an efficient and effective effort of the total membership of his institution toward its purposes. The leadership function is a stimulating, prodding, and sometimes disruptive influence, while the management function has a smoothing and stabilizing influence. The first emphasizes creative planning, initiative, and future-facing boldness; the second stresses efficiency and productivity through teamwork and consideration of others. (*18,* pp. 1–2)

We are examining leadership in the organizational setting, discussed in chapter 4, where a formal organization is perceived as a hierarchy of superordinate-subordinate relationships within a social system. This hierarchy of relationships serves to facilitate the allocation and integration of roles and resources to achieve the goals of the organization.

Leadership in this organizational context implies the initiation of new structures or procedures for accomplishing the organizational goals and objectives. The emphasis is upon initiating change. The leader is a "change agent." The administrator, on the other hand, may be identified as the person who utilizes existing structures or procedures to achieve institutional goals or objectives. The administrator is frequently concerned with maintaining rather than changing established structures.

Let us examine leadership further. Webster defines a leader as "a person or animal that goes before to guide or show the way, or one who precedes or directs in some action, opinion or movement." Ordway Tead, author of *The Art of Leadership,* says, "Leadership is the activity of influencing people to cooperate toward some goal which they come to find desirable." Organization leadership is the process of influencing an individual or a group in efforts toward the achievement of organizational goals.

Leadership has been the subject of much research by psychologists, sociologists, and political scientists. Lipham (*17*) reviewed the psychological and sociological studies of leadership and concluded that neither discipline alone could explain leadership adequately. Both the individual dimension (psychological) and the group or organizational dimension (sociological) must be considered together. Most of the recent studies of leadership do consider both the individual and the organizational dimensions and the interaction between the two. Gibb recognized the complexity of the concept when he stated:

> Any comprehensive theory of leadership must incorporate and integrate all of the variables which are now known to be involved, namely (1) the personality of the leader, (2) the followers with their attitudes, needs, and problems, (3) the group itself both as regards to (a) structure of interpersonal relations, and (b) syntality characteristics, (4) the situation as determined by physical setting, nature of task, etc. Furthermore, any satisfactory theory must recognize that it will not be these variables *per se* which enter into the leadership relation, but that it is the perception of the leader by himself and by others, and the shared perception by leaders and others of the group and the situation with which we have to deal. (*11*, pp. 913–14)

What appears to be one of the more useful approaches to research on leadership is a series of studies focusing upon leadership *behavior* in organizational environments.

Leadership Behavior

Many of the studies of leadership behavior have resulted from and are based upon the work of Stogdill and others (*23*) at The Ohio State University. Two dimensions of leader behavior were identified and defined as follows:

1. *Initiating structure* refers to the leader's behavior in delineating the relationships between himself and the members of his work group, and in establishing clear organizational goals, communication channels and procedures for accomplishing group tasks.

2. *Consideration* refers to the leader's behavior indicative of friendship, mutual trust, respect, and warmth in the relationships between himself and the group members.

In a number of studies in which these two dimensions were used, the effective leaders were those who scored high on both dimensions. A study by Halpin (*12*) of school superintendents and another by Everson (*6*) of high school principals revealed that effective or desirable leadership behavior was characterized by high scores on both initiating structure and consideration.

Cartwright and Zander (*5*, p. 496), based on research done at the Research Center for Group Dynamics at the University of Michigan, have pointed out that most group objectives may be accomplished through behaviors which can be classified as either "goal achievement behaviors" or "group maintenance behaviors." The kinds of leadership behavior directed toward goal achievement are those in which the leader "initiates action . . . keeps members' attention on the goal . . . clarifies the issue . . . develops a procedural plan . . . evaluates the quality of work done and makes expert information available." The types of leadership behavior which serve the function of group maintenance are those through which the leader "keeps interpersonal relations pleasant . . . arbitrates disputes . . . provides encouragement . . . gives the minority a chance to be heard . . . stimulates self-direction and increases the interdependence among members." While these conclusions were based upon research with small informal groups and the research reported earlier was done in more formal social organizations, the similarity in findings is interesting.

Katz and Kahn (*14*) identified two major modes of behavior among supervisors in business and industry. They claim that some supervisors are *production-oriented* while others are *employee-oriented.* Employee-oriented supervisors focus primarily on employee motivation, satisfaction of employee needs, and the building of employee morale. Production-oriented supervisors, on the other hand, emphasize increased efficiency, greater production, and institutional goal attainment.

The Getzels and Guba (*9*) model of behavior in social organizations is widely recognized and has particular significance for vocational education administrators. It is based upon the theory that administration is a social process in which behavior is conceived as a function of both the individual and the institution. In this model administration is structurally the hierarchy of subordinate-superordinate relationships within a social system; and functionally the locus for allocating and integrating roles and facilities in order to achieve the goals of the social system. The social system is comprised of two dimensions: the nomothetic which consists of institution, role, and expectation; and the idiographic which consists of the individual, his personality, and his need-dispositions. The term *institution* is used to designate agencies established to carry out institutionalized functions for the social system as a whole and *roles* are the dynamic aspects of the positions, offices, and statuses within an institution. Roles are defined in terms of role expectations, and roles complement one another. It can be seen that a given act is derived simultaneously from both the nomothetic and idiographic dimensions; that is, behavior is the product of both the role and the personality of the role incumbent. The proportion of role and personality factors determining behavior will vary greatly from one situation to another.

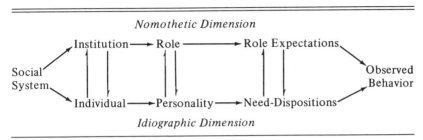

FIGURE 5-1

MODEL SHOWING THE NOMOTHETIC AND THE IDIOGRAPHIC
DIMENSIONS OF SOCIAL BEHAVIOR

From J. W. Getzels and E. G. Guba, "Social Behavior and the Administrative Process," *School Review* 65 (1957): 429. Copyright 1957 the University of Chicago Press.

The Getzels and Guba concept and assumptions are presented in figure 5–1. In this diagram each term on the two horizontal axes is the analytic unit for the term preceding it. In the nomothetic dimension, for example, institution is defined as a set of roles, and role as a set of expectations which influence behavior. Similarly, on the idiographic dimension the individual is seen as having certain personality characteristics or needs which influence behavior. It can be seen that a given act is derived simultaneously from both the nomothetic and idiographic dimensions; that is, behavior is the product of both the role and the personality of the role incumbent. The proportion of role and personality factors determining behavior will vary greatly from one situation to another.

Campbell and others (*4*) have related the Getzels and Guba model to the role of the school administrator. They feel that the administrator gets his power both from his institutional role (formal authority) and his personality (informal authority). The administrator has power and authority as a result of the position (role) he occupies, but he can also get status and power through the personal dimension. Position authority and power is vested in the administrator holding the office but the power and authority which is derived from the personal or ideographic dimension must be earned and entrusted to the administrator and can be withdrawn. The effective administrator has and uses both kinds of power.

Conflicts frequently occur when there is a discrepancy between the pattern of role expectations and the personality of the individual in that role. Conflicts can also develop when roles are not clearly defined or when the person is expected to conform to contradictory or inconsistent roles. Conflicts among roles and between roles and persons filling them are symptomatic of administrative failure. It is the responsibility of the vocational education administrator to bring the institutional roles and the individual personality dimensions into harmony. The success of a leader in administration is determined largely by his ability to satisfy institutional goals and at the same time meet the individual's needs.

Bowers and Seashore (*3*) have identified four types of leadership behavior which are:

1. *Support*—behavior which serves the function of increasing or maintaining the individual member's sense of personal worth and importance in the context of group activity.
2. *Interaction facilitation*—behavior which serves the function of creating or maintaining a network of interpersonal relationships among group members.
3. *Goal emphasis*—behavior which serves the function of creating, changing, clarifying, or gaining member acceptance of group goals.
4. *Work facilitation*—behavior which serves to provide effective work methods, facilities, and technology for the accomplishment of these goals.

They conclude that these four dimensions of leadership, even though developed initially to describe formal (position) leaders, appear to be equally applicable to the description of leadership by the members of the group. Furthermore, they claim that group members do engage in behavior which can be described as leadership and that in these groups it appears likely that "the total quality of peer leadership is at least as great as the total quality of supervisory leadership."

One can make a strong case for group-centered leadership in a democratic society. This, however, does not preclude the need for leadership through formal administrative positions; it merely changes the role of the administrator.

LEADERSHIP IS SITUATIONAL

The Getzels and Guba model helps us understand that there are at least three major modes of leader behavior: (1) behavior that stresses the nomothetic (task-achievement) considerations; (2) behavior that emphasizes the idiographic (needs-satisfaction) considerations; and (3) behavior that utilizes a judicious combination of the two. The proportions of individual (personality) and institutional (role) factors determining leader behavior will vary according to the situation. For example, in a military organization the behavior of a leader would be influenced more by role than personality, while in an organization of artists, personality would dominate over role.

A leader in a typical vocational education role would probably be most successful if he were to use a judicious combination of role and personality factors.

Fiedler (7) studied leadership in the organizational context and in relation to organizational effectiveness. He defines leadership as a problem of "influencing and controlling others," and leadership effectiveness must therefore be measured on the basis of the performance of the leader's group. He takes the position that different situations require different leadership; that is, the same leadership style or the same leadership behavior will not be effective in all situations. He accepts the two major modes of behavior identified by leadership research which may be characterized by terms such as (1)"nomothetic," "task-oriented," "initiating structure," and (2)"idiographic," "people-oriented," and "consideration." Both of these modes of leader behavior have been effective in some situations and not in others; neither of them works in all situations.

Fiedler identifies three major situational factors which determine whether a leader will find it easy or difficult to influence his group: (1) the degree to which the group accepts and trusts its leader; (2) the leader's position power, that is the power which the organization rests in the leadership position; and (3) the degree to which the task of the group is structured or unstructured. But these factors by themselves do not determine group performance. Just as there is no one style of leadership which is effective for all groups, so there is no one type of situation that makes an effective group. Liked leaders do not, on the average, perform more effectively than do disliked leaders; and powerful leaders do not perform better than leaders with low position power. Effective group performance, then, requires the matching of leadership style with the appropriate situation.

Fiedler has worked out a system for classifying how much influence the situation provides the leader and then matching the situation with the style of leadership required. Fiedler and others who have worked with this Contingency Model of Leadership Effectiveness have concluded that the effectiveness of the leader depends on the favorableness of the group as well as on his own particular style of leadership. For example, task-oriented leaders perform best in very favorable and very unfavorable situations, while the human relations-oriented leaders performed best in intermediate situations. The training of persons for leadership roles can be effective, according to Fiedler, only if it teaches the individual to diagnose the situation correctly and then either adapt his leadership style to fit the situation, or change the situation to fit his leadership style.

THE MANAGERIAL GRID

The two dominant modes of leadership behavior identified by Stogdill and others (23) at The Ohio State University—initiating structure and consideration—and supported by others who have used terms such as task-oriented and people-oriented, have been put together by Blake and Mouton (2) into a formulation which they call "The Managerial Grid." They have taken the two variables—task and people—labeling the former "concern for production" and the latter "concern for people," and placed them on horizontal and vertical axes with scales from a low of 1 to a high of 9. The grid has eighty-one cells which could be used to show the many styles of behavior in managerial roles as indicated on these two crucial dimensions of leadership.

Applications of Research

The administrator of vocational and technical education programs should be both a leader and a manager. But regardless of how he prefers to classify his behavior—as leader behavior or as manager behavior—he should use the results of research on leadership, management, and organization done by social scientists during recent decades. In this section we will report what appear to us to be the most useful and practical findings of behavioral research as applied to administration. Although most of this research was done in social organizations other than educational institutions, it is equally applicable to administration of vocational schools and colleges.

MCGREGOR'S "THEORY Y"

McGregor (20) advocated the integration of organizational and individual goals in what he called Theory Y. He felt that too many managers still operate on the traditional view of direction and control, and he labeled this Theory X.

Theory X—Traditional View of Direction and Control.   McGregor contends that behind every managerial decision or action are certain assumptions about human nature and human behavior. A few of the more pervasive of these assumptions are implicit in most of the early literature on organization and in much current managerial policy and practice.

1. The average human being has an inherent dislike of work and will avoid it if he can.
2. Because of this human characteristic of dislike of work, most people must be coerced, controlled, directed, threatened with punishment to get them to put forth adequate effort toward the achievement of organizational objectives.
3. The average human being prefers to be directed, wishes to avoid responsibility, has relatively little ambition, wants security above all. (20, pp. 33–34)

Theory Y—Integration of Individual and Organizational Goals.
Under this theory McGregor suggests that managerial decisions and actions are dominated by a different set of assumptions.

  1. The expenditure of physical and mental effort in work is as natural as play or rest.
  2. External control and threat of punishment are not the only means for bringing about effort toward organizational objectives. Man will exercise self-direction and self-control in the service of objectives to which he is committed.
  3. Commitment to objectives is a function of the rewards associated with their achievement.
  4. The average human being learns, under proper conditions, not only to accept but to seek responsibility.
  5. The capacity to exercise a relatively high degree of imagination, ingenuity, and creativity in the solution of organizational problems is widely, not narrowly, distributed in the population.
  6. Under the conditions of modern industrial life, the intellectual potentialities of the average human being are only partially utilized. (*20,* pp. 47–48)

Vocational administrators can enhance their leadership capability by working toward the integration of individual and organizational goals; that is, by making decisions and taking actions which are dominated by the assumptions underlying Theory Y.

McGregor's Theory Y is based upon the results of motivational research. McGregor states:

Man is a wanting animal—as soon as one of his needs is satisfied, another appears in its place. This process is unending. It continues from birth to death. Man continuously puts forth effort—works, if you please—to satisfy his needs. (*20,* p. 36)

Motivations.   In chapter 2 we discussed the human need to work as it relates to education for work. The leader-manager should understand why humans work so that he can structure the work group for which he is responsible in order that both the individuals and the organization will derive maximum benefits.

According to Maslow (*19*) human needs tend to arrange themselves into a hierarchy. At the lowest level are the physiological needs—food, rest, exercise, shelter, protective clothing—which are extremely important when they are not satisfied. But when the physiological needs are satisfied, then the needs at the next higher level tend to dominate human behavior. The point should be made that a satisfied need is no longer a motivator of behavior. The next higher level of needs are in the area of safety—protection against danger, threat of deprivation. When man is no longer concerned about his physiological needs and his physical welfare, his social needs become important motivators of behavior. These include the need for belonging, for association, for acceptance by one's fellows, for giving and receiving friendship and love. Here again the leader-manager can structure the work situation so that when these social needs are dominant they can be satisfied.

Above the social needs in the Maslow hierarchy of importance are two kinds of egoistic needs: those that relate to one's self-esteem, including the need for self-respect, self-confidence, autonomy, achievement, competence or knowledge; and those that relate to one's reputation, which include the need for status, recognition, appreciation, and the deserved respect of one's fellows. Unlike the lower needs the egoistic are seldom satisfied. Once these needs become important to an individual, he seeks indefinitely to satisfy them. However, they do not become significant motivators until the physiological, safety, and social needs are reasonably satisfied.

Finally, at the top of the hierarchy are the needs for self-fulfillment; the need to realize one's potential, for continued self-development, for being creative in the broadest sense of the word. The point should be reiterated that needs which are satisfied are no longer motivators of behavior; for practical purposes satisfied needs exist no longer.

Referring to Theory X, McGregor states:

> The philosophy of management by direction and control—*regardless of whether it is hard or soft*—is inadequate to motivate because the human needs on which this approach relies are relatively unimportant motivations in our society today. Direction and control are of limited value in motivating people whose important needs are social and egoistic.
>
> People, deprived of opportunities to satisfy at work the needs which are *now* important to them, behave exactly as we might predict—with indolence, passivity, unwillingness to accept responsibility, resistance to change, willingness to follow the demagogue, unreasonable demands for economic benefits. It would seem that we may be caught in a web of our own weaving. (*20,* p. 42)

LIKERT'S "SYSTEM 4"

Likert (*16*) developed the "principle of supportive relationships" which provides a "formula for obtaining the full potential of every major motive which can be harnessed in a working situation." He stated the principle as follows:

> The leadership and other processes of the organization must be such as to ensure a maximum probability that in all interactions and all relationships with the organization, each member will, in the light of his background, values, and expectations, view the experience as supportive and

one which builds and maintains his sense of personal worth and importance. (*16*, p. 47)

The relationship between the superior and subordinate should be one which is supportive and ego-building. To the extent that the superior's behavior is ego-building rather than ego-deflating, his behavior will have a positive effect on organizational performance. But the superior's behavior must be perceived as supportive by his subordinates, viewed in the light of the subordinate's values, background, and expectations. The subordinate's perception, rather than that of the superordinate, determines whether or not a particular experience is supportive.

The Likert research also provides support for the concept of team or group decision making and supervision. In the traditional organization, as we saw in chapter 4, the interaction is on a one-to-one basis between superordinate and subordinate. But in System 4 management the interaction and decision making rely heavily on group process. This concept is illustrated in figure 5–2.

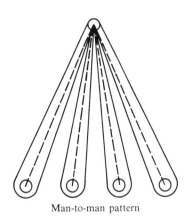 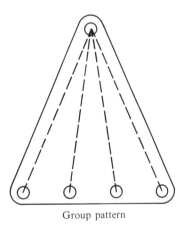

Man-to-man pattern   Group pattern

FIGURE 5–2

Man-to-Man and Group Patterns of Organization

From Rensis Likert, *New Patterns of Management* (New York: McGraw-Hill, 1961).

If the director of vocational education in a city school system were to implement this concept he would avoid dealing with a single member of his professional staff in making a decision which would ultimately affect other members of the staff and the programs for which they are responsible. Instead, he would use group decision-making processes whenever practicable. The community college dean of occupational education would use his division directors or department chairmen *as a group* to solve problems and make important decisions rather than solve problems and make decisions unilaterally with individual staff members.

Likert also uses an overlapping group form of structure in which each work group is linked to the rest of the organization by means of individuals who are members of more than one group. Persons who hold overlapping group membership are called "linking pins." If the linking pin concept were employed in the illustrations given above, the director of vocational education might be on the superintendent's administrative council consisting of top staff members and the dean of occupational education would serve on the community college president's top administrative team.

The group method of decision making and supervision should not be confused with committees. The group method holds the supervisor accountable for the quality of all decisions, for their implementation, and for the results.

To be effective, persons in leadership positions should have high performance aspirations for the organization. But this is not enough. Every member of the organization should have high performance aspirations. The group method of decision making is a mechanism through which the members of the organization can participate in the goal-setting process. In this way they become the organization's goals and not merely the leader's goals. Likert feels that any time these high performance aspirations do not exist, there is a deficiency in the interaction process of the organization.

Likert's System 4 management is based upon *participation:* that is, the formal involvement of members in the exercise of control, usually through decision making in small groups. He developed a scheme for analyzing different management systems in terms of their organizational and performance characteristics on the basis of a number of variables. Scales have been designed and widely used to classify organizations on each of the variables, ranging from system 1 (exploitive authoritative) through system 2 (benevolent authoritative) and system 3 (consultative) to system 4 (participative). For example, under the leadership variable there is an item dealing with the extent to which superiors have confidence and trust in subordinates. Where there is *no* confidence and trust the organization would be classified (on that item) as "system 1," but in organizations where superiors have complete confidence and trust in all matters the organization would be classified as "system 4." Eight organizational variables are used in Likert's scheme: leadership, motivation, communication, interaction-influence, decision making, goal setting, control, and performance goals. For additional information, see Likert's book *The Human Organization: Its Management and Value* (*16*).

The Need for Leadership

Vocational education in the United States, unlike general education, was initiated largely on the basis of a national concern. When the Smith-Hughes Act was passed in 1917 there was very little evidence of concern about or interest in vocational education on the part of local educational leaders. It was to be expected, therefore, that the leadership for the development of vocational education emanated from the national level, then to the states, and subsequently to the development of programs at the local level. This pattern of operation continued and was reinforced through amendments to the Smith-Hughes Act until the passage of the Vocational Education Act of 1963. The 1963 Act gave support to the idea of placing more responsibility on the states and through the states on the local community.

Unfortunately, after forty-five years of federal leadership, the states and local school districts were either not ready or not willing to accept the leadership responsibilities for vocational education. They continued to look to Washington for leadership. The 1968 Amendments to the Vocational Education Act gave states and local communities more responsibility for program planning and evaluation. The federal leadership role was shifted with more emphasis on administrative and statistical responsibilities and the programming role was given to the states, with a high degree of local involvement made mandatory. For example, in order to participate in state and federal funds for vocational education, local communities are required to submit plans to the state which reflect the programs to be operated in the local school district.

Furthermore, for the first time the local school district was given the right to appeal decisions of the State Board for Vocational Education in regard to the allocation of funds. Such appeal takes the form of a hearing and if the results are not satisfactory, the local district can go to the courts. The 1968 Amendments also make it mandatory that each State Board for Vocational Education appoint an advisory council which reflects the interests of lay persons as well as professional educators and not only advises the state board but also evaluates vocational and technical programs in the state.

This shift in responsibility from the federal to state and local units of school administration creates a need for an increased number of local vocational education leaders who have the competence to plan, operate, and evaluate vocational programs on the secondary and post-secondary levels. But not only do we need *more* leaders for administrative roles, we need a "new breed" of leaders—persons who have conceptual, technical, administrative, and human relations skills needed to develop dynamic vocational education programs which will serve the needs of individuals and society.

Most vocational administrators are recruited from teaching positions and vocational teachers generally have a high degree of competence in a particular occupational field. Leaders in vocational education can no longer follow their specialized roles exclusively; they must be both specialists in vocational education and behavioral scientists as well. They must be able to understand and assess the trends of environmental and social change. They must be able to relate vocational and technical education to business and industry, to government, and to education in general. They must be able to conceptualize the new and emerging relationships and set new goals for vocational education.

REFERENCES

1. Bennis, Warren G. *Changing Organizations.* New York: McGraw-Hill, 1966.

2. Blake, Robert and Jane Mouton. *The Managerial Grid.* Houston, Texas: Gulf, 1964.

3. Bowers, D. G. and S. E. Seashore. "Predicting Organizational Effectiveness with a Four-Factor Theory of Leadership." *Administrative Science Quarterly* 11 (1966): 238–63.

4. Campbell, Roald F., Edward M. Bridges, John E. Corbally, Jr., Raphael O. Nystrand and John A. Ramseyer. *Introduction to Educational Administration.* Boston: Allyn and Bacon, 1971.

5. Cartwright, Dorwin and Alvin Zander, eds. *Group Dynamics: Research and Theory.* Evanston, Ill.: Row, Peterson, 1960.

6. Everson, Warren L. "Leadership Behavior of High School Principals." *National Association of Secondary School Principals Bulletin* (NASSP, National Education Assn.) 43, September 1959.

7. Fiedler, Fred E. *A Theory of Leadership Effectiveness.* New York: McGraw-Hill, 1967.

8. Georgopoulous, B., and Arnold S. Tannenbaum. "A Study of Organizational Effectiveness." *American Sociological Review* 22 (1957): 534–40.

9. Getzels, Jacob W., and Egon G. Guba. "Social Behavior and the Administrative Process." *School Review* 65 (1957): 423–41.

10. Getzels, Jacob, James M. Lipham and Roald R. Campbell. *Educational Administration as a Social Process.* New York: Harper & Row, 1968.

11. Gibb, Cecil A. "Leadership." In *Handbook of Social Psychology,* ed. Gardner Lindzey. Cambridge, Mass.: Addison Wesley, 1954. Pp. 877–920.

12. Halpin, Andrew W. *The Leadership Behavior of School Superintendents.* Chicago: Midwest Administration Center, University of Chicago, 1960.

13. Hersey, Paul and Kenneth H. Blanchard. *Management of Organizational Behavior—Utilizing Human Resources.* 2d ed. Englewood Cliffs, New Jersey: Prentice-Hall, 1969.

14. Katz, Daniel and Robert Kahn. *The Social Psychology of Organizations.* New York: John Wiley, 1966.

15. Likert, Rensis. *New Patterns of Management.* New York: McGraw-Hill, 1961.

16. Likert, Rensis. *The Human Organization: Its Management and Value.* New York: McGraw-Hill, 1967.

17. Lipham, James M. "Leadership and Administration." In Sixty-third Yearbook of the National Society for the Study of Education, Part II *Behavioral Science and Educational Administration,* ed. Daniel E. Griffiths. Chicago: NSSE, 1964.

18. Little, Kenneth. "Leadership as Viewed by a Psychologist." Unpublished paper.

19. Maslow, A. H. *Motivation and Personality.* 2d ed. New York: Harper & Row, 1970.

20. McGregor, Douglas. *The Human Side of Enterprise.* New York: McGraw-Hill, 1960.

21. McGregor, Douglas. *The Professional Manager.* New York: McGraw-Hill, 1969.

22. Sergiovanni, Thomas J. and Robert J. Starratt. *Emerging Patterns of Supervision: Human Perspectives.* New York: McGraw-Hill, 1971.

23. Stogdill, Roger M. and Alvin E. Coons, eds. *Leader Behavior: Its Description and Measurement.* Research Monograph No. 88. Columbus, Ohio: Bureau of Business Research, The Ohio State University, 1957.

24. Tannenbaum, Arnold S. *Social Psychology of the Work Organization.* Belmont, Calif.: Wadsworth, 1967.

25. Wenrich, Ralph C. "Professional Development and Leadership Roles." In *Contemporary Concepts in Vocational Education.* First Yearbook of the American Vocational Association, ed. Gordon F. Law. Washington, D.C.: American Vocational Association, 1971.

Chapter 6   DECISION - MAKING PROCESSES

The essence of administration is in making decisions. Katz and Kahn delineate four categories of decision making:

(1) policy making as the formulation of substantive goals and objectives, (2) policy making as the formulation of procedures and devices for achieving goals and evaluating performances, (3) routine administration, or the application of existing policies to ongoing operations, and (4) residual, ad-hoc decisions affecting organizational space without temporal implications beyond the immediate event (7, p. 260).

In chapter 3 we discussed the major influences and groups involved in the formulation of generalized substantive goals and objectives for vocational and technical education. The purpose of this chapter is to review the remaining aspects of decision making, particularly the development of operational policies for achieving the goals of the organization, as they relate to the formulation of those goals and objectives. In so doing, we recognize that general policy formulation and operational decision making are interactive processes and in practical application can hardly ever be separated. Virtually every operational decision in some way defines, modifies, tempers, repudiates, or strengthens formulated policy.

The purposes of this chapter are to help the reader:

1. to understand the differences and interrelationship between policy making and operational decision making in vocational education;
2. to understand and explain the problem-solving process and the pressures which affect it;
3. to understand the management-by-objective approach to decision making;
4. to analyze how decisions are made in an organization, and to improve the decision making process.

Decisions are made at every level of any organization by every member of the organization. Decisions made at the highest executive level of an institution are modified by every employee in the way in which he helps implement these decisions. Our major concern in this chapter, however, focuses on decisions related to the development of procedures and techniques for achieving the overall goals and objectives of the institution. For our purposes, goals are the generalized statements about the specific ends of the institution; and objectives are the intermediate steps through which the general goals are achieved.

Decision making, as used here, refers to the process by which intermediate objectives are determined and implemented. The level of decision making can be classified in terms of three basic dimensions outlined by Katz and Kahn: "The level of generality or abstraction of the decision; the amount of internal and external space affected by the decision; and the length of time for which the decision will hold" (*7,* p. 259).

While these dimensions are illustrative for abstract analysis, in practice it is usually difficult to distinguish among many kinds of decisions, and between decision making and policy making. One decision affects many others, and procedural decisions generally affect overall institutional policy. Nevertheless, the three dimensions suggested by Katz and Kahn provide some basis upon which to judge the relative importance of a given decision. Important decisions tend to affect the whole institution in a general framework, tend to have effects on external relations as well as internal functioning, and tend to endure for an indefinite time period. Conversely, lesser decisions tend to affect one segment of the institution, tend to be related only to internal relations, and tend to be time-limited. It should be noted, however, that limited decisions are always tenuous because they come back to haunt the administrator as case precedents.

Policy Making and Management Decision Making

We differentiate between policy making as the development of the major overall goals of the institution, and management decision making as the development of intermediate objectives and means for achieving long-range goals. The role of various groups in making policy for vocational-technical education has been discussed in chapter 3. One of the major problems in this field is the lack of sufficient involvement of local administrators in overall policy formulation. A major goal of every vocational administrator should be to maximize his influence in the policy making process—in the definition and formulation of the overall goals and purpose of his institution.

It is readily apparent to any administrator that day-to-day decisions affect policy, and that every decision he makes in some way defines, modifies, or alters a given policy. However, many administrators fail to see their role as formally involving policy development. Robert Taylor, Director of the Center for Vocational and Technical Education at Ohio State University, effectively illustrates this problem when he talks about the farmer who was so busy rounding up his pigs that he did not have time to build a pigsty. Vocational-technical educators often get so bogged down in minutia that they fail to be concerned with overall policy. Part of the administrator's job is to concern himself with policy and with the major constituency groups who affect policy. Simultaneously, he must understand the internal decision making process and what forces are likely to affect it and him. This chapter analyzes these forces and suggests some approaches for improving decision making.

Forces that Affect Decision Making

PERCEPTION

Most decision makers prefer to think that their decisions are based on rational analysis of plausible alternatives and the selection of actions or solutions which optimize the consequences to their school. Plausible alternatives, however, are perceived in terms of a variety of pressures supporting and opposing them. Consequently, most decisions are made in an atmosphere of conflicting forces and trade-offs. In this milieu decision making often becomes essentially the fine art of compromise. Thus, as Herbert Simon pointed out many years ago: "In an important sense, all decision is a matter of compromise. The alternative that is finally selected never permits a complete or perfect achievement of objectives, but is merely the best solution that is available under the circumstances" (14, p. 6). Thus, the administrator decides to take a given course of action, depending on perceived social forces, his own definition of the problem he is confronting, and the relationship of that problem and those forces to the ideological principles to which he adheres.

In analyzing the forces that affect decision making, a critical factor is the recognition that there is a problem and the perception of the pressures auguring for one solution or another. There may be many compelling and logical reasons for taking a certain course of action, but the question is whether or not the administrator is aware of them. Information feedback is at the heart of effective decision making. The administrator may overemphasize some factors simply because they infringe on him (i.e. the squeaky wheel gets oiled), while he totally ignores other more important factors which have not been brought to his attention. Few decisions are based on optimum rational analysis of all aspects of a problem. Simon noted: "It is impossible for the behavior of a single, isolated individual to reach any high degree of rationality. The number of alternatives he must explore is so great, the information he would need to evaluate them so vast that even an approximation to objective rationality is hard to conceive" (*14*, p. 79).

PROBLEM DEFINITION

One hindrance to rational decision making is that the way a problem is defined tends to determine the way in which it is resolved. The definition may determine what actions are taken as well as what ones are not taken, or apparently need not be taken. Perhaps more important, problem definitions tend to persist and resist redefinition or replacement, thus perpetuating a variety of less than optimal solutions. The way a problem is defined, and resolved, depends on a variety of sociopsychological factors operative in the given situation context including: the reliability and validity of the information used to define the problem and potential solutions, the amount of information, the emotional state of the decision maker at that instant, the social-hierarchical relationships of people involved in defining the problem, the relative success the individual or institution has had in the past in defining and resolving similar problems.

In many decisions there may be a conflict of pragmatism with principle. Even accepting the premise that every decision is a form of compromise, ultimately there comes a point of principle which a given administrator is not willing to compromise. Most decisions are made from a viewpoint of practicality, taking into account the perceived, if not real, forces operative at the time. But there is always the issue of what is "right"—i.e. academically honest, in the best interests of students and the public in general, and acceptable in light of the ethical values held by the administrator himself. It is a wise practice for an educational administrator to ask himself almost continually, Does this decision compromise my integrity or the educational principles to which this institution is dedicated? Failure to do this can mean the gradual diminution of the principles on which the institution is founded.

BENEFIT/COST RATIOS

A common approach used by industry and many agencies in government in making decisions is the determination of a benefit/cost ratio of a given action. Simply put, the probable benefits, direct and indirect, of a given alternative action or project are given a dollar value. Similarly, the expected costs, direct and indirect, are calculated in dollar terms. Each alternative action can then be evaluated by dividing the total dollar benefits by the total dollar costs. If an alternative has a benefit/cost ratio of less than one, then it is discarded. Of all plausible alternatives, the one with the highest benefit/ cost ratio is presumably selected. While this approach seems reasonable, the problem is of course in the perception and measurements of benefits and costs. Stromsdorfer pointed out:

> Little or no reliable knowledge of the relative investment gains of voca- tional courses or program areas exists. The estimates of benefits of pro- gram areas are still inconclusive and sound cost measures are yet to be done. Benefit-cost measures which compare sets of vocational skills on which one would be willing to stake millions of dollars simply don't exist. The benefit measures are ambiguous at best and are of no use in any case in the absence of measures of relative costs. (*15,* p. 102)

The point of this illustration is that any system or model of decision making ultimately comes back to the judgmental qualities of human beings—about what is possible, what is optimal, and what is probable.

PERSONALITY DIMENSIONS

To study and understand decision making in a given organization, one necessarily has to understand the people involved and their personality characteristics. Katz and Kahn note four of the more important personality dimensions related to policy and decision making:

> (1) their orientation to power versus their idealogical orientation, (2) their emotionality versus their objectivity, (3) their creativity versus their con- ventional sense, and (4) their action orientation versus their contemplative qualities. (*7,* p. 291)

In addition to these more enduring personality dimensions, there are usu- ally a host of other more immediate psychological factors operative in specific decisions. These relate to perceived time pressures, information overload, personal prejudice, emotional mood, individual values or needs, and other variables active at a given time.

While administrators vary significantly in the extent to which their decisions are rational as judged by others, it is clear that no one will make perfectly rational decisions all the time. This is one reason for involving more people in the decision making process, although crowd psychology amply illustrates that mass irrationality is always a potential danger.

The Problem-Solving Approach to Decision Making

One approach to reduce irrational decision making is to follow a problem-solving model, to view each decision as a problem which has several viable alternative solutions. Decision making as a problem-solving process involves: (1) identification and analysis of the problem; (2) search for alternative solutions; (3) anticipation of consequences of alternative solutions; (4) selection and implementation of the best alternative solution; and (5) review of actual consequences and possible remedial steps. This approach is an optimistic one, viewing problems as opportunities. Conversely, the administrator may be confronted with what he views as dilemmas rather than problems. Dilemmas exist when no viable alternative solution is to be found.

IDENTIFYING PROBLEMS

The problem-solving process does not begin until the administrator perceives a problem. In some cases, this is not difficult; if a new vocational education policy is determined, the problem becomes how to implement it. The problem may be more complex, however, if it requires reevaluation of current policies or review of unsatisfactory implementation. In this case, the administrator may not even be aware that there is a problem. Further, when a felt need is perceived, it may merely be a manifestation of the real problem. For example, parental or student criticism of the content of a given occupational program may really be related to the adequacy of the instructor. A comprehensive management information system facilitates early identification of problems. The vocational educator needs early feedback about graduates who are not finding jobs, unsatisfied employers, new technology requiring changes in curriculum, new laws and regulations related to his institution or its occupational programs, student or faculty dissatisfaction, trends in enrollments or in the local economy, and perceptions of his institution by individuals and groups who interact with it.

One major difficulty for senior administrators is isolation or insulation from realistic information and data about their school or college. Subordinates tend to gloss over unpleasant news and elaborate on successes. Even if the information being fed back is substantially correct, the administrator himself may internalize only those pieces of information which fit his preconceived notions. For example, suppose a traditionally excellent occupational program which the administrator himself helped develop is now finding fewer matriculants and even fewer jobs for those who complete the program. The administrator, because of his past involvement, may look for new recruiting or placement opportunities, as opposed to reviewing the curriculum for relevance and possibly terminating the program.

The most effective way to insure early and correct problem identification and analysis is to develop multiple systems of feedback and management information which can be compared and contrasted. Concomitantly, it is helpful to have several people or work groups analyze the same problem from different perspectives. There are, of course, two dangers in this process: (1) too much data, or badly structured and poorly retrieved data, can result in information overload for the administrator—to the point he is unable to make a judgment on any of it; and (2) too many individuals or groups concentrating on a given problem area can result in unproductive duplication of effort. Nevertheless, an adequate information system is at the heart of the problem-solving process. Even with an adequate feedback system, problem definition is not complete until the problem has been analyzed in light of the major goals of the institution. How it relates to these goals will in part shape potential alternative solutions.

SEEKING SOLUTIONS

The search for alternative solutions, once a problem is defined, is the most creative part of the problem-solving process. As noted earlier, the definition of a problem often structures potential solutions. An additional difficulty is that most people tend to repeat and transfer solutions which have worked previously under other circumstances. Often incorrect analogies have been made or conditions are sufficiently different, so that the previously successful solution is not applicable. At this stage in the problem-solving process it is always worth having a devil's advocate or an assistant principal for heresy. For example, in a booming machine tool program, the program director asks for more equipment and student station space, and all available information indicates the need for graduates is acute and student interest is high. The answer may not be to build new shop facilities and acquire more equipment. The solution may be to contract the use of a local plant for the third shift if it is not running twenty-four hours a day. While this may or may not be feasible, the point is that we tend to think of educational solutions in terms of school buildings, day-time programs, and semi-artificial atmospheres. In seeking solutions, it is best to solicit input from as many sources as possible, but particularly from those people who will be affected by the decision most directly.

ANTICIPATING CONSEQUENCES

Anticipating consequences of alternative solutions to problems is perhaps the most difficult aspect of problem-solving, partly because of the variety of factors which must be considered. Every decision has consequences, some of which are planned, and some of which may be totally unforeseen. One fact that administrators sometimes forget is that not making a decision or taking an action is a form of decision making, as is delaying making a decision. Thus, there are the consequences of no decision or a delayed decision which must be analyzed along with consequences of various alternative decisions.

Many simulations and gaming models have been developed for school and public administrators. Some of these are computer-based and some are not. Gaming simulation may help the vocational educator to see the potential consequences of various interrelated decisions, and it also helps develop his general decision making ability. Because of the complexity of the problems, the multiplicity of variables involved, and the lack of quick, reliable feedback (like a profit-and-loss statement in business), educational simulation tends to be better as a heuristic device than as a predictive one. Nevertheless, in many areas educational decision makers are attempting to develop predictive simulation models.

During the technological revolution of the last two decades, it has become clear to scientific observers that society has generally failed to predict the social consequences of technical innovation. For example, educational television has not lived up to the predictive assertions of its earlier supporters, yet the effects of Saturday morning cartoon brutality on kids' attitudes and Sunday afternoon televised sports events on family life patterns are becoming more apparent. Since most educational consequences are social and complex, the predictive validity of educational judgments is seldom likely to be high. However, it is precisely this step in the problem-solving model which deserves the most considered administrative attention.

SELECTING THE BEST ALTERNATIVE

Following the anticipation of possible consequences of alternative solutions, the administrator must make a judgment about which alternative is maximally beneficial to his school or college. The determination of benefit can only be made in light of the basic goals and priorities of the institution. Few solutions are optimal; most are trade-offs of bad and good consequences. Few decisions are totally acceptable to all parties affected by them. For example, the decision to use limited financial resources to equip one program may mean that another does not get the support which the staff, students, or community constituents feel it deserves. Once an alternative solution is selected, it *should be implemented as quickly as possible*. Usually, delays in implementing a decision create staff anxiety about the decision and the administration's commitment to it.

REVIEWING CONSEQUENCES AND POSSIBLE REMEDIAL STEPS

Few decisions are irrevocable, and virtually no decision can be made and then forgotten. Implicit in the problem-solving approach to decision making is a continuing review of decisions made and how actual consequences compare to expected consequences. Here again, multiple channels of information feedback are of paramount importance in the maintenance of an adequate management information system which will keep the administrator apprised of results of decisions. If feedback indicates that the consequences of the decision are not as anticipated, the administrator should be willing to modify the action, or in extreme cases reverse it. While administrative consistency in planning and decision making is important, it is equally important for vocational administrators to acknowledge errors and miscalculations and to take remedial action. It is fallacious to assume that decisions once made and implemented need no further review. A monthly or periodic review of all major decisions made in the institution and a follow-up analysis of perceived consequences stimulates continued feedback. In addition to improving decision-making effectiveness, this also facilitates intra-institution communication so that staff who inadvertently have not participated in or been advised about some decision at least become aware of it.

In practice, the problem-solving model of decision making seldom functions optimally. As Braybrooke and Lindbloom (*2,* p. 113) have pointed out, the ideal model does not adapt to such factors as man's limited intellectual capacities, limited available information and knowledge, the costliness of analysis, the interdependence of facts and value judgments, unforeseen and uncontrolled variables, interrelationships of various problems and decisions, and diversity of forms in which problems arise. They propose that the actual decision making process follows a model of "disjointed incrementalism," in which the decision maker attempts to bring about small changes which are only incrementally different from the status quo, and where decisions tend to focus on successive proximation of a problem solution. Even given the seriousness of their critique, Braybrooke and Lindbloom acknowledge that "problem solving as successive approximation is a practical and sophisticated adaptation to the impossibility of attaining the synoptic ideal" (*2*, p. 123).

The Management-by-Objectives Approach to Decision Making

During the past decade a popular concept has developed among managers in both industry and education. Suggested by Peter Drucker and amplified by George Odiorne, management by objectives (MBO) has received fairly wide acceptance as one administrative approach to decision making. Odiorne defined MBO:

> In brief, the system of management by objectives can be described as a process whereby the superior and the subordinate managers of an organization jointly identify its common goals, define each individual's major area of responsibility in terms of the results expected of him, and use these measures as guides for operating the unit and assessing the contribution of each of its members. (*10*, p. 55)

IDENTIFYING GOALS AND OBJECTIVES

The most important step in MBO is the identification of the major goals and the intermediate objectives of the organization. Within certain degrees of tolerance, there must be staff agreement on these goals and objectives. How this agreement is achieved and the extent of staff participation is a subject for some disagreement. In describing MBO, Odiorne says: "It also presumes that while participation is highly desirable in goal setting and decision making, its principal merit lies in its social and political values rather than its effects on production, though even here it may have a favorable impact, and in any case seldom hurts" (*10*, pp. vii–viii). Other management theorists (Likert, McGregor, Blake and Mouton) feel that staff participation in determination of goals and objectives is crucial. They hold that people are more likely to accept and internalize as their own those objectives which they have discussed and had some significant input in determining.

In vocational education, goal setting is in part a societal policy making process involving a broad spectrum of inputs. Presumably, professional people employed by vocational schools and colleges agree with the basic institutional goals and priorities before they accept teaching or administrative appointments. The real problem is how best to involve them in formulation of intermediate objectives and means for achieving long-range goals.

Once agreed-upon objectives have been established, there are several additional key factors operative in MBO: (1) measures of success must be determined, (2) a time schedule must be outlined, and (3) a communications process must be structured which will allow review and reformulation.

MEASURING ACHIEVEMENT

For Odiorne and others, a critical difference between private enterprise and public bureaucracy is the element of risk. If a manager in private enterprise fails consistently to achieve objectives, he is likely to suffer personal loss—in his salary or his job itself. In education there has been a tendency not to hold the educator responsible for failure to achieve objectives, partly because the objectives have not been stipulated in quantitative, measureable, behavioral terms. In a management by objectives approach to decision making, a subordinate is not told how to achieve the agreed-upon objectives, but he must be fully aware of what measures are to be used to determine whether in fact he has achieved them. This aspect of decision making is obviously critical to program planning and evaluation. It is probably easier to set measurable behavioral standards in vocational and technical education than it is in more abstract educational areas.

In the MBO approach a vocational educator could easily lay out, for example, specific objectives for an automotive service two-year program: (1) that a certain number of students will enter and complete the program; (2) that attrition will be no more than a certain percentage; (3) that a certain percentage of graduates will be able to pass the new nationally normed competency examination of the National Institute for Automotive Service Excellence; (4) that a certain percentage will be employed directly upon graduation in the automotive field; (5) that evaluation of training of students by employers on predetermined measurement instruments will achieve a certain level, and so on.

TIME-ORIENTED REVIEW

Directly related to the question of behavioral measurement is the fact that MBO is time-oriented. Goals and measurements must be time-related so that there are agreed times for review. Depending on the level of goals or objectives, the time frame for review may be from almost daily to annually. The important point is that both superior and subordinate understand what the time frame is to be. For example, review of admissions quotas for any program should be as frequent as the entry points to the program, depending on whether this is once a year or every academic term. Review of an objective to reduce attrition might require almost daily checks of class absences.

COMMUNICATIONS

The nature of the communications process for review and reformulation of objectives is important. The subordinate must feel he can do his job without being under continual surveillance by his boss. On the other hand, he must also be able to get support and feedback from him on problems or changes in objectives. Educational administrators, like other managers, must be prepared to review and reformulate objectives when unrealistic levels have been set. The communications review process must allow staff to reassess levels upward or downward, and to realign their own priorities in light of reformulated objectives. In turn, this system must allow the supervisor enough advance information so that he can provide suggestions for remedial action in areas where his subordinates are falling short or where objectives were not set high enough.

MANAGING BY EXCEPTION

In the management by exception approach, the agreed-upon objectives are still stipulated in quantitative, behavioral terms. It is then the subordinate's responsibility to report any area where objectives are likely to be missed by some fixed amount, say twenty percent. Thus, if the subordinate's operation exceeds or falls short of expected outcomes by twenty percent, the problem is reported and reviewed. For example, if a vocational program in welding technology is planned to accommodate twenty students, and by some circumstance twenty-four students are admitted, the program coordinator and his supervisor would have to reevaluate the current situation— in terms of work station availability, need for consumable supplies, instructional assistance, potential for running two sections, etc. Conversely, if the dental assisting program fails to place eight of its forty graduates in the dental field, then an analysis is required of manpower needs in the field of the geographic area, of the curriculum, of the placement service, or of other related variables.

The management by exception approach obviously must structure different levels of exception required for reporting. The admissions office cannot afford an overall twenty percent error factor downward since virtually all educational and financial planning depends on projected levels of enrollment. What both management by objective and by exception offer is an alternative to a decision making pattern of administrative firefighting. Without this kind of institutional planning of goals and objectives, decision making tends to be based on the exigency of the moment, i.e. who is screaming the loudest. As every administrator knows, some of this kind of decision making is inevitable; the trick is to reduce it to a minimum.

Network Analysis

The quantity of exigency decisions can often be reduced by the use of flow charts and other methods of program network analysis. The most popular of these methods are the Program Evaluation and Review Technique (PERT) and the Critical Path Method (CPM). PERT and CPM are planning and management tools which depict on a graphic network the events and activities required to achieve an established goal or goals. In both techniques, the decision maker analyzes the events or actions required to reach the goal and breaks down the specific tasks and points of accomplishment into discrete entities. A graphic network is then constructed to illustrate the relationship between the various activities. PERT is a probabilistic method which identifies various time options. In PERT, the time required to complete each event is estimated in terms of the most optimistic possible time, the most likely time, and the most pessimistic. In the Critical Path Method, the minimum time path is sought and the approach is essentially deterministic. Both systems assign responsibility for activity or event completion to a given office or individual. CPM and PERT can be useful techniques to improve decision making because they force consistent planning, clarify the interdependent relationships of various activities, reveal the probable location and timing of future problems, and pinpoint action responsibility. CPM, particularly, identifies critical activities and potential bottlenecks.

A similar network approach to structuring complex problems is the decision tree. The emphasis in the decision tree technique is upon decision points, rather than activities as in CPM, or events as in PERT. It provides graphic illustration of the timing sequence and the interrelationship of various decisions, as well as the interception point of results due to chance or uncontrollable circumstances.

The advantages of various forms of network analysis are that they develop disciplined planning and provide some indication of subsequent decisions and activities which will be required, given a current decision. However, as has been pointed out:

> Network analysis is not the solution to all management problems. It is not a substitute for the manager's knowledge, intelligence, experience, and judgment. (6, p. 16)

Network analysis is no panacea for the problems of decision making; it is merely a planning tool. Too frequently, enthusiastic supporters of network analysis approaches like PERT and CPM become so engrossed in the form, in developing graphic depictions, that they forget the substance, the human elements in decision making which are the most essential. Nevertheless, for the vocational educator network analysis can be a most useful tool, especially in planning, designing, and implementing instructional programs. For detailed discussion of methodology, the reader should refer to Cook (*3*) and Handy and Hussan (*6*).

Some Guides for
Decision Making

A basic tenet of the democratic process is that people should have the right to participate in making decisions that directly affect their lives. In the education process, presumably this right would extend to faculty, staff, students, and the community at large. The problem is complicated by the complexity of the educational decisions to be made and the variety of factors which must be considered. It is virtually impossible for even the best informed lay citizens to be fully aware of all aspects of educational administration and the technical intricacies of a given problem. Unfortunately, as educators we often fail to differentiate between technical judgments and value judgments. The educator is paid to make technical decisions, to determine how value judgments, once agreed upon, should be implemented to achieve maximum effectiveness. His technical competence should also provide significant input into the decision making process about overall goals and objectives, but that competence does not warrant giving the educator the singular responsibility for determining institutional goals. Nevertheless it is imperative that vocational educators use their technical competence to help the constituency at large make meaningful value judgments about institutional goals.

It is almost axiomatic that to achieve both optimal organizational morale and effectiveness in implementation, decisions should be made at the level closest to the people who will be affected by them. A participative management philosophy, similar to Rensis Likert's "System 4," is likely to generate more rational and effective decisions in schools and colleges. The creative contributions of staff at all levels will be maximized where a participative, team management approach is used in making decisions.

> System 4 management, in contrast (to the traditional superior-to-subordinate organizational structure), uses an overlapping group form of structure with each work group linked to the rest of the organization by means of persons who are members of more than one group. These individuals who hold overlapping group membership are called "linking pins." The interaction relies heavily on group processes. Interaction occurs also, of

course, between individuals, both between superiors and subordinates and among subordinates. At each hierarchical level, however, all subordinates in a work group who are affected by the outcome of a decision are involved in it. (A work group is defined as a superior and all subordinates who report to him.) (*8,* p. 50)

Related to the issue of participation in decision making is the importance of communication about decisions. Once determined, the decision should be communicated as clearly and broadly as possible. Above all, the faculty, students, and staff should be the first to hear about important decisions and developments. The use of common courtesy in making decisions and communicating them is often the difference between acceptance and rejection by those affected.

In vocational-technical institutions a primary question about every decision is how will it affect the instructional process. In resolving day-to-day problems and making decisions about critical issues administrators sometimes forget that the only reason for the existence of their institution is the instruction of students. It is imperative that all people consulted about a given decision understand both that guiding principle and the specific way in which their advice or counsel will be used. If people's expectations about their role in the decision-making process vary from reality, then their frustration may hazard the effectiveness of implementation.

Another principle in administrative decision making is to view every decision in light of its long-term consequences. This requires a continuing futuristic point of view, a continual examination of long-term consequences of each decision. For example, the decision to hire a thirty-year-old faculty member at a starting salary of $10,000 a year is not a $10,000 decision. Given potential tenure and retirement rules, this may be regarded from a futuristic viewpoint as a $250,000 to $300,000 decision, at least. A decision to build certain kinds of shop facilities that have limited transferability means a very long-term commitment to a specific kind of occupational program over the lifetime of the building. The futuristic viewpoint is especially critical in manpower planning and curriculum development.

Effective decision making requires understanding the sociopsychological dynamics involved in each problem. Every decision is ultimately a human judgment. Accordingly, sociopsychological factors are involved. The administrator should become a student of people and of the reasons they have for making specific decisions. This means that the administrator should be able to empathize with and anticipate the reaction of key individuals and groups to a given decision. Effective decision making depends substantially on understanding people.

REFERENCES

1. Blake, R. R. and Jane S. Mouton. *The Managerial Grid.* Houston, Texas: Gulf, 1964.

2. Braybrooke, David and Charles E. Lindbloom. *A Strategy of Decision.* New York: Free Press, 1963.

3. Cook, Desmond L. *Program Evaluation and Review Technique.* Washington, D.C.: U.S. Office of Education, 1966.

4. Getzels, Jacob W., James M. Lipham, and Roald F. Campbell. *Educational Administration as a Social Process: Theory, Research, Practice.* New York: Harper and Row, 1968.

5. Hale, James A. *Review and Synthesis of Research on Management Systems for Vocational and Technical Education.* Columbus; ERIC Clearinghouse on Vocational and Technical Education, The Ohio State University, Information Series No. 51, December 1971.

6. Handy, H. W. and K. M. Hussan. *Network Analysis for Educational Management.* Englewood Cliffs, N.J.: Prentice Hall, 1969.

7. Katz, Daniel and Robert L. Kahn. *The Social Psychology of Organizations.* New York: John Wiley, 1966.

8. Likert, Rensis. *The Human Organization.* New York: McGraw-Hill, 1967.

9. Magee, John F. "Decision Trees for Decision-Making." *Harvard Business Review* 42 (July–August 1964).

10. Odiorne, George. *Management by Objectives.* New York: Pitman, 1965.

11. Pharis, William L., Lloyd E. Roleson, and John C. Walden. *Decision Making and Schools for the 70's.* Washington, D.C.: National Education Association, 1970.

12. Phi Delta Kappa National Study Committee on Evaluation. *Educational Evaluation and Decision Making.* Bloomington: Phi Delta Kappa, 1971.

13. Richards, Max D. and Paul S. Greenlaw. *Management Decision Making.* Homewood, Illinois: Richard D. Irwin, 1966.

14. Simon, Herbert A. *Administrative Behavior.* 3d ed. New York: Macmillan, 1957.

15. Stromsdorfer, Ernst W. *Review and Synthesis of Cost-Effectiveness of Vocational and Technical Education.* Columbus: ERIC Clearinghouse on Vocational and Technical Education, The Ohio State University, Information Series No. 57, August 1972.

Part III   ADMINISTRATIVE STRUCTURES AND FUNCTIONS

Chapter 7 ADMINISTRATIVE STRUCTURES

Historically, the federal government has had a dominant role in policy making regarding vocational and technical education. Federal legislation provided the structure for a federal-state cooperative relationship which has endured since the passage of the Smith-Hughes Act in 1917. We concluded our discussion on policy making (see chapter 3) by suggesting that there should be a balance of power, but that the states and local administrative units must take more responsibility for policy making and program planning. The major responsibility for establishing vocational and technical programs and determining priorities should rest with local schools and colleges. Consequently, the discussion in this chapter on structure for the organization and administration of vocational and technical education will give particular attention to local structure.

The purposes of this chapter are to help the reader:

1. to understand the basic legal framework for public education in the United States;
2. to understand, in general terms, the administrative structures designed by the states to carry out their responsibility for public education, including vocational education;

3. to understand how local school districts and individual schools carry out their responsibility for vocational and technical education;
4. to detect weaknesses in administrative structures.

The administration of vocational and technical education takes place within a framework or structure which, in many respects, is similar to education generally; consequently, the vocational administrator should be familiar with this structure. In addition, he must also understand those characteristics of the administration structure which are uniquely associated with vocational and technical education.

The Legal Structure

The United States Office of Education, from its inception in 1867 until about 1950, was concerned mainly with gathering statistics on "the condition and progress of education in the several states and territories." But in the case of vocational education, with the passage of the Smith-Hughes Act in 1917, the Office of Education had the additional responsibility for the administration of the act. This included allocating funds to the several states according to a prescribed formula and "making studies, investigations, and reports to aid in the organization and conduct of vocational education. . . ." More recently, the federal government has become more directly involved in education in all fields and at all levels.

The federal government's authority to expend funds for the support of education stems from the "general welfare" clause contained in Article I, Section 8 of the United States Constitution. As interpreted by the courts the "general welfare" clause grants the Congress rather broad authority to appropriate funds for education as well as for other programs that it judges to be necessary for the welfare of the nation as a whole. Federal authority does not extend to control over the states' educational policies.

States and local school districts are not legally required to participate in the provisions of the vocational acts or other federal programs, but if they do, they must comply with federal regulations regarding the use of federal funds. Few people would expect Congress to appropriate funds for any purpose without attempting to guarantee that the monies be expended for the purposes intended. Therefore, federal expenditures for vocational education have of necessity affected the degree to which the federal government has exercised control. Since the states and local school districts spend eight or ten dollars for vocational education for every dollar spent by the federal government, the states and local schools should and do have major control of vocational education.

The question of federal control of vocational education is of far less concern to school administrators today than it was years ago. Most school administrators now recognize the desirability of a federal-state partnership in the support of public education. However, the first federal act giving support for vocational education (1917) was viewed with suspicion; during the intervening years, the federal government has respected the states' responsibility for education and the relationship has been generally quite satisfactory to the states. In fact the federal-state cooperative arrangements for the support of vocational education are sometimes cited as a model for other federal support programs. A study by Cardozier (4) indicates that the amount of control the U.S. Office of Education has depends upon how much state and local administrators are willing to allow. Vandiver (13) found, in a study of selected aspects of federal guidelines and state plans for vocational education as they related to the administration of Vocational Education programs, that the federal guidelines do not inhibit the development of state plans and, furthermore, that most states have not exercised leadership by using the degrees of freedom permitted by federal guidelines. Steps have been taken to develop state (and local) leadership so that in the years ahead we can expect much more initiative to come from the states. A number of states have developed leadership training programs, and The University of Michigan Leadership Development Program in Administration of Vocational and Technical Education was one of the first.

The primary authority in the legal structure for education is the state and, except for specific limitations on the legislature's power which may be contained in the state's constitution and the limitations imposed by the United States Constitution, the state legislature has complete and absolute authority over education. Theoretically, the state legislature may exercise so much power that local school authorities would be mere puppets. On the other hand, the state may limit itself to determining broad educational policies and may grant equally broad powers to other agencies or to local school districts to implement these policies. The choice is in the hands of the state, or more specifically in the hands of representatives of the people, the state legislature. Therefore, whatever structure currently exists in any state is not fixed; the state legislature can change the structure at any time. In the past, local boards of education have been granted rather broad authority for decisions at the local level. The state legislature has the right to rescind any authority which local boards of education now have or to expand such authority. There are no inherent rights in the operation of schools which the state may not abrogate.

In most states some special government structure for education has been set up. All states have chief state school officers, generally called state superintendents of public instruction. The chief state school officers are elected by popular ballot or appointed by state boards of education or by the governor. If elected or appointed by the governor, the chief state school officer is legally an officer of the state and as such exercises the authority of the state; if appointed by a state board of education he is legally an employee serving as the board's executive officer, and he is not then an officer of the state, because sovereignty is usually lodged with the state board. Most boards are either appointed by the governor or elected by the people.

The state department of education is the administrative arm of the state board of education. The size of state departments of education varies widely ranging from a few people to several hundred professionally qualified individuals. The development of this structure for the governance of education does not remove education from general government, since the state legislature controls education. State boards and state superintendents may recommend to the governor a budget for the schools of the state but neither the governor nor the legislature is required to accept such recommendations.

State departments of education are generally organized into divisions, such as administration and finance, curriculum and instruction, research, teacher education and certification, vocational and adult education, community college and higher education, and vocational rehabilitation. The designated divisions in a particular state suggest the areas in which the state department is staffed to provide services to the schools of the state. The emphasis in many states has shifted from supervision to services but in most states personnel are still preoccupied with needed regulatory duties, leaving little time for educational leadership; this is especially true of vocational and technical education.

The division within the department of education responsible for the administration of the state-wide program of vocational and technical education is generally directed by a person with the title of state director of vocational education. In some cases he also has the title of assistant or associate superintendent of public instruction. Figure 7–1 is an organization chart of a state department of education and figure 7–2 shows the organization of a division of vocational education in a state department of education.

Divisions of vocational education traditionally were organized by occupational fields, such as agricultural education, office and distributive education, trade and industrial education, home economics and homemaking education, health occupations education, etc. Now many vocational divisions are organized along more functional lines, such as programs for high school youth, programs for post-secondary youth, programs for out-of-school youth and adults, programs for youth with special needs, career development services, and research services. Some states have organizations based on both field and function.

States generally make decisions about (1) the instructional program, (2) certification of personnel, and (3) building standards, to the extent that

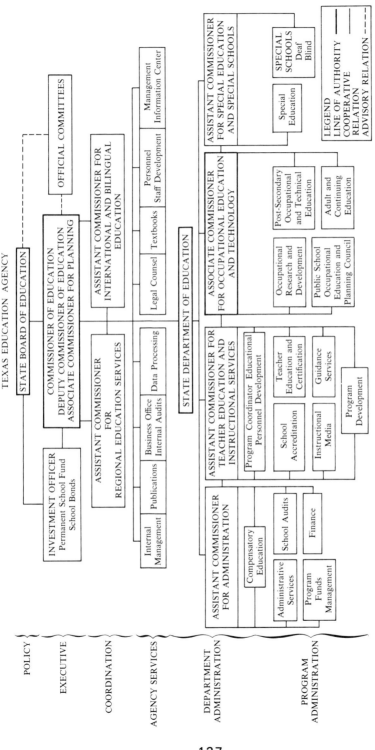

FIGURE 7-1

ORGANIZATION CHART FOR A STATE DEPARTMENT OF EDUCATION

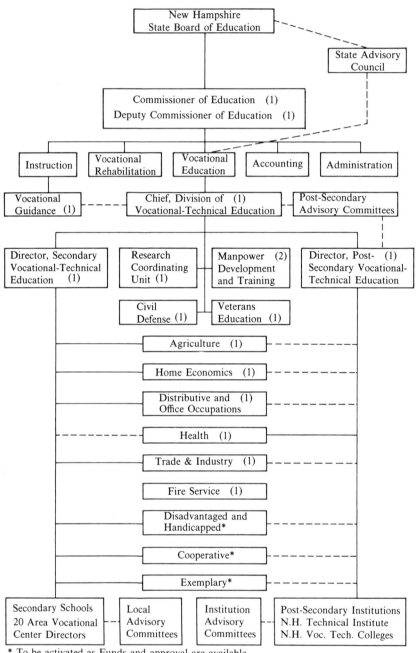

FIGURE 7–2

Organization Chart for a Vocational-Technical Education
Division in a State Department of Education

these matters are prescribed in state laws. There is a wide variation in the amount of state control exercised over curriculum and instruction, especially in vocational education.

The scope or the extent of the program is determined by states; in some states the program is limited to grades 1–12; the kindergarten is optional. A few states now have permissive junior college legislation, including some elements of state financial support; in other states, aid to community colleges is provided through separate appropriations, but generally with some programmatic controls.

States have legal functions to perform. They have a regulatory function which cannot be avoided. Minimum standards need to be established and enforced. Some states operate special schools such as schools for the deaf and blind, or for slow learners, although there appears to be a tendency to distribute these special school functions among existing school districts. Generally, school administrators feel that states should get out of the business of operating schools and direct their efforts toward planning and research, providing leadership and direction for the local school districts of the state.

It should be pointed out that, traditionally, the states are responsible for the administration of the federal vocational education acts. Any state wishing to participate is required by law to designate or create a state board (for vocational education) and to submit and have approved a state plan for vocational education. This federal-state relationship is discussed in chapter 3.

Local school districts are the creation of the state and serve as the basic government unit through which the exercise of local control is effected. School districts are therefore instrumentalities of the state and are, in effect, extensions of state government. They are created to implement the mandates of the state and to ensure the rights and privileges of a free education to all people. The state legislature has full authority over school district organization. It can modify, consolidate, reorganize, or destroy school districts. It can classify districts and then differentiate duties, obligations, or amount of authority among the classes of districts it creates. But generally legislatures are reluctant to modify the existing school district structures because of public opposition. This may account for the fact that in the United States in 1970 there were nearly 18,000 separate school districts. While local control of public education is essential, many local units of school administration are too small to provide the educational services needed by children, youth, and adults living in those districts. Larger units of administration are needed to provide the breadth and quality of vocational and technical education programs demanded by society. The area vocational school or center, serving youth and adults from a number of local school districts, has been a partial solution to this problem, as we shall see later.

School District Organization

The school district is the basic unit of government created by the legislature and designed to achieve local control of public schools. School districts have quasi-corporate powers and are empowered by state law to administer a public school or public school system. A school district is controlled by a governing board which has taxing power and the right to make contracts; it may sue or be sued. School districts vary greatly in size and function. The American Association of School Administrators' Commission on School District Reorganization (*1,* p. 122) describes school districts in terms of the scope of programs they provide and in terms of their geographic characteristics. Since we are most concerned about program, let us examine the five categories under this classification: (1) elementary school districts, (2) secondary school districts, (3) unified school districts, (4) community or junior college districts, and (5) non-operating school districts.

Elementary school districts comprise a majority of the school districts in the United States but they serve only six percent of the total public school enrollment. Most of these districts operate one-room rural schools with varying lengths of programs—K-6, K-8, 1-6, 1-8—although there are some elementary districts in metropolitan areas. Reorganization of school districts in rural areas is reducing the number of elementary districts. The range in program quality in these elementary districts is great.

Secondary school districts overlay elementary school districts and provide only secondary education, receiving their students from the "feeder" schools in the elementary districts. These, too, represent a wide range in quality and size. In 1966–67 there were 883 such districts serving more than 1.5 million high school students.

By far the most common is the unified, K-12, school district. In some cases these districts also operate community or junior colleges. Some states have special districts for community and junior colleges. Approximately eighty percent of the enrollments in public schools are unified districts.

In 1961–62 there were still over 4,000 non-operating K-12 school districts, which had no program at all; but this category has been reduced greatly and should be eliminated as soon as possible since it serves no useful purpose. Boards of education in non-operating districts usually contract with other districts for the educational services of their children and youth.

Community junior college district organization varies widely by state. As indicated above, in some states unified secondary districts are empowered to operate community college programs. Other states permit the formation of unique community college districts, frequently coterminous with county boundaries, which are essentially autonomous. The most prominent approach is that of California, Illinois, Colorado, and Maryland, where locally controlled district institutions are coordinated and in part supervised by a state-wide community college board. In some other states, the community colleges are part of the state university system (administered through the authority of the governing board of the university).

Organization of Schools and School Systems

School districts are also categorized by geographical or area characteristics: (1) community districts are those organized around "natural" communities and labeled as such in the law; (2) city districts are those coterminous with city boundaries; (3) county districts—in some states the county is the basic unit of school government; (4) towns or townships—many school districts follow town or township boundaries; and (5) common schools which include the remaining rural schools. Attention has been called to the great variations in school district organization between states, and even within some states. For this reason it is important that the vocational administrator become familiar with the administrative structure created in his state to deliver educational services to the people of the state.

Since vocational and technical education is specialized education for employment, it is generally provided only through school districts which operate high schools and/or community colleges. We will therefore examine the administrative structures of such districts and the schools within them.

DISTRICTS OPERATING HIGH SCHOOLS

As mentioned earlier, the school district is the basic governmental unit through which the exercise of local control of schools is implemented. Although the number of local school districts has been reduced from nearly 100,000 to less than 20,000 in twenty years (1948–1968), only about half of the existing districts operate high schools. Most of these districts provided some vocational and technical services for high school youth and adults, and some provided vocational and technical education through community college or K-14 programs.

Since the size of these school districts and the scope of services provided vary greatly, the administrative structures vary greatly also. The extent of the vocational and technical education programs provided would obviously be reflected in the administrative arrangements. Many of these local school districts, even though they operate a high school, are too small to make more than a token effort to meet the vocational education needs of youth and adults. Most certainly they cannot afford to employ specialized personnel to give administrative leadership and direction to the planning and operating of vocational and technical education programs. Therefore, the following discussion will be concerned with the organization of larger districts.

Larger school districts with one or more high schools have a superintendent of schools, who is the executive officer for the board of education, and an administrative hierarchy of generalists and specialists on the central office staff. Superintendents, regional superintendents in a large city, and some associate and assistant superintendents, by the very nature of their assignments, are generalists. That is, their responsibilities cut across the entire school system; they must put together all of the purposes and programs of the school system in order to serve the educational needs of the community and to carry out the mandates of the board of education most effectively. These are usually considered "line" positions.

In addition to the line positions, large school systems have established positions which are essentially "staff" or advisory in nature. Administrators who fill these positions are usually specialists. Examples are the director or assistant superintendent for business affairs who is a specialist in budgeting, accounting, purchasing, and other business functions; the assistant superintendent or director of personnel is a specialist in recruiting, salary and fringe benefit plans, negotiations, and other personnel functions; and the assistant superintendent or director of vocational education is a specialist in the "world of work," in the business and industrial community, including relationships with both labor and management, and knows how to translate these community needs into relevant programs. The generalists have the responsibility to relate the schools to the larger society as a whole while the vocational specialist should have the responsibility to relate the school system to the work life of the community. Just as the general school administrator is needed to help establish viable instructional programs, procure competent personnel, give appropriate motivation to the staff, help provide suitable physical facilities and the needed financial resources, so the specialized vocational administrator is needed to provide similar services as they relate to programs for the world of work. Most general school administrators are familiar with educational institutions to which their students progress, but they are not equally familiar with the world of work into which many of their students go after graduation or even before. Furthermore, the general school administrator should not be expected to function as a vocational specialist; he needs a staff person who by virtue of his training and experience is qualified to perform these functions. Any school system large enough to provide a comprehensive education program, which considers preparation for employment a valid purpose of public education, should have a full-time vocational specialist on the superintendent's staff.

In larger school systems the vocational specialist will need a staff of assistants who may be even more specialized than he.

What level in the administrative hierarchy is most appropriate for the director of vocational education? In many school systems the vocational specialist reports to the associate superintendent for curriculum and instruction and in some systems he is responsible to the director of secondary education. Since the vocational specialist is expected not only to plan instructional programs but also to procure competent personnel, to help provide appropriate facilities and needed financial resources, and maintain relationships with business and industry in the community (and since each of these functions when applied to vocational education requires special competencies which most general school administrators do not possess), it seems appropriate to place him in a position where he can perform these specialized functions most effectively. Also, if he is responsible for vocational education on all levels, including adult occupational programs, it seems inappropriate to have him report to the director of secondary education.

The need for the vocational specialist on the superintendent's staff lies in the fact that all of the functions he is expected to perform, while they may be similar to functions performed by other specialists—curriculum and instruction, personnel, facilities, finances, community relations, etc.—have features which are unique to vocational and technical education. These unique characteristics will be discussed in chapters 8 through 14.

Campbell and others (3), in an excellent chapter on "The Administrative Hierarchy," make a case for more specialization because of the increase of knowledge and new functions being taken on by the schools as a result of new demands in the larger society. They predict that much more use will be made of vocational and technical schools or vocational and technical programs in comprehensive high schools as a result of these societal demands. Also, they predict that the schools of the future will be extended into the community college and adult education fields with particular emphasis on training and retraining for work. They claim that as schools take on more diverse functions, school systems and individual schools will be larger. The result will be larger and more complex central office staffs. They add:

> Perhaps an even greater contributor than size to the increased complexity of school organizations of the future is the increased diversity of people employed by school districts. Many of these people . . . may have as much orientation toward social work as toward education. Numerous school personnel of the future will probably be strongly oriented toward the world of work. Teachers of adults cannot employ the same sanctions as do teachers of children and youth and this will increase the diverse viewpoints of faculty members in schools of the future. (p. 253)

In chapter 4 we identified four variables which account for organizational effectiveness. One of these dealt with external flexibility, meaning that the organization must cope with the external environment and be able to adapt to it, because the organization (as a social system) gets its resources from the environment, and therefore must be concerned about environmental conditions and means. This factor is important for all of education, but it is absolutely critical in the planning and operation of vocational and technical programs. The vocational specialist on the superintendent's staff should have this function as one of his primary responsibilities.

In our opinion the education goal of preparing youth to enter the world of work and keeping youth and adults viable in the work force through continuing vocational and technical education will be given higher priority in the future than it has had in the past. To carry out this function adequately requires a high caliber of leadership from administrative specialists who should be equally knowledgeable about both education and the world of work. The vocational specialist must have one foot firmly planted in the schools and the other in the work life of the community. He should occupy a position high enough in the administrative hierarchy of the school system so that he has visibility and positional authority sufficient to carry out his responsibilities. In our judgment, this position on the superintendent's staff should warrant the title of assistant or associate superintendent.

INTERNAL ADMINISTRATIVE STRUCTURES FOR HIGH SCHOOLS

High schools vary widely in size, grades taught, and programs offered. More than half of the public high schools in the United States enroll fewer than 500 students. At the other extreme, some large cities have high schools which accommodate 5,000 or more youth in the daytime and an equal number of youth and adults in the evening. Some high schools include grades 7-12 (junior and senior high schools combined), others grades 9-12, and 10-12. The trend has been toward the high school with the upper three grades, 10-12, but the concept of the middle school might change this. Middle schools are generally organized around 5 or 6 through 8, resulting in a 5-3-4 or 4-4-4 grade level organization pattern.

While high schools vary greatly in size and grade levels served, there is even more variation in programs offered. Small high schools (500 or less) can offer little more than a college preparatory curriculum, some general education courses, and a few specialized vocational programs, usually limited to agricultural occupations, home-related occupations, and office occupations. The industrial programs, when offered, are usually more appropriate for general education and recreational purposes than they are as preparation for a vocation. (See chapter 1 for a discussion of the differences between the practical arts and vocational education.) Anderson and VanDyke (2) compare the advantages and disadvantages between large and small high schools and conclude that the advantages, with the exception of close personal relationships, are with the large high school.

Conant (5) divided all high schools into two general categories: specialized high schools found in certain large cities and comprehensive high schools "in communities of all sizes." He defined a comprehensive high school as one "whose programs correspond to the educational needs of *all* youth of the community" while a specialized high school "offers a program adapted to a special group of students and usually requires evidence of certain aptitudes on the part of candidates for admission." He concluded that the enrollment of many American high schools is "too small to allow a diversified curriculum, except at exorbitant expense," and that the number one problem in many states is the elimination of the small high school by district reorganization. But the number of small high schools eliminated or combined to form larger ones during the decade since Conant's report is insignificant. It was obviously not an acceptable solution. The area vocational center may be a partial solution; it serves to make small high schools (as well as larger ones) more comprehensive. Area vocational and technical centers will be discussed in the context of intermediate school districts since they generally serve youth and adults from an area larger than a local school district.

While the process of organizing administrative structures may be thought of as an administrative task or function (and indeed it is), we are concerned here with both the product (how we are organized) and the process of organizing. Chapter 4 was devoted to a review of the literature on organizational concepts which have implications for the structuring of educational organizations. We would reemphasize the point made in chapter 4 that too little attention is given by school administrators to the structuring (or restructuring) of schools. The goals and purposes of high schools particularly have changed, but the structures have not changed to accommodate them. The administrative structure of any organization should be designed to facilitate the achievement of the organization's goals or purposes. Although we will be concerned primarily with the formal dimensions of administrative structures this should not be interpreted to mean that the informal or human relationships aspects are not important also.

High schools in the Untied States have been and still are dominated by the traditional function of preparing youth for college, even though only sixty percent of the youth who graduate from our high schools go to college and approximately twenty-five percent of our youth never graduate from high school. The early American high school and its antecedents—the Latin grammar schools and academies—were *strictly* college preparatory institutions. To this original and primary purpose of secondary education has been added a second function; that of preparing youth for employment. Most high schools wish to be considered "comprehensive," which implies that they are concerned about and endeavoring to serve the needs of all youth in the community. Conant (*5*, p. 17) defines the three main objectives of a comprehensive high school as:

> (1) to provide a general education for all the future citizens
> (2) to provide good elective programs for those who wish to use their acquired skills immediately upon graduation
> (3) to provide satisfactory programs for those whose vocations will depend upon their subsequent education in a college or university. (*5*, p. 17)

But even though the purposes of secondary education have been broadened, the internal administrative structure of most high schools is still the same today as it was more than a hundred years ago when the high school had a single purpose. If we agree that organizational structures should be designed to facilitate the achievement of the goals or purposes of the organization, "form follows function," then it appears obvious that the structures which were designed for a single purpose high school should be examined in light of the new goals of comprehensive high schools.

The basic unit in the administrative structure of most high schools is the department, and departments are organized on the basis of subject matter. The departments generally represent the academic subjects which have traditionally been a part of the high school curriculum, such as English, mathematics, science, social studies, and foreign languages. Later the organization was expanded to include departments of art, music, health and physical education, home economics, business education, industrial education, and agricultural education. There is some evidence to suggest that the departments added more recently do not enjoy the same status as the more traditional academic departments. This may be a part of the conflict between the liberal arts and the more practical subjects in the curriculum. The point is that this structure puts the emphasis on subject matter, and teachers in the various subject areas tend to be more concerned about their subject than they are about students, each group defending its own piece of intellectual terrain. We tend to teach subjects for their own intrinsic value and lose sight of the functional benefits to be derived from a mastery and application of these subjects. It seems to us that school subjects are a means to an end.

We propose that the administrative structure for the high school be built around the major goals or objectives of education on that level. If a school desires to be comprehensive and accepts Conant's definition, it might have an organization with three divisions—one for each major purpose. The formal organizational chart in this illustration is diagrammed in figure 7–3.

Other high schools might identify other goals and objectives to form the basis of their structures, but we believe structures which are based upon goals will be more likely to achieve those goals and objectives than structures which are based upon means. Each of the above units (divisions) would have an administrative head who would be responsible and accountable for programs designed to achieve the objective of that division. Students would *not* be grouped by divisions, but would take courses in any or all divisions depending upon their career goals and academic interests. Teachers might teach in two or more divisions since virtually all subject matter has a contribution to make to the objectives of all divisions. The difference is that teachers would now be encouraged to teach their subjects with a specific function in mind.

The team concept of management might be implemented in our hypothetical example by forming an administrative council consisting of the principal, the assistant principal, and the three divisional directors. Proposals for changes in school programs and policies would be subjected to the scrutiny and approval of this council before being implemented.

The concept of structuring a human organization around purposes or goals is supported by the research of social scientists on organizational effectiveness. It is not a new idea in education. The idea was expressed by French and others (*6*) who felt that if the comprehensive high school is to be effective, departmental teaching (subject matter) must be subordinated to the purposes of the secondary school. They proposed that high schools should be "purpose-organized," but said there first must be a "more forth-

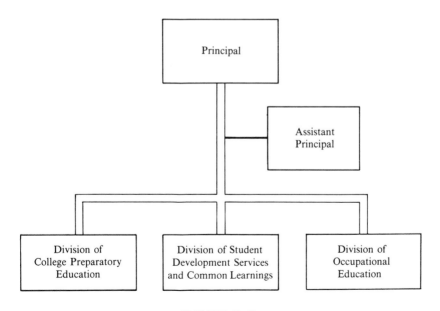

FIGURE 7–3

HIGH SCHOOL ORGANIZATION CHART BASED ON THREE MAJOR PURPOSES

right acceptance of basic purposes as determinants of high school organization." The early American high school was a single purpose high school while the modern comprehensive high school is a multipurpose institution; in order to function effectively and to achieve its new purposes a new administrative structure is needed.

Kazanas (9) did a study of seventy-six large high schools in Michigan to determine the relative effectiveness of schools which were organized by subject-matter departments, which he called "process-based," and those which were organized in terms of goals or purposes, which he called "purpose-based." While he found no schools which were totally organized on the basis of purpose, he concluded that those schools which reflected some purpose orientation in their organization were more effective in their achievement of the objective of preparing youth for employment.

Since two-thirds of the youth enrolled in high school vocational programs in the United States are in so-called comprehensive high schools it is important that steps be taken to make these high schools more comprehensive. We believe that the administrative structures found in most high schools tend to obstruct rather than facilitate the development of functional and meaningful programs for employment-bound youth.

McCleary and Hencley (10), in a chapter on "Organization and the Secondary School," discuss three dimensions of organization: purposes, structure, and climate. Their treatment of purposes is particularly relevant to this discussion. They think the crucial function of a high school principal in regard to organization is "welding an increasingly divergent team of specialists into a functioning unit at the point at which institutional purposes are translated into operational practice."

The comprehensive high school must diversify its programs so as to serve the needs and interests of both college-bound and employment-bound youth in our schools. To do this, high school principals need the help of a vocational staff specialist. A number of studies of Michigan high school principals suggests that they, too, feel the need of such help. A study by Wenrich and Shaffer (14) identified the areas of responsibility which principals thought should be assigned to an assistant principal for vocational education. They included:

Pupil personnel services, such as establishing and operating a student job-placement service, conducting follow-up studies, and providing career guidance services;

School-community relations, such as developing relations with relevant community agencies, establishing and working with lay advisory committees, and determining local occupational education needs;

Instructional-program development, such as evaluating existing programs, developing new and innovative programs and improving instruction;

Business functions including budgeting, equipment requisitioning, etc.;
Professional personnel services, such as inservice teacher education and
assistance with recruitment, selection and orientation of new teachers.

INTERMEDIATE SCHOOL DISTRICTS

Intermediate school districts must be considered in any discussion of
school organization and administration because they are important components in many states. The function of the intermediate district is being
critically examined and in some states it is assuming a new role.

The intermediate unit of school administration is an office or an agency
of school government between the state departments of education and the
local school districts. The county superintendent's office in many states
served the function of communication between the state department of
education and the great number of local school districts. It was an extension
of the arm of the state department of education. But the intermediate
district should not be confused with the county school districts which
operate in some states (particularly in the South) as basic units of school
administration, because they do not stand in an intermediate position.
Although intermediate school districts may often be coterminous with
county boundaries, they frequently do not follow county lines or may be
larger than a county.

Originally the justification for the intermediate unit was that many local
school districts were too small and inadequately staffed to provide all the
needed educational services. While many of the smaller school districts have
become a part of larger districts, the functions of the schools have expanded
and are more complex so that even relatively large districts are not able to
provide many essential services, including vocational education. It appears
unlikely that we will have in the foreseeable future local school districts all
of which are large enough to do an adequate job of vocational and technical
education, for example.

Two alternatives are being considered. One is for state departments of
education to set up regional offices throughout the state, and the other is
to create intermediate school districts to provide certain services. Campbell
and others (*3,* pp. 136–37) believe that a reconceived form of the intermediate unit would be desirable for both rural and urban areas. They believe
intermediate districts should have the following functions:

1. Planning for local district reorganization
2. Determining the location of school plants
3. Providing supplemental financing designed to further equalize educational opportunity
4. Offering specialized instructional programs such as technical and
   junior college programs

5. Providing specialized educational services such as psychiatric help to pupils in local school districts

6. Providing educational leadership to local school districts.

Intermediate districts serving these functions already exist in a few states. New York State is organized into fifty-five supervisory districts which have general supervision over the services to be provided to component school districts. Each of the districts is governed by a Board of Cooperative Educational Services (BOCES). Each BOCES elects a district superintendent who is responsible to the State Commissioner of Education, but as executive officer of the BOCES, he also has a responsibility to the area.

Michigan has a system of intermediate school districts, some of which are the size of a county, but others cover a larger geographical area; there were sixty such districts in 1972, each with an elected board which appoints the district superintendent. Services provided by these intermediate districts vary greatly but they include audio-visual, library services, data processing, special educational services for the physically and mentally handicapped, and vocational education services through area vocational centers.

Twenty-six of the states have some type of intermediate district and many of them have a superintendent with a staff of specialists. We believe the intermediate district has an important role in the development and operation of vocational and technical education programs. Through cooperative efforts the intermediate district staff member can bring together the resources already in the district, or area vocational-technical schools or centers can be established.

AREA VOCATIONAL-TECHNICAL SCHOOLS AND CENTERS

The federal vocational education acts have encouraged the development of area vocational and technical education school facilities by authorizing funds to be used in the construction of such facilities. The Vocational Education Act of 1963 defines the term "area vocational education school" to include:

1. A specialized high school used exclusively or principally for the provision of vocational education

2. The department of a high school used exclusively or principally to provide vocational education in no less than five different occupational fields

3. A technical or vocational school used exclusively or principally to provide vocational education to persons who have completed or left high school

4. The department or division of a junior or community college or university which provides vocational education in no less than five

different occupational fields, under the supervision of the State Board, and leading to immediate employment but not necessarily leading to a baccalaureate degree.

With the support and encouragement of federal legislation the number of area schools and centers has expanded rapidly; in 1972 there were approximately 1900 in operation. Some of these area schools and centers are for secondary school youth and adults (approximately 500) while others serve post-secondary youth and adults (more than 900) and the remainder cover the whole spectrum.

A distinction should be made between a school and a center. An area vocational-technical school has its own student body and a complete program of studies; it operates as any other school with complete student services, including athletics and other extracurricular activities. The area vocational center provides only the specialized vocational education services. It is a shared-time program for students regularly enrolled in neighborhood high schools who come to the center for two or three hours each day for their specialized training only. Area centers like area schools are generally used at night for adult vocational-technical education.

The problems in the organization and administration of area vocational centers are somewhat unique since the students attending the centers have a dual enrollment but maintain their primary identity with the "home" school, get their general education and participate in sports and other extracurricular activities in their home school, and are graduated from it. The center serves two or three groups of high school students each day who are bused from their home high schools to and from the center.

COMMUNITY COLLEGES

Community colleges are touted by some as unique American institutions. During the 1960s they were clearly the fastest growing organizations in higher education. By 1972, over 2 million Americans were enrolled in more than 1100 public community and junior colleges, operating in every state of the union (*11,* pp. 17–22). As noted earlier, the state system and organization varies greatly, but all states now have some kind of community college operation.

Several experimental versions of the community-junior college began in the latter half of the nineteenth century, usually under the auspices of a major university like Michigan or Chicago (*12,* pp. 46–50). California was one of the first states to pass legislation authorizing community colleges. In 1907, it authorized the board of education of local districts operating high schools to offer post-graduate courses, which were to approximate the first two years of university study, and to charge tuition for these courses. For several decades the development of the new two-year colleges, in California and in other states, was usually accomplished through the upward extension of the high school to include grades 13 and 14. Appropriately, they were referred to as junior colleges. Later, junior or community colleges were organized as separate institutions, but often operated as part of larger city school systems. Within the past twenty years, the two-year college movement has focused on the diverse functions it performs, and increasingly these institutions are referred to as comprehensive community colleges.

While the programs in two-year colleges were originally aimed at preparing youth for upper-division work in four-year colleges and universities, there has been an expansion of their purpose so that most community colleges offer some vocational and technical programs. In addition, the comprehensive community college usually accepts as its functions terminal general education, adult education, community service, counseling, and remedial programs. The commitment to this functional diversity in one respect has caused a crisis of identity for the comprehensive community college, in that it has difficulty being all things to all people. In practice, however, the emphasis in most community colleges is still on academic, college transfer programs. This is partly because these programs are less expensive, and easier to organize and operate. Recently, occupational education has grown substantially in community colleges, because of increasing interest on the part of students and greater state and federal support for vocational and technical programs.

Since social organizations tend to pursue the purpose for which they were created, it is usually more difficult to restructure an existent junior college to accommodate a different or additional purpose than it is to build such purposes into the original structure of a new comprehensive community college. Thus, in established junior colleges it is difficult to develop occupational programs on an equal basis with academic transfer programs. Comprehensive community colleges, especially newer ones, have the advantage of an organization designed to serve several purposes. Community colleges committed to the purpose of preparing youth and adults for careers in occupations requiring less than a baccalaureate degree require an administrative structure which will facilitate the development and operation of vocational, technical, and semiprofessional programs.

A comprehensive community college offering occupational programs should have a key line administrator assigned singular responsibility for the organization and operation of these programs. The unique problems of vocational and technical education programs require competencies not required in the development and management of general education or academic programs. The chief occupational education administrator should be on a par with officials administering other basic functions of the college. His appropriate title may be dean or director, but his status and responsibilities must be equivalent to those of the administrator in charge of general academic programs. In addition to this designation of line responsibility, successful occupational programs require total institutional commitment and support from the chief administrator. The president must be as informed, concerned, and involved in vocational programs as he is in any other aspect of the college. Harris (8) asserts that it is of *utmost importance* that the quality of leadership for occupational education programs be equal to the leadership provided for the academic programs.

One critical unresolved issue is whether there should be a separate line organization for occupational departments and academic departments, or whether college departments or divisions should have responsibility for both general academic and vocational-technical programs. The advantage of developing separate occupational departments is the direct line hierarchy to the occupational dean and the clear division of program responsibility. On the other hand, giving departments responsibility for both occupational and academic programs provides better institutional integration, reduces potential status differences, and makes the entire organization responsible for career education. Thus, the social science department has responsibility for occupational programs in various human service vocations; the natural science department assumes responsibility for allied health occupational training; math and pre-engineering responsibility is integrated with program direction in drafting, surveying, etc. For some trade and industrial occupations, it is difficult to integrate responsibility. Depending on the nature and history of the particular community college, either of the structural models in figures 7–4 and 7–5 or a variation of them may be appropriate.

This chapter has described a variety of legal and organizational structures and levels under which occupational education programs operate: comprehensive high schools; specialized vocational secondary schools, including both area vocational schools and area vocational centers; comprehensive community colleges; and technical institutes, whose singular purpose is occupational education. These technical institutes are based on legal and jurisdictional structures which are usually similar to community colleges; the difference is that they are not multipurpose institutions. One final form of public institution offering occupational education is the four-year college which provides less-than-baccalaureate program options. These colleges may be relatively autonomous or function as part of a state-wide higher education system.

Whatever the level and however structured, institutions offering vocational and technical programs share unique problems and concerns not common to general education. The following chapters in this section describe the major functions of every school or college, but with specific emphasis on the aspects unique to occupational education. Each of the

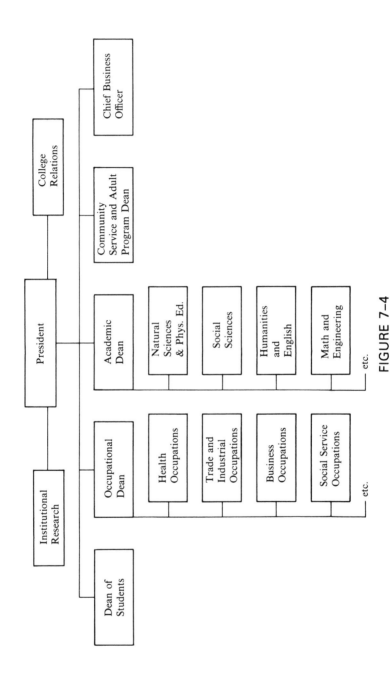

FIGURE 7-4

SEPARATE OCCUPATIONAL–ACADEMIC STRUCTURE
IN A COMMUNITY COLLEGE

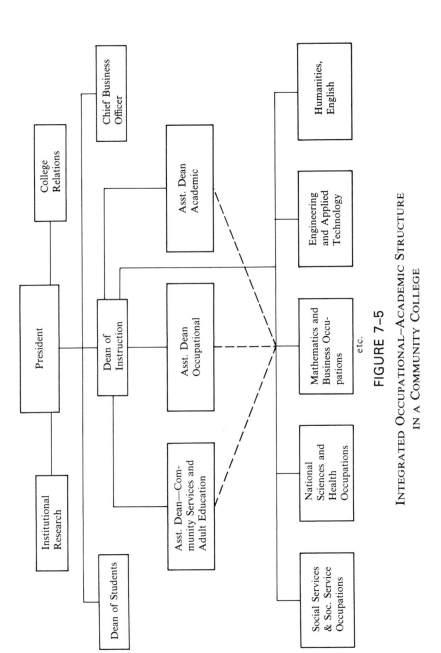

FIGURE 7-5

**INTEGRATED OCCUPATIONAL–ACADEMIC STRUCTURE
IN A COMMUNITY COLLEGE**

functions is viewed from the perspective of the vocational educator: curriculum and program planning, management of instruction, student development services, personnel administration, fiscal and physical planning and management, building a public constituency, and evaluation.

REFERENCES

1. American Association of School Administrators. *School District Organization.* Washington, D.C.: The Association, 1958.

2. Anderson, Lester W. and Lauren A. VanDyke. *Secondary School Administration.* Boston: Houghton Mifflin, 1972.

3. Campbell, Roald F., Luvern L. Cunningham, Roderick F. McPhee and Raphael O. Nystrand. *The Organization and Control of American Schools.* 2nd ed. Columbus, Ohio: Charles E. Merrill, 1970.

4. Cardozier, V. R. "Vocational Education and Federal Control," *The American School Board Journal* 150, No. 4 (April 1965): 30–32.

5. Conant, James B. *The American High School Today.* New York: McGraw-Hill, 1960.

6. French, Will, J. Dan Hull and B. D. Dodds. *American High School Administration.* New York: Rinehart, 1960.

7. Griffiths, Daniel E., David L. Clark, D. Richard Wynn and Laurance Iannaccone. *Organizing Schools for Effective Education.* Danville, Illinois: Interstate, 1962.

8. Harris, Norman C. *Technical Education in the Junior College—New Programs for New Jobs.* Washington, D.C.: American Association of Junior Colleges, 1964.

9. Kazanas, H. C. "A Model for Reorganizing the Comprehensive High School." *Journal of Industrial Education Teacher Education* 9 (Winter 1972).

10. McCleary, Lloyd E. and Stephen P. Hencley. *Secondary School Administration.* New York: Dodd, Meade, 1965.

11. Medsker, Leland L. and Dale Tillery. *Breaking the Access Barriers. A Profile of Two-Year Colleges.* The Carnegie Commission on Higher Education. New York: McGraw-Hill, 1971.

12. Thornton, James W., Jr. *The Community Junior College* 2d ed. New York: John Wiley, 1966.

13. Vandiver, Robert E. *An Evaluation of Federal Guidelines and State Plans for Vocational Education.* Doctoral dissertation University of Oklahoma. Ann Arbor, Michigan: University Microfilms, 1968.

14. Wenrich, Ralph C. and Earl W. Shaffer. *High School Principal's Perceptions of the Rules and Responsibilities of Persons Who Would be Charged With Responsibility for Leadership in the Development of Occupationally Oriented Programs in High Schools.* Ann Arbor, Michigan: The University of Michigan, 1965.

Chapter 8   CURRICULUM AND PROGRAM PLANNING

As the bridge between man and his work, vocational and technical education programs must be the result of a carefully planned design. All educational planning takes place within a complex series of systems, relating value preferences to technical possibilities and institutional capabilities.

Since curriculum and program planning is the foundation of the teaching-learning process, it is a most important task of the vocational education administrator. The purpose of this chapter is to review some of the problems and processes of curriculum and program planning which are unique to vocational education. Since by logic and by law curriculum planning in vocational education is related to manpower planning, this chapter also deals with basic issues in manpower need analysis.

The purposes of this chapter are to help the reader:

1. to understand and use the basic tools of manpower analysis;
2. to assess student occupational interests and employment needs;
3. to relate needs, as defined by manpower analysis and student interests, to curricular planning;
4. to understand and use basic approaches to vocational curriculum development: local-regional manpower surveys, curriculum advisory committees, student interest inventories, etc.;

5. to set up a system for continuing review and renewal of curriculum, programs, and courses.

Definition of Terms

The term curriculum is used liberally by educators to mean all learning experiences provided by the school or college. Most laymen view the curriculum as that aggregate of courses provided in a school or college. To be sure, formal courses (or some other unit of instruction) are the core of the curriculum; but these organized learning experiences are often supplemented and enhanced by other less formal and sometimes less structured activities. "Extracurricular" or "cocurricular" activities include athletics, dramatics, musical organizations, social events, and special interest clubs. Also included might be experiences outside the school in the community, such as field trips and work experience. While some of these extracurricular activities relate directly to preparation for employment, we are concerned primarily with those structured learning experiences of the more formal type, generally called programs and courses.

The terms curriculum, program, and course are too often used interchangeably without being adequately defined. We define *curriculum* as the entire spectrum of educational experiences made available to students through a given institution. The curriculum is made up of many programs, and each program consists of an aggregate of courses. Determination of curriculum in vocational education then is a problem of broad policy definition related to the overall career needs of students and manpower needs of a given geographic region. Curriculum development in vocational education has to do with determining which occupations should be covered by the institution's educational efforts, and in what priority order resources should be allocated. In this macro sense, curriculum is the responsibility at least of the top level administrators and the controlling body of the institution.

Program refers to the aggregate educational offerings of a school or college related to a specific occupation or occupation cluster. It covers all the knowledge, values, attitudes, and manipulative skills associated with job entry in a given occupational area. A *course* is a discrete segment of a program which covers specific, measurable behavioral objectives of knowledge, attitudes, or practices related to a given discipline or occupation. Thus, an integrated series of courses comprises a program, and the sum total of programs offered by a school or college comprises its curriculum.

Curriculum planning is essentially a policy-making process that determines which programs should be initiated, revised, updated, or terminated. *Program planning* is a combination of policy planning, i.e. what should be done, and work planning, i.e. how it should be done. *Course planning* is essentially work planning. Course planning should be the responsibility of faculty who are competent in the given occupational area. Curriculum development, program planning, and course planning require input from a wide variety of sources, and the coordination of this input is an administrative responsibility.

Approaches to Curriculum Planning

Although we are concerned primarily with curriculum planning as it relates to specialized education as preparation for careers, most vocational administrators work in school systems or in educational institutions which are engaged in both general and specialized education. The processes and approaches to curriculum development in vocational and technical education, while in some respects unique, have a great deal in common with the processes and approaches used in general education. Tyler (*15*) and Taba (*13*), two recognized authorities in curriculum development, seem to agree that the first step in the process is to determine needs. Taba claims that needs must be determined before objectives are formulated, and that these needs must include the needs of society, the needs of the individual student, and the demands of the disciplines of knowledge. The vocational curriculum developer should be able to accept the validity of recognizing the needs of society and the individual, but he may be reluctant to accept the notion that the "demands" of the basic disciplines must be respected.

After needs have been diagnosed and objectives formulated, Taba (*13*) lists five more steps in the process of curriculum development: selection of content, organization of content, selection of learning experiences, organization of learning experiences, and evaluation. Content selection and organization are matters of program planning and lead to course structuring, while selection and organization of learning experiences are the problems of course planning and teaching. Our concern in this chapter centers on the former.

The administrator of vocational programs in comprehensive institutions must be able to mesh the specialized vocational program with any general education requirements of the institution and with other specialized programs. In some secondary schools the vocational administrator may find opposition to any program of specialized education (other than preparation for college). In most schools where general and specialized programs operate side by side they tend to complement one another. Because of this close relationship between general and specialized programs, administrators and curriculum planners in such schools should understand general curriculum principles and practices but they also should understand those unique features of curriculum development and program planning associated with vocational and technical education. We are concerned here with a few of the most important features and some of the problems of curriculum and program planning in vocational education as they relate to administration. For a fuller understanding of curriculum processes and procedures, consult the references at the end of this chapter.

In the past a frequent criticism of vocational and technical education programs was that they were developed solely to meet the needs of the "establishment" for cheap manpower. It was alleged that program and curriculum development occurred in response to local business and industrial needs, not in response to the real needs of students. Obviously, vocational and technical education must be responsive both to manpower needs and to student preferences, as well as to economic and sociopolitical requisites.

While a variety of approaches to curriculum planning exist, they can usually be categorized as one of the following types, or a combination of them: social demand, manpower requirements, or benefit/cost (5). The social demand approach attempts to forecast and assess consumer preference and demand for education, i.e. what students, parents, and the taxpaying community want. Presumably, in vocational education consumer demand is related to perceived employment opportunities. The manpower needs approach to curriculum planning attempts to relate program development to future economic demands for the production of goods and services. The benefit/cost approach attempts to insure maximum achievement of a given goal, or minimum use of resources to achieve that goal. It takes the position that there is a given amount of resources, which should be used to achieve an optimal rate of return. In practice, curriculum planning is a composite of these three approaches and includes in-depth study of demands, resources, and the cultural-intellectual level of the probable student population. Curriculum planning is a process which ultimately is political, in the broadest sense of the word.

Arnold and Ferguson (1) identified four considerations of major importance in determining which occupational areas should be emphasized in a local secondary school vocational program: (1) local and national manpower needs; (2) student needs as perceived by community representatives and school staff; (3) student occupational aspirations; and (4) parental occupational preferences for their children. Figure 8-1 shows the relationship of their criteria for selection of occupational areas and some other community considerations and constraints which must be taken into account as decisions are made. They identified thirty-nine occupational areas and then developed techniques which would enable a local community school district to rank the thirty-nine areas relative to each of the four

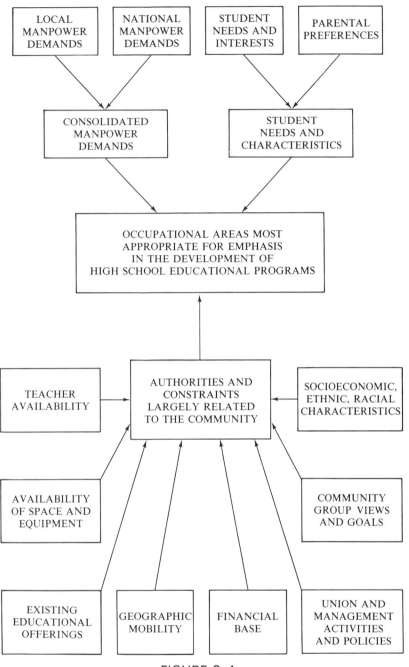

FIGURE 8-1

CRITERIA FOR SELECTION OF OCCUPATIONAL AREAS APPROPRIATE
FOR EMPHASIS IN THE DEVELOPMENT OF HIGH SCHOOL
EDUCATIONAL PROGRAMS

considerations. The methodology was tried out in eighteen school districts where, through interviews, information was obtained from school administrators, curriculum and guidance personnel, parents of eleventh graders, eleventh grade students, and local business and community planners. Although this approach was used to determine appropriate high school programs, it is believed to be equally valid for post-secondary program determination. For information related more specifically to planning occupational education programs on the community college level, see Teeple (*13*).

While curriculum planning must take into account this broad array of social forces, it is our contention that the student must be the focal point. The whole career education thrust of awareness, exploration, and preparation for the world of work must ultimately respond to the self-fulfillment needs of the student. Thus a vocational-technical program must incorporate manpower needs analysis, but not limit that analysis to a local geographic area. As long as there are existent jobs within the practical mobility potential of the student, preparation for those jobs should be considered as a possibility by curriculum planners. A case which illustrates this philosophy involves the school district in Alpena, Michigan, a small town in the northeast corner of the state on Lake Huron. There, vocational educators search out job opportunities within a 500-mile radius and then train students to meet specific employer needs. Because of its rural, out-migration population pattern and general lack of industry, Alpena found too many of its high school graduates jobless. The vocational program now actually prepares them to leave the area. While the migration pattern may be unfortunate, the school district is planning its curriculum to meet students' needs.

Manpower Analysis

Even a student-oriented curriculum in vocational and technical education still requires manpower need analysis. Since vocational education is education for employment and since the Vocational Education Acts of 1963 and 1968 state that training and retraining shall be provided "which is realistic in the light of actual or anticipated opportunities for gainful employment" (Public Law 90-576), those responsible for curriculum planning must necessarily analyze manpower supply and demand.

Unfortunately, manpower need forecasting is not used as widely or vigorously as it should be by educators in general and by vocational-technical educators in particular. As Young et al. pointed out:

> Opinion that forecasting makes a net positive contribution to educational planning is not universal. Doubt concerning this contribution arises, first,

from the fact that forecasts often are disappointingly inaccurate and, second, from the fact that these inaccurate forecasts may then result in misallocated resources. (*18*, p. 21)

The results of poor manpower analysis are frequently quite visible. In forecasting the need for professionals at the national level, it is now apparent that the emphasis on science and engineering in the later 1950s and 1960s resulted in a temporary oversupply of Ph.D. scientists and engineers, many of whom have recently been unemployed and/or retrained. In the last two to three years it became apparent to educators and legislators alike that too many elementary school teachers were being produced. Better curriculum planning, based on correct manpower need analysis, might have prevented this.

Four basic techniques have been identified and are most commonly used in manpower forecasting (*18*, p. 25): (1) employer surveys, (2) extrapolation of trends, (3) econometric techniques, and (4) job vacancy-occupational outlook approach. The employer survey, often referred to as "Area Skills Survey" or "Training Needs Survey," is a technique for determining local-regional needs. Correctly administered, it identifies from 50 to 150 occupations which have relatively high levels of employment in the area. A scientific sample of employers in these occupations is then surveyed to determine their current manpower needs and their expected needs two years and five years hence. The employer survey is the approach most used by local vocational administrators, since it is relatively easy to administer, has a low cost, and is quickly implemented. The reliability and validity of employer responses may be questionable, however, since many firms have not done the necessary planning to project their own needs with any degree of accuracy; but this approach has the distinct advantage of incorporating the ideas and preferences of local employers who are significant constituents of the school or college.

A second approach to manpower forecasting is that of extrapolation, which attempts to forecast future needs on the basis of past trends. Extrapolation may, of course, be done on a local-regional, state-wide or national basis. Like the employer survey, extrapolation is relatively quick, easy, and inexpensive. However, given the technological knowledge explosion and rapid changes in production patterns and occupational requirements, the predictive validity of extrapolation becomes more questionable the further it is extended into the future.

A more sophisticated and futuristic approach to manpower forecasting is the econometric technique used by the Bureau of Labor Statistics of the U.S. Department of Labor. The BLS econometric approach yields a national ten-year demand analysis based on projections of population, labor force, productivity, consumption, and overall output. It provides estimates of new openings by occupation, but not necessarily by educational need category. The econometric model also has its limitations of accuracy since it is hard to forecast economic activity, technological change related to productivity, and specific needs in given labor market areas which change due to labor and capital mobility. The BLS model has been advocated for state and regional level planning. The implementation of the model would be difficult for a vocational educator, since it requires reasonably extensive knowledge of labor economics and statistics. On the local-regional level, however, it could be carried out by various manpower and employment agencies of the state and federal governments, and then be applied to vocational education planning.

A fourth approach, the job vacancy/matrix approach, attempts to build local input into a modification of the econometric model. It takes data from the BLS matrix analysis and also examines local employment service listings of unfilled job openings. Jobs unfilled for thirty days are compared with national trends and analyzed in terms of casual characteristics. This finally results in a priority listing of jobs with apparent shortages which the educator must then analyze in terms of probable persistence, trainability, and benefit/cost return. The job vacancy/matrix approach is relatively inexpensive, can be programmed on a local-regional basis, builds in up-to-date trends, and can be implemented by the vocational educator.

The best manpower approach is an eclectic one which utilizes elements from all of the above. Burt (*3*) gives a variety of survey examples which local administrators might find helpful. The problem, however, is one of determining how much effort and resources a school or college can afford to put into manpower forecasting. It is argued that in many areas shortages of trained manpower are so acute in some fields that the introduction of a new educational program will only begin to dent the need, and thus there is little need for an expensive, sophisticated forecasting effort.

Whatever approach the educator elects to use, it is important that it be consistent, explainable to constituents, and constantly checked for predictive validity. Manpower forecasting related to curriculum planning is obviously a constant, continuing process, and cannot be limited to a one-time snapshot of the local labor market. Kidder indicated six critical requirements for a manpower forecasting model which can be used by vocational educators:

(1) The technique should be replicable at different times and in different places. This requirement concerns costs as well as technical complexity of the model.
(2) All *assumptions of the model should be reasonable,* and should be explicitly and clearly stated.
(3) The structure of the model should be thoroughly explained, in language understandable to potential users of the model.

(4) Forecasted estimate errors should be included.

(5) Forecasted subtotals should be internally consistent, and should be cross-checked to prove consistency.

(6) Accuracy analysis should be an integral part of the forecasting process. (*6*, p. 5)

Determining Consumer Preferences

Most educators would agree that informed consumer (students, parents, community) preferences should be the highest priority factor in curriculum and program planning. The problem is in defining the consumer and then making sure his preferences are based on informed analysis.

STUDENT PREFERENCES

The first problem is in ascertaining the composition of the consumer population. For the comprehensive high school and the area vocational center this may not be a substantial problem. Their primary consumer is the day-student; and this population is generally well-defined geographically and in terms of age group. However, most area vocational centers run adult vocational and manpower training programs and most comprehensive high schools have adult evening classes. The adult and out-of-school youth population is a more difficult population to analyze.

Comprehensive community colleges can define their consumer population in terms of geography, but age span, even for full-time students, is another matter. Many people tend to think of the community college as a junior college serving freshmen and sophomores in the 18–20 age bracket. To the contrary, community college students on the average are older than their freshmen and sophomore counterparts in four-year colleges. In some community colleges attendance in the evening far outdistances day class enrollment. Community colleges widely regard their clientele as the entire age spectrum of the community over age 18. Four-year technical colleges may draw students from multicounty, state-wide, or multistate regions. They frequently offer a variety of both pre-employment and inservice training programs to adults of all ages. Thus, the problem of clientele identification is more difficult for post-secondary vocational and technical education.

A second, but related problem is making sure that consumer preference is founded on an adequate knowledge of occupational options and career possibilities. There seems to be a fairly wide communications gap regarding job skill requirements and status in many occupations, and more importantly, in availability of jobs and the wage-income potential. The fact that many skilled technicians now earn two to three times what some professionals earn is just beginning to be understood by the public, and while a Ph.D. chemist may not be able to find a job in his field, a medical technologist may have many open options. Ascertaining clientele preferences may itself also become an educational process. An illustration of the occupational opportunity information gap is the frequent reluctance of minority students, particularly in urban areas, to enter vocational and technical programs at the secondary and post-secondary levels. For years these people were pushed into secondary vocational programs which they regarded as inferior (and which often were!). As a result, attending college means having nothing to do with technical or occupational training, except at the professional level.

Finally, the problem of informing the potential clientele about career possibilities has to do not only with currently available options, but with a sense of the future. A rational choice about vocation must consider current employment opportunities and the probable future developments in technology, supply and demand, income levels, requirements for retraining, and perhaps most importantly, the ladder relationship of the career choice. By ladder relationship we mean the opportunity, through further education and/or experience, to enter another career phase in the same general discipline or career field. In the future the United States will see a growth of new technician careers which perform specialized and limited functions in traditionally professional fields. The question the informed potential student must be able to answer is: How much career mobility does my chosen occupational field permit me? An important and continuing task of educators, prominently noted by career education proponents, is the diffusion of information about vocations. Based on that diffusion, then and only then can consumers make rational inputs about vocational curriculum preferences.

Ascertaining consumer preferences can be achieved through a variety of information-gathering mechanisms. Direct survey questionnaires can be administered to large numbers of potential vocational-technical students through high school classes, at public employment offices, at military release centers, or through the mail. Educational and vocational guidance counselors can provide reasonably valid feedback about students with whom they deal. Industrial personnel offices often have interest inventory information on the people who have applied for jobs in their companies, as do Veterans Administration Offices, Vocational Rehabilitation Offices, State Employment Security Offices, and a host of other governmental agencies, including various offices of the U.S. Department of Labor.

Related to the problem of ascertaining student perferences is the issue of reconciling these preferences to realistic ability levels of the student population. Attempting to prepare people for careers for which they are temperamentally, culturally, or intellectually unsuited can be an economic waste and a tragedy of human frustration. One of the most important things a vocational educator must study and understand is his student population. McMahon summed up the challenge of curriculum development:

> Curriculum must be developed to meet the needs of the student rather than the desires of the developer. No textbook theories or calculated formulas can replace the in-depth study of local interests, resources, economy, industry, finances, and the cultural and intellectual level of the student population. (*10*, p. 2)

PARENT AND OTHER CONSUMER PREFERENCES

While the student is the primary concern of any educational program, there are other groups which must be considered because of their influence on both students' decisions and program approval. Parents, of secondary school youth particularly, might be surveyed to determine their attitudes toward specialized vocational programs in general, but also to get their perceptions of the kinds of occupational programs appropriate for their children. In the final analysis parents and other taxpayers in the community must be convinced that whatever programs are to be initiated are indeed needed and appropriate. For them to be involved in the process of arriving at decisions to make curriculum changes or additions may assure their support.

Critical Factors in Curriculum and Program Planning

FEDERAL AND STATE GOVERNMENT INVOLVEMENT

Given the need to evaluate manpower needs and consumer preferences, there is still a question about at what level curriculum and program planning should take place. Where should priorities be determined? To observers of the education scene it is clear that there is significant influence from the national level; the expenditures of the U.S. Office of Education (*16*, p. 117) at all levels have increased substantially over the past decade, rising from $547 million in 1962 to over $4.7 billion in 1972. The Educational Amendments of 1972 created the post of Deputy Commissioner for Adult, Vocational and Technical Education, and placed heavy emphasis on career education. In fact, the career education thrust received strong support on the national level, particularly from the then U.S. Commissioner Sidney Marland. While the U.S. Office of Education has generally resisted the temptation to impose specific curricula and programs on state and local school systems, its influence has certainly determined many curricular priorities. Money talks, as can be amply demonstrated by the effect of research and development grants awarded by the federal government. Many local administrators have applied for various kinds of research and development grants only to rue the day when they found that local priorities had in effect been determined by the grant regulations, that indeed the tail was wagging the dog. Under the Vocational Education Acts of 1963 and 1968, the federal government has distributed federal revenue for use by state vocational education agencies, but it has partly shaped state and local priorities by levying certain requisites:

> The U.S. Office of Education has required that states distribute their federal vocational education funds to local education planning agencies through a system reflecting (1) manpower needs, (2) vocational education needs, (3) relative ability of the district to pay, and (4) excess costs. (*18,* p. 125)

While one may agree or disagree with federal priorities or requisites, the fact is that they exist. But above all, the federal government has insured the establishment of state-wide planning, development, and coordinating agencies for vocational and technical education. The involvement of these state agencies ranges widely from loose coordination and distribution of federal and state monies to specific determination of curricular and program offerings in given areas, even including the delineation of course outlines and objectives. Thus, the parameters regarding curriculum development vary greatly from state to state for local vocational and technical education administrators.

LOCAL DETERMINATION

While the development of a state master plan for vocational education helps to delineate priority areas of concern, the final decision about curriculum for locally based institutions (comprehensive high schools and community colleges, and area vocational schools or centers) should be left for local determination. While information about state-wide manpower needs and about potential manpower supply from other educational institutions (public, private, and industrial) is crucial for rational decision making at the local level, the choice should nevertheless remain there. Thus, which occupational programs are to be offered is a local educational-political decision, based in part on inputs and influences from state and national agencies. However, the problem of determining the substantive composition of a program becomes more complex. Who should determine what knowledge, attitudes, and skills are required in a given occupational area? Should not a program for the training of auto mechanics at a comprehensive high school be approximately equivalent to one offered at an area vocational center in the same state? Should not a degree in automotive service technology at one community college cover essentially the same substantive material as that in another? Program parity across similar institutions virtually requires some sort of state coordination. Licensing and professional certification agencies guarantee some level of proficiency of graduates in those occupations where such examinations are required. State-wide or even nationwide competency examinations are needed in technical and vocational areas to measure behavioral outcomes. Such examinations would reduce the need for state agency coordination or control of program planning and development.

By the same token, determining courses should be done at the local level by the faculty member, with review and assistance of supervisory personnel and non-educators. It is extremely difficult to prepare a standardized occupational course outline at the state level which is appropriate for different geographical areas. Furthermore, good pedagogical theory dictates that the teacher be integrally involved in determining what is to be taught and how it is to be taught. McMahon has pointed out that

> State-developed material can be used as an interim course of study if the beginner has no older colleague willing to share his. It can supplement and complement teacher-developed material but it should not be used as a permanent substitute for one's own analysis and course-building activities. (*10,* p. 23)

Thus, local education institutions should control *course* planning at one end of the spectrum, and overall curriculum planning (i.e. determination of what programs should be offered) at the other end. In the middle, the question of program outcomes or student competencies requires some sort of coordinating and regulating mechanism beyond the economics of the local labor market and student interests.

ARTICULATION

One of the reasons for this need for program coordination and equivalency is the problem of institutional articulation. Recognition of the need to link programs of different level institutions is growing. For example, how does the student who graduates from a surveying program in an area vocational center program fit into the associate degree program in a community college or subsequently into a baccalaureate program in surveying or civil engineering of a four-year institution? When schools and colleges are unable to accept credits from other institutions or recognize certificates, diplomas or degrees conferred, there is obvious economic inefficiency and individual frustration. Meaningful articulation between different level programs and across similar institutions will shortly become a public mandate which educators can ill-afford to disobey.

Articulation is a problem for community colleges and four-year technical colleges, but in addition, they are obligated to review their entire curriculum more carefully in terms of state-wide priorities since most of them are state-supported institutions. Thus, curriculum planning decisions, as well as program development ones, must consider state manpower needs and the program offering of other institutions. As their students are matriculated from a wide geographical area or sometimes the entire state, and on graduating tend to seek employment throughout the state or region, these institutions should have their curriculum proposals reviewed by a state vocational education planning agency.

FIXING INSTITUTIONAL RESPONSIBILITY

At the local level, a critical question involves how the curriculum is to be developed, and by whom. As noted earlier, curriculum decisions are policy decisions and should involve the governing board and chief administrator of the institution. However, none of these people operate in a vacuum. The question is what other individuals and groups should have input. As the elected or appointed responsible officials, the board members must be concerned with all aspects of the operation of the school or college. While they should approve the curriculum, the impetus for initiation, redirection, or termination of programs or courses must come from the chief administrator and people who advise him.

Curriculum planning and development is the responsibility of the chief vocational administrator. In large or new and growing institutions he may have an assistant who has unique responsibility for vocational curriculum development and coordination. At the secondary level he may be called a vocational curriculum coordinator; at the collegiate level he may be an assistant dean for occupational education planning. This person is responsible for investigating possible program areas, conducting manpower or area skills surveys, inventorying student and community preferences, analyzing job skill requirements, reviewing the curricular offerings of other institutions, formulating new occupational program proposals, evaluating the effectiveness of current programs, and proposing revision or termination of current offerings. Beyond the curriculum coordinator the most important institutional resource for curriculum development is of course the faculty. While faculty must have final responsibility for course construction, which includes selection and organization of content and learning experiences, they are also major participants in the development of entire program areas, and have a legitimate voice in overall curriculum decisions. Faculty should be knowledgeable about job skill requirements in their own occupations and about the emerging occupation trends which will lead to new program offerings.

OCCUPATIONAL ANALYSIS

Occupational education content is derived from occupations. Therefore there must be a close link between vocational and technical education programs in the schools and occupations as practiced in the world of work. To strengthen this link between vocational education and the world of work, the two relevant departments in federal government—the United States Department of Labor and the United States Department of Health, Education and Welfare—published jointly in 1969 a report titled *Vocational Education and Occupations.* It outlines a system which is used to define and classify vocational and technical instructional programs offered by states and local school systems, and links the programs to occupations found in all areas of the economy; it is a tool which educational planners should find most helpful. This publication is referenced here to emphasize the close relationship between occupational *practice* and occupational *education* which must exist if vocational and technical programs are to be viable. Another useful tool in relation to program planning is the United States Employment Service *Dictionary of Occupational Titles* (DOT) (1965) which is based upon occupational analysis, presents a classification system for occupations, and shows relationships among them; a total of 21,741 separate occupations are defined. A teacher in an occupational program should be able to identify by DOT number and definition the occupations in which students completing that program might expect to find employment.

If a school or college decides to offer a program aimed at preparing workers for a particular occupation or family of occupations, the next step is to determine the actual work performed in that occupation and the performance requirements of workers. Occupational analysis is the process used, and consists of identifying by observation, interview, and study the technical and environmental factors of a specific occupation and reporting the significant activities and requirements of the worker. Occupational analysis determines what the worker needs to know and be able to do in order to function effectively in a particular occupation; it should also result in information regarding attitudes, values, working conditions, etc. associated with the occupation. It is the basis for determining content for specialized vocational and technical education programs because undergirding each skilled, technical, paraprofessional, or professional occupation lies a substantial set of relatively stable behaviors which can be described and taught. Qualified vocational teachers are generally familiar with occupational analysis techniques, and teachers are primarily involved in this process. School administrators should at least be aware of the fact that content for vocational and technical programs is derived from occupations and that occupational analysis is the process used.

Having determined the occupational characteristics and requirements, the next step is to determine the education and training needed by the worker for successful performance in the occupation. This is a matter of determining teachable content, organizing this content into units of instruction—courses and lessons—and then selecting and organizing learning experiences, followed by evaluating the instructional program. These functions are clearly the responsibility of teachers because they are specialists, each in his occupational area.

Occupational and job analysis is used for a variety of purposes, but we are concerned here only with its use in determining content for instructional purposes. Also, it should not be assumed that in developing a new program in a high school or in a community college we must necessarily do a complete analysis of the occupations for which the program is to prepare youth and adults. More frequently, analyses done by others are used as a base and then modified to fit the local situation. In some states analyses have been done and courses of study prescribed *by the state,* but in any event the instructional program should be adapted by the teacher to meet local conditions and needs.

ADVISORY COMMITTEES

In addition to faculty, administrative staff, and governing board members, other people need to be involved in curriculum development. The chief administrator should have a general occupational adivsory committee of lay citizens representing industry, labor, local government, public service agencies, and education consumers. This committee must be active, not just window-dressing. It can provide vital information about evolving occupational needs, entree to local industry and labor organizations for manpower studies, faculty recruitment, cooperative education placement, possible equipment donations, and available space for training programs, as well as providing general moral support and information dissemination in the community. Most educators feel they are already overburdened with committees which serve no useful purpose. Nevertheless, there is an overriding and compelling need for a general curriculum advisory committee to give a balanced perspective to questions about the institution's overall educational mission. Advisory committees can play an invaluable role in gaining grassroots community support for vocational-technical programs. This curriculum advisory group can provide a perspective on the political viability of proposed programs, the appropriateness of the proposed program for the institutional level and for the sophistication of the student body, and whether the economic benefits (including indirect or secondary benefits to the community) warrant the cost.

With respect to development of occupational programs within the overall curriculum, involvement of an active advisory committee for each specialized vocational program is indispensible. Experienced practitioners and employers within the particular career field are needed to provide job skill requirement analyses, information about new technologies being employed in the occupation, changes in manpower requirements, adequacy of material provided in courses, resource participants for particular aspects of courses, information about possible donations of equipment, materials or space from industry, availability of cooperative education training slots, and assistance in placing program graduates.

Both program and general curriculum advisory committees should include a wider range of people than just employers, experienced professionals in the occupation, and representatives of labor. Recent graduates can provide feedback about the applicability of what they learned in their particular program or at the school in general as it relates to their entry job needs. Local representatives of state employment offices or the U.S. Department of Labor can be most useful members. Current students, provided they are not intimidated, can be a source of creative ideas for programs. Instead of incorporating students into regular program or curriculum advisory committees, some schools and colleges actually set up a separate student advisory committee for the various programs. The mantle of the committee structure often permits students to express concerns or criticisms which they are unable or unwilling to express individually.

One additional kind of vocational advisory committee which can be important for the local administrator is the Joint Apprenticeship and Training Committee (JATC). JATCs are formed, through voluntary agreement of management and labor in collective bargaining, for the purpose of selection, training, education, and placement of apprentices in a given trade. Composed of equal representatives of management and labor, JATCs can have significant influence in improving overall manpower training in a given area. The JATC usually works with local vocational schools and colleges in developing both skills courses and related education courses. The JATC also can provide meaningful advice about changing employment trends, job skill requirements, and applicability of program content to job needs.

An Illustration

We have discussed alternative approaches and critical factors in curriculum and program planning. How these approaches and factors interrelate and are sequenced is shown in figure 8–2. This figure summarizes a model of program planning and development proposed by Battelle Columbus Laboratories (*2*, p. 89). The first part of the model relates primarily to the problems of planning discussed in this chapter, while the second part focuses on what we call management of instruction, as discussed in the following chapter. The total process, however, is integrated and continuing, and cannot be disjointed.

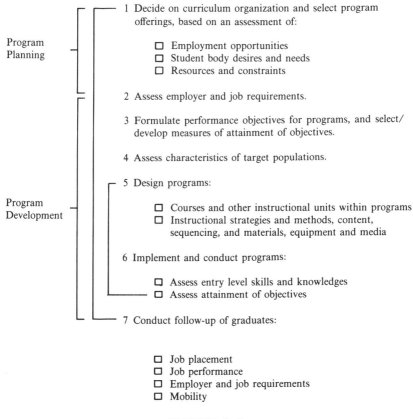

Program
Planning

1 Decide on curriculum organization and select program offerings, based on an assessment of:

☐ Employment opportunities
☐ Student body desires and needs
☐ Resources and constraints

2 Assess employer and job requirements.

3 Formulate performance objectives for programs, and select/develop measures of attainment of objectives.

4 Assess characteristics of target populations.

5 Design programs:

☐ Courses and other instructional units within programs
☐ Instructional strategies and methods, content, sequencing, and materials, equipment and media

Program
Development

6 Implement and conduct programs:

☐ Assess entry level skills and knowledges
☐ Assess attainment of objectives

7 Conduct follow-up of graduates:

☐ Job placement
☐ Job performance
☐ Employer and job requirements
☐ Mobility

FIGURE 8–2

STEPS IN CURRICULUM DEVELOPMENT, REVISION, AND UPDATING

From Battelle Columbus Laboratories Study reported in *American Vocational Journal,* November 1972.

The following example illustrates the curriculum and program planning process which a community college might use in developing a new occupational program preparing people to be legal assistants. The legal assistant is an emerging career, usually requiring two years of post-secondary education, which enables people to perform technical duties in a law office, business, or governmental organization. Specific tasks of a legal assistant might include preparing materials for director and shareholder meetings in business; preparing materials for compliance/regulatory agencies; indexing documents for trials; researching legal problems and preparing reports of the findings; managing the office of a law firm; managing records relating to estates and trusts, taxes and insurance; and assisting lawyers in investigating criminal cases.

The first step in curriculum planning is recognizing the possibility of the need for a given program. This recognition might come via a board member, a faculty member, educational literature, or any number of sources. The vocational administrator must then undertake a survey of the local-regional manpower market to determine whether or not employment possibilities might exist in the area for persons prepared as legal assistants. This survey would necessarily include lawyers' offices, local business, government agencies, and municipal and district courts. If potential employers are found to be interested, and perhaps enthusiastic, the next step is surveying the interests and preferences of students or potential students within the jurisdiction of the college. This might be done formally or informally on the campus, through high school vocational counselors, through parent-teacher associations, and through local employment agencies.

Assuming positive student response, the next step would be forming a program planning advisory committee representing the major employer groups surveyed, and including some vocational educators (potential faculty) and students. This committee would help the vocational administrator:

a. review any state or federal guidelines or studies related to the legal assistant occupation;

b. assess what other educational institutions have developed in legal assistant programs;

c. assess employers' requirements and conduct an occupational task analysis;

d. assess the characteristics and needs of the potential student body; and

e. in light of the above, formulate the tasks which a legal assistant should be able to perform and the kinds of educational inputs which local students would require to be able to perform them;

f. design specific courses and other experiences within the legal assistant program framework, taking into account pedagogical methods, content, sequence, and materials, equipment, and media required.

Based on the advisory committee's analysis, a program coordinator should be assigned specific implementation responsibility. In the legal assistant program, this faculty member would have a legal background and experience in one or more of the kinds of employing organizations. The advisory committee continues to aid him during the implementation of the program and provides review and critique of possible program changes. As the first graduates complete the program, the committee helps place them and evaluates their effectiveness. Based on the placement and related measures of effectiveness and satisfaction, the coordinator and advisory committee make recommendations about program revision, expansion, or termination.

Special Problems

INITIATING NEW PROGRAMS

New program development is the lifeblood of any technical or vocational education institution. As technology expands and the composition of the labor force changes, manpower demands are altered. Futurologists chide educators for training people for jobs which may not exist in five to ten years, and certainly will be extinct by the turn of the century. Schools and colleges must develop new programs for new careers. The impetus for new programs may come from many sources: concerned employers or consumers, legislators, state coordinating boards, the local governing board, program or curriculum advisory committees, faculty, or the administration. The issue is not so much who suggests a new program, but rather how a program idea is processed or given consideration in the planning effort once it has been suggested. The curriculum development process should be carefully spelled out so that it is clear to all concerned what factors must be considered in recommending a new program. Such a process should include: a review of manpower needs and job availability in the occupational area; analysis of required and institutionally available space and equipment; a review of the availability of qualified potential faculty; and finally a dollar benefit/cost analysis utilizing the previous data to compare the proposed program with existent programs and other proposed alternatives. Programs should not be established capriciously; on the other hand, any legitimate suggestion should receive serious consideration.

ASSOCIATED ACADEMIC REQUIREMENTS

A second major issue in vocational-technical education curriculum development is the amount of "general education," "academic," or "related" courses that should be required in a given occupational program. The question of how many and what kinds of courses in related fields (i.e. mathematics, science, English, or other courses necessary for successful entry in the occupation but not dealing with specific behavioral job skills) is less difficult than the more philosophic question about what kind and how many general education courses a student should be required to take. Too many vocational-technical institutions are criticized for preparing a student only to enter a job, rather than to prepare him to cope with the technical and social change which will most likely require him to continue his education or be retrained for a vocation which currently does not exist. While there is no easy answer to this persistent issue of substantive blend in a given occupational program, we would argue for flexibility expressed in terms of the individual student's needs. The problem must be worked out at each school or college in the context of its own sociopolitical milieu.

Most comprehensive community colleges as well as many four-year technical colleges have open door admissions policies which permit any resident citizen constituent over eighteen to matriculate in the institution, regardless of his past academic record. This "second-chance" open door policy was, until recently, a relatively unique characteristic of the community colleges, but one which has some inherent problems. Some students with general academic deficiencies cannot succeed in vocational-technical programs because they lack general communication and arithmetic skills. Thus, post-secondary curriculum development planning must give adequate consideration to what kind and how extensive a remedial education program the institution should offer in conjunction with its vocational programs. Not providing some remedial courses in English, mathematics, and science may preclude any chance of program success for a large number of students. The decision about remedial course offerings must obviously consider the kinds of students the institution is attracting and the specific needs they have. Better articulation with the secondary schools which serve as "feeders" can help solve this problem.

REQUIRED WORK EXPERIENCE

Cooperative education programs, designed to give students training through experiences in real-life situations, are widely accepted in both secondary and post-secondary vocational-technical education. To what extent is cooperative education experience desirable or required in each specific program? Is an internship, a clinical experience, or a work experience requirement an integral factor in preparing people for a job entry in a given occupation? For example, most teacher training institutions hold that there is no substitute for student teaching experience. This is similarly true in many allied health occupations, and increasingly accepted in business and trade-technical programs. The benefits of an extensive cooperative education program extend beyond the learning experiences of students to improved graduate placement, development of grassroot community support, and improvement of program content. Each institution must determine the extent to which its programs should involve cooperative on-the-job education.

REVISING THE CURRICULUM

A final problem related to curriculum is revision. Curriculum revision has to do with updating course and program content to incorporate new technology and practices related to changing job needs. It also has to do with the development of new programs to meet new needs or provide training for new careers. However, new program development in a time of stabilizing enrollments is virtually dependent on the elimination of existent non-productive or less desirable programs.

Program advisory committees are the best mechanisms for revising and updating course content and adding new courses. They can be helpful in weeding out substantive material which is no longer germane. However, when it comes to program termination in the process of curriculum revision, the program advisory committee is likely to be resistant. They have become the built-in constituency which supports the continuation of the program even when other factors indicate it should be discontinued. The decision to terminate a program is usually difficult. Faculty teaching in the program may become cases of human agony unless alternatives positions can be found. Alumni of the program may become incensed. Friends of the institution see its traditions crumbling, particularly if the program is one of long standing. Nevertheless, if program evaluation (see chapter 14) indicates that there are no jobs for graduates, or that lesser trained people can adequately perform the work, or that costs are skyrocketing without sufficient benefit to the institution or the community (i.e. all graduates migrate to other regions), or that other institutions can do the job better, then it may be time to terminate the program. When such a decision is made, it is important to communicate the rationale for eliminating the program to all people involved, within the institution and outside it. Adequate curriculum planning should permit a gradual acceptable phasing out process which will alleviate or avoid many of the headaches of precipitous change. Planned change is vital to the life of the total institution.

REFERENCES

1. Arnold, Joseph P. and Edward T. Ferguson, Jr. *Determining Occupational Emphases for High School Program Design.* Columbus, Ohio: The Center for Vocational and Technical Education, 1973.

2. Battelle Columbus Laboratories. "Developing, Revising and Updating Curriculum To Meet On-the-Job Needs," *American Vocational Journal* 49, No. 8 (November 1972): 89–98.

3. Burt, Samuel M. *Industry and Vocational-Technical Education.* New York: McGraw-Hill, 1967.

4. Fibel, Lewis R. *Review and Synthesis of Literature on Occupational Preparation in the Community College.* Columbus: ERIC Clearinghouse on Vocational and Technical Education Information Series, No. 55, March 1972.

5. Harmon, W. G. *Three Approaches to Educational Resource Allocation.* Toronto: Institute for the Quantitative Analysis of Social and Economic Policy, December 1968.

6. Kidder, David E. *Review and Synthesis of Research on Manpower Forecasting for Vocational-Technical Education.* Information Series No. 54. Columbus: The Center for Vocational and Technical Education, The Ohio State University, 1972.

7. Larson, Milton E. *Review and Synthesis of Research: Analysis for Curriculum Development in Vocational Education.* Research Series Number 46. Columbus: The Center for Vocational and Technical Education, The Ohio State University, 1969.

8. Law, Gordon F., ed. *Contemporary Concepts in Vocational Education.* Washington, D.C.: American Vocational Association, 1971. See particularly:
   O'Kelley, George L., Jr. "Approaches to Curriculum Planning," pp. 112–117.
   Olivo, C. Thomas. "Philosophical Bases for Curriculum Development," pp. 126–29.
   Moss, Jerome, Jr., and Brandon B. Smith. "Some Steps in the Curriculum Development Process," pp. 130–37.

9. Malinski, Joseph F. *Planning Techniques for Local Programs of Vocational Education.* Columbus: ERIC Clearinghouse on Vocational and Technical Education, Information Series 63, July 1972.

10. McMahon, Gordon G. *Curriculum Development in Trade and Industrial and Technical Education.* Columbus: Charles E. Merrill, 1972.

11. McNamara, James F. "A Mathematical Programming Approach to State-Local Program Planning in Vocational Education." *American Educational Research Journal* 8, No. 2 (March 1971): 335–63.

12. Olson, Jerry C. "Decision Making Power: Signs of Articulation." *American Vocational Journal* 46, No. 7 (October 1971): 39–42.

13. Taba, Hilda. *Curriculum Development: Theory and Practice.* New York: Harcourt, Brace and World, 1962.

14. Teeple, John B. "Variables in Planning Occupational Education Programs." *American Association of Junior Colleges Journal,* February 1970.

15. Tyler, Ralph. *Basic Principles of Curriculum and Instruction.* Chicago: University of Chicago Press, 1950.

16. U.S. Department of Health, Education and Welfare. *Digest of Educational Statistics.* 1971 Edition, DHEW Publication No. (OE) 72-45. Washington: U.S. Government Printing Office, 1972.

17. U.S. Department of Health, Education and Welfare. *Standard Terminology for Curriculum and Instruction in Local and State School Systems.* Washington, D.C.: U.S. Government Printing Office, 1970.

18. Young, Robert C., William V. Clive and Benton E. Miles. *Vocational Education Planning: Manpower, Priorities and Dollars.* Research and Development Series. No. 68. Columbus: The Center for Vocational and Technical Education, The Ohio State University, 1972.

Chapter 9 MANAGEMENT OF INSTRUCTION

All curriculum and program planning efforts are useless unless they are effectively implemented in the instructional process. While the basic actors in the instructional process are the teacher and the learner, the responsibility for the management of instruction rests with *both* administrators and faculty. Management of instruction involves supervision and evaluation of the instructional process, coordination of scheduling, development of course sequences, incorporation of appropriate educational technology in courses and programs, coordination of outside experiences, and the use of community resources.

The purposes of this chapter are to help the reader:

1. to understand how all professional personnel are involved in the management of instruction;
2. to appreciate the shift in emphasis from the teacher as a dispenser of knowledge and skill to the teacher as manager of the learning environment;
3. to understand why it is important to give students more responsibility in decision making regarding their learning experiences;
4. to understand why it is necessary to have in every school or college one person who is responsible for coordinating instruction in vocational and technical education;

5. to explore and use outside resources for instructional support in a given occupational field;
6. to make use of the advancements in educational technology and innovative approaches to programming and scheduling.

If we accept the research on leadership and organizational effectiveness discussed in chapters 4 and 5, we should structure schools and colleges in full recognition of these concepts. For example, we know that leadership is widely diffused in any organization; it is not limited to persons in administrative or supervisory positions. Furthermore, we know that participatory management has certain advantages in terms of achieving organizational goals. These and other related concepts suggest that the management of the instructional processes should involve all persons engaged in the process—students and staff alike. In this chapter we will consider ways in which the administrator can structure and use the community and school environment to enhance learning. Considerations which are unique to specialized vocational and technical education will be emphasized since our primary interest is in instruction which is aimed at imparting specific knowledges, skills, and attitudes to others for the purpose of employability.

The Teacher as Manager of the Learning Environment

A vocational teacher has three distinctly different roles to play. One is as the key person working with groups of students in a classroom, shop, or laboratory; another is as a professional working with other teachers, supervisors, and administrators in the department, division, school, or college; and the third is in his role in the community with workers in the occupation which he is teaching. In each of these roles the teacher may function as a leader, but in the first and second he has, in addition, certain managerial responsibilities.

IN THE CLASSROOM

The classroom, shop, or laboratory is a social system with most of the characteristics of any other social organization. The environment in the learning laboratory is dependent to a large extent upon the leadership behavior of the teacher. Likert (6) applies the criteria used in "System 4" (described in chapter 5) to the classroom situation. He points out that the classroom of today is different because of pressures created by external social and technological conditions and by internal pressures brought about by a new type of teacher and a new type of student. He states:

> Psychologically, the teacher is finding less satisfaction in being a central authority figure. Children are more likely to resent direct authority today than to obey it.

The result is a discernible change in the ways schools operate. Principals are relying less and less on direct orders and more and more on team participation of teachers. Teachers in turn are seeing themselves in a new role and are working to create a democratic environment with abundant opportunities for self-direction by children.

Such a setting calls for a balance between control by the teacher and the exercise of initiative by the children. Good teachers are working to find realistic ways to combine centralization and decentralization of authority and responsibility.

Likert then gives the teacher a scale which can be used to rate his classroom and his performance as an instructional leader. Likert believes that the more opportunity there is in any social organization for meaningful involvement in goal setting, planning and operating the system, the greater will be the productivity of the group.

Vocational teachers can enhance their roles as instructional managers and leaders in the classroom by showing more confidence in students and using their ideas in planning, thereby making them more responsible for achieving instructional goals. Vocational teachers can also improve the effectiveness of their efforts in the classroom to the extent that they know the problems faced by individual students and have created a climate in which two-way communication is facilitated. Teachers should make decisions on the basis of school policy *and* student considerations, and they should involve students in decision making, especially those decisions related to students' classroom obligations. Both teachers and students should participate in the evaluation of classroom performance. Vocational administrators can help teachers acquire those competencies which will make them more effective leaders in the classroom, shop, or laboratory, because the behaviors of successful administrators and successful teachers have a great deal in common.

Basically, teachers are managers of a specific learning environment. They control the specific inputs necessary for the learning process, and plan, direct, and coordinate the specific activities of students in the classroom setting. They may also control various resources required for instruction. In effect, the teacher also plans, coordinates, and sets instructional priorities, even if these decisions are limited to a specific course or program. Vocational programs will be most effective if faculty view themselves as managers who control a variety of resource inputs and whose goal is to provide an optimal learning environment for a group of people with widely diverse abilities and characteristics.

IN THE INSTITUTION

Teachers are demanding a larger share in the administration of schools and colleges. College and university faculties have for some time exercised considerable control over instructional matters. High school and community college faculties will continue to organize primarily for purposes of negotiating economic benefits, but we can expect that ultimately matters of instructional management will be negotiated also. Vocational administrators should encourage teachers to take an active role in professional organizations, including teacher unions, where unions are already certified as bargaining agents. Through their professional organizations teachers can be a significant force in improving the quality of vocational education.

Teachers can also influence decisions made through the formal administrative structure of the school or college. If vocational administrators involve teachers in the decision-making process as fully as they should, the pressure for teacher unions to become active in school administration will be greatly reduced. The vocational administrator can involve teachers in the management of instruction through departmental or divisional meetings, through committees which cut across departmental or occupational lines, through the creation of special task forces, and in workshops.

IN THE COMMUNITY

The vocational teacher must have the confidence and respect of workers in the occupation for which he is preparing youth and adults. To do this he should be encouraged to maintain his relationships with the business or industry in which he was involved prior to becoming a teacher. Personnel policies should support the practice of vocational teachers returning periodically to their prior occupation for the purpose of updating their skills, learning about new practices, and maintaining occupational contacts. In some schools and colleges the vocational teacher's continuing involvement with the world of work is assured by making him responsible for job placement of students completing the program.

Student Involvement

There is a growing interest in involving students in the management of the school. This interest and, in some cases, concern stems from the fact that students are demanding more meaningful involvement. Students in two- and four-year colleges have been most vocal but secondary schools are also beginning to feel student pressures.

Student government organizations have traditionally provided the opportunity and mechanism for students to participate in organizing and operating certain social services for students, such as dances and other special events. But some students want more from their student government; they have ideas about changes they would like to see made in curricular as well as extracurricular matters and they desire political access to school authority so that their ideas might be heard.

Students' involvement in decision making can be on two levels: in making *governing decisions* and in making *individual choices.* In making governing decisions they share authority and influence in setting limits and conditions on behavior, while in making individual choices they select from options which have been defined. Student involvement may concern itself with non-academic decisions—student dress, hair styles, smoking, discipline in halls, student meetings, and social affairs—or academic decisions which concern the program of instruction—courses, teachers, grading methods, etc.

A study done at the Center for Social Organization of Schools by McPartland and others (*12*) reports some interesting findings on student participation. In reference to participation in non-academic decisions they found that

> When students feel they have a share of real authority in making governing decisions for non-academic behavior, there will be a greater respect for the resulting rules and regulations (even though they may be strict) both by the student representatives who helped make the decisions and by the other students in the school. . . . Student participation in making governing decisions (setting the rules) was consistently more important for school stability than degree of student choice under the rules (the permissiveness of the rules). School stability is more likely with strict rules which the students help draw up, than with permissive rules which students had no part in deciding. (*12*, pp. 16–17)

The study also looked into participation in academic decisions; one school in the study gave an unusual degree of choices in such matters as course content, academic obligations, time allocations, choice of teachers, and choice of grading methods. They describe this school as follows:

> At this school there are four terms in each nine-month academic year. At the beginning of each term, the students are presented with a catalog of course offerings and permitted to choose their own courses and teachers from this unusually rich set of offerings. There are required "areas" from which students must select one of several offerings, and these are frequently prerequisites for admission to advanced courses. Nevertheless, students and teachers in this school recognize that students have an unusual amount of say in deciding their academic program. (*12*, p. 21)

The researchers then compared the students in the "academic-choice school" with the students in the other thirteen high schools in the study as related to some important academic outcomes and school goals. They found that students from the academic-choice school gave significantly higher ratings of how well the courses were taught and their teachers' ability. The students with more choice were also significantly more satisfied with the course offerings and course assignments. The researchers claim that "providing students with greater academic choice might be expected to produce less hostility and more trust and respect between students and teachers" (*12*, p. 23). The students in the academic-choice school were found to be significantly higher on important attitudes toward responsibility which was positively related to academic performance as measured by school grades. While additional research is needed, this study would suggest that students in a school where they have more opportunity for participation in decision making do as well or better than students in schools which do not involve students.

Some people view student involvement in decision making as a means of reducing student dissension and disruption. It may indeed serve this purpose, especially if the options available to youth are broad enough. It is interesting to note that the study cited above found that

> The students who are most certain about their occupational destination, or who see the main purpose of schooling to prepare one for a job, have the least desire to get involved in school decisions. (*12*, p. 9)

NATIONAL VOCATIONAL STUDENT ORGANIZATIONS

Students who have made a tentative career choice and are enrolled in a specialized vocational education program are generally more interested in becoming involved in student organizations related specifically to their occupational interests. Through these organizations youth can become deeply involved in their own educational experiences. Of the several national organizations, the Future Farmers of America (FFA) is perhaps the oldest and best known. Local chapters of FFA have programs which are an integral part of the instructional program and through FFA activities, vocational agriculture students participate in making decisions regarding their education. Similarly, in other occupational areas there are national student organizations with which state and local units can affiliate. A partial list of student organizations and areas of occupational interest follows:

> DECA: Distributive Education Clubs of America for students taking marketing, merchandising, and management courses in the secondary and post-secondary schools.
>
> FBLA-PBL: Future Business Leaders of America-Phi Beta Lambda is a national organization serving students preparing for careers in business.
>
> FFA: Future Farmers of America for students preparing for careers in agricultural production, processing, supply and service, agricultural mechanics, natural resources and environmental science, horticulture, and forestry.

FHA: Future Homemakers of America for students enrolled in consumer homemaking and home economics-related occupations courses in the secondary schools.

OEA: Office Education Association for students enrolled in office occupations education in the secondary and post-secondary schools.

VICA: Vocational Industrial Clubs of America for students taking trade, industrial, technical, and health education courses in the secondary and post-secondary schools.

A new organization designed to serve students in health occupations is operating in some states.

Vocational education administrators should encourage and assist teachers in the development and use of vocational student organizations. Through such organizations vocational students can be involved in the decision-making process at a point where they are most directly affected. Local chapters of these organizations can be a powerful influence in bringing the world of work and the school into a closer working relationship, resulting in more realistic vocational instruction.

Improvement of Instruction as a Function of Administration

If we think of *curriculum* development as producing plans for further action and *instruction* as providing the conditions and resources needed to put plans into action and *teaching* as the interaction between the teacher and the learner, it becomes obvious that curricular decisions, while they should have input from all segments of the school and community, are the primary responsibility of the chief administrator and the governing board. Instructional decisions are the primary concern of middle management, with inputs from teachers, students, lay advisory committees, and others. Determining content and planning learning experiences is clearly the responsibility of the teacher, but hopefully with considerable student involvement.

Administration and supervision are the two terms traditionally used in education to describe the roles of instructional management. Administration includes the development and determination of institutional priorities: the marshalling of financial, physical, and human resources; and the function of planning and programming. Supervision refers more specifically to the direction and critical evaluation of instruction. In fact, administration and supervision have come to be used interchangeably to describe the role of educational management. Virtually every professional involved in a vocational program performs some administrative and some supervisory functions. It is our contention that both faculty and administrators in vocational and technical education must be regarded as instructional managers. Depending on the type of institution and the level of the position, the specific management functions will vary.

The internal administrative structures for high schools and community colleges were discussed in chapter 7. Traditionally, high schools have a principal, one or more assistant principals depending on the size of the school, and a number of departments which are generally organized along subject-matter lines. Often the principal and his assistants constitute the administrative council. Sometimes the subject-matter department heads are involved as a group in instructional decisions. More frequently department heads function as instructional managers for their own content areas. Many high schools use committees which cut across subject-matter interests. In the typical high school the administrative responsibility for instruction in vocational education rests with the principal and the department heads in areas such as business education and industrial education. But instruction aimed at preparation for employment must involve aspects of the whole school program and therefore this purpose of education cannot be served by the vocational or practical arts teachers alone.

Consequently, there should be on the administrative team of every comprehensive high school principal a specialist in vocational education who is responsible for giving leadership to the development and operation of programs for employment-bound youth. A leader on the principal's staff in the role of curriculum specialist for occupational education would help teachers of all subject-matter fields see the relationship of their subjects to occupations and would assist them in developing learning experiences which are relevant to the needs of employment-bound youth.

The administrative structure for the management of vocational and technical education in community colleges generally has an arrangement similar to that recommended for high schools. The person responsible for curriculum and instruction, as it relates to employment, is generally a dean for occupational education who reports to the president or an assistant dean who in turn is responsible to the dean of instruction. This person generally serves on the president's administrative council where decisions regarding instruction and related institutional problems are made. The dean of occupational education has on his team a number of division and/or department directors.

The administrative responsibility for instruction in vocational and technical education in specialized vocational high schools, area vocational schools, and technical institutes is less complex than it is in comprehensive high schools or community colleges. The single purpose institution has a faculty and administrative staff, all of whom are working toward the purpose of preparing youth for employment.

Regardless of the type or level of institution or the kind of administrative and supervisory structure, the fact is that any school or college wishing to provide functional occupational programs for youth and/or adults should centralize the responsibility for this major purpose of public education in one person. In a smaller high school this function may be performed by the principal, but in larger schools the principal should have an assistant who is especially qualified by education and experience for this role. Community colleges have recognized this need and almost without exception have an occupational education dean or assistant dean to provide leadership and direction in this area.

McMahon (*11*) advocates employment of a curriculum coordinator for vocational education on the school level whose responsibility it would be to give leadership to curriculum, program, and course development in all occupational programs in that school. His duties would be to supervise program development and course construction, to assist in the formulation of course objectives and in the preparation of instructional materials, to evaluate instructional programs, and to assist in revising and updating instruction where necessary.

Improvement of Instruction through the Use of Community Resources

The administrator of vocational and technical education must develop and maintain close working relationships with all elements of the community served by the school or college, but he must be intimately associated with the world of work and especially the people who control employment including both labor and management. The administrator should also help his teachers establish a close relationship with the particular occupation in which each is involved. The need for and benefits to be derived from close contact with the community are discussed in chapter 13. We will consider here some specific instructional values and needs.

COOPERATIVE VOCATIONAL EDUCATION

Programs in which the student receives a portion of his instruction in a real-work situation have grown rapidly during recent decades. Sometimes these experiences in the workplace are used to complete the training received in schools and colleges such as internships and other clinical experiences; in other situations much of the specific training is provided on the job. On-the-job experience, as a part of vocational and technical education programs, varies widely in amount and timing sequence.

On the high school level particularly, cooperative vocational education programs have been viewed as one of the most successful forms of vocational education. Cooperative programs are developed through an arrangement between the school and employers in the community in which students alternate in-school academic and vocational instruction with entry level employment in any occupational field. Students' programs are individually planned and coordinated by a teacher-coordinator who is a school employee, and the individual's learning experiences are supervised and evaluated by both the coordinator and the employer or his representative. School attendance and on-the-job training may be on alternate half-days, days, weeks, or other periods of time. Student learners are paid at least statutory minimum wages but generally the starting wages are fifty percent of the wages of an experienced worker in the particular occupation and increased at a prescribed rate during the training program. Cooperative programs are offered in many different occupations; the important consideration is that there must be a suitable work station and an employer willing to participate as a partner in the training of youth. Larger schools may have a teacher-coordinator for each occupational category, but in smaller schools one coordinator may operate a combination program with students in diversified occupations.

Where cooperative programs have been in operation for some time they are well accepted by students, parents, and employers. School administrators and board members are also generally quite supportive of cooperative programs. In many ways, as Butler and York (3) have pointed out, cooperative education epitomizes the qualities sought in optimal occupational education. Cooperative vocational education relates theory to practice, responds to individual differences and student preferences, provides individual attention in a real world-of-work situation, involves non-school resources in the instructional process, contributes to the relevance of the in-school instructional component, extends school-community relations, and eases the students' transition from school to work.

OTHER WORK-EXPERIENCE PROGRAMS

While cooperative vocational education is an excellent arrangement for certain occupations which lend themselves to this approach and in those communities where there are available appropriate training stations, it is not a panacea. Training for some occupations can best be provided in educational institutions where the primary purpose is instruction. But even in situations where most of the competencies needed for employment are developed in school shops or laboratories, there is still a need to supplement the in-school preparation with on-the-job experiences.

All vocational and technical education programs should include at least one work-experience component. The most desirable arrangement includes less-formal exploratory work experiences in the occupation near the beginning of the program and a concentrated period of weeks or months near the end of the program in a real-world situation as an employee, but with considerable supervision and some instruction. For the health and medical occupations, a clinical experience should be provided. Work experiences are needed to give the learner an opportunity to do some reality testing. Just as it is important for an M.D. to serve an internship or a future teacher to do student teaching, so it is important for other skilled workers to have work experiences in their chosen occupations as a part of the preparatory program.

Apprenticeship is another form of on-the-job training, in which the apprentice is a full-time employee. As a part of the apprenticeship agreement he is required, on a part-time basis, to attend classes in related instruction, such as mathematics and science. Apprenticeship is an important method of training highly skilled workers in certain trades in manufacturing and construction, even though it is applicable to only a small percentage of the total labor force. The vocational administrator is frequently involved in apprentice-training programs since the public schools—secondary and/or post-secondary—usually provide the related instruction.

A blending of learning experiences in the more formal educational setting with learning activities in an actual employment situation is needed in all vocational programs so that the two sets of experiences will be mutually reinforcing and enriching.

Initiation and operation of work experience programs for all students in vocational and technical education programs, including students in cooperative programs, requires competencies in instructional management which are different from and an extension of those required of most academic teachers or general school administrators. The teachers and teacher-coordinators who are expected to actively participate in the management of these programs must be carefully selected in terms of personal qualifications and special preparation for such roles.

QUALIFIED WORKERS ARE RESOURCES

The vocational and technical education instructors should be encouraged to use skilled workers in the community as resource people and visiting instructors. People who have special competence in a particular phase of some occupation are frequently available to the schools for an hour or two on a voluntary basis. Or they can be employed, if not during the day, perhaps for an evening school program. Vocational and technical programs will be enhanced if persons currently employed in an occupation are brought into the school setting as "teacher for the day" or any fraction thereof.

JOB PLACEMENT AND FOLLOW-UP

Job placement is discussed in chapter 10 as a service to students; we are concerned here with job placement and follow-up as it relates to the improvement of instruction.

It is absolutely imperative that the schools take responsibility for job placement, if not alone for the direct benefit to the student, then certainly as a means of getting feedback from the places of employment; such information is needed to revise and improve vocational and technical programs. In areas where local branch offices of the United States Employment Service and state employment services are interested in providing placement services for high school and college graduates, school administrators tend to relinquish this function. By doing so they are cutting off one of the best means of continuous input to keep vocational programs viable and relevant. School and college administrators should work with public employment agencies, but they should not deny teachers access to the kinds of information which can come only through regular and frequent contacts with the occupation and the business or industry into which their students go for employment. For this reason we favor a decentralized system of job placement involving at least one teacher in each specialized program, with time allocated for this important function.

Follow-up studies of vocational and technical program graduates and dropouts are another source of information for the improvement of instruction. They can also be useful to educational planners and administrators in making decisions on questions of priorities among types, levels, and fields of training programs and the allocation of resources to these programs. For additional information, consult a report done by Little (7) on placement and follow-up of vocational and technical students.

Improvement of Instruction
through In-School Resources

Persons most closely associated with a particular program (teachers and students) are best able to determine what could be done to improve the quality of that program. We will discuss some considerations which might be useful to administrators in helping others improve vocational and technical programs.

INDIVIDUALIZED INSTRUCTION

The traditional image of the teacher dispensing information is being replaced by the role of directing, guiding, and stimulating learning. The focus of instruction in the past rested primarily upon the teacher, but it is now shifting to the learner. The vocational teacher, as manager of the instructional environment, is the central figure in bringing about this change, but teachers need the assistance and support of the vocational administrator.

Curricula, programs, and courses are planned for *groups* of learners, rather than for *individual* learners. In order to accommodate the wide range of individual differences, many schools have organized students into ability groups on the assumption that they will then have "homogeneous" sections. A review of the literature on ability grouping reminds us of its futility. Ability grouping may be more detrimental than helpful, if we assume that we have dealt adequately with the problem of individual differences.

While differences are important, we must also guarantee the knowledge and skill which is a *common* necessity. Having identified these common or essential elements, we tend to behave as though everyone in that program must acquire these components in a roughly identical fashion; this concept is the principal obstacle to individualized instruction. Wilhelms (*14*) takes the position that the essential common element in a program or curriculum is purpose, "and the moment we so conceive it, we are free to reach toward the individual." He further states:

> The goal is essential; the particular means are optional. Similarly, to every important human goal there are many roads and, if not all of them are royal, neither are all of us kings. The fundamental error in curriculum thinking has been to equate content with goal; or worse, to redouble our zeal as to content just because we have forgotten the goal. (*14*, p. 68)

Instructional content should be viewed as means to an end and not the end itself. In vocational and technical education programs the common group element is the purpose—to prepare for employment in a particular occupation or family of occupations. Vocational teachers should be encouraged to explore the wide range of ways to help unique individuals toward their purposes.

Individualized instruction requires organization and management of the learning environment so that the learning activities will meet the needs of each student in terms of that student's ability to learn, his needs, interests, motivation, educational background, and experience. Instruction meets the student where he is and on his own terms. Also, individualized instruction gives the learner some choices as to what, how, and with whom he studies, and how fast he proceeds.

INSTRUCTIONAL OBJECTIVES

There is a current growth of interest and activity in the area of formulating instructional objectives. This movement has been accelerated by the interest in programmed instruction and by the writings of people concerned about the improvement of instruction. Mager (*9*), Mager and Beech (*10*), and others have contributed to the emerging popularity of instructional objectives by preparing aids on how to write them. Vocational and technical education is moving steadily and positively toward systematizing instruction, which makes the development of instructional objectives an absolute necessity. Furthermore, it now becomes necessary to express instructional objectives in measurable terms.

The literature on instructional objectives is directed largely toward formulation of *behavioral* objectives. Since instruction is designed to modify the learner's behavior, it follows that these intended changes in behavior must be described in terms of measurable learner behaviors—either an observable behavior of the learner *or* a product resulting from the learner's behavior. Mager (*9*) believes that behavioral objectives should also specify the conditions under which the behavior occurs and the desired minimum level of learner proficiency.

Vocational and technical educators may be more inclined to use behavioral or performance objectives than other educators because the concept is particularly relevant and useful in specialized education. Many educators have avoided writing measurable performance objectives either because they think it unimportant or because they lack the knowledge needed to do it. Some teachers may resist because considerable time is involved in the formulation of measurable objectives. The vocational administrator should help teachers overcome whatever reasons they have for failure to state objectives in measurable terms. Larson (*5*) takes the position that success in teaching is dependent upon instructional planning as well as performance in the teaching process itself, and devotes a major portion of his book to building a performance base and developing performance goals.

It is a well-known principle of program evaluation that the measurement of achievement must be based upon the intended goals or objectives. If supervisors and teachers have done a good job of defining the goals of programs and courses in terms of measurable performance objectives, the task of evaluation will be relatively simple. Program and course evaluation is discussed in chapter 14.

PROGRAM MANAGEMENT OBJECTIVES

The vocational administrator or supervisor should help his teachers develop measurable instructional objectives, but he should also develop performance objectives for his own guidance and direction. Borgen and Davis (*1*) have developed a set of management strategies to be used in local planning and evaluation of occupational education courses and programs. Included in their materials is a packet of forms and suggestions designed to help the local vocational and technical education administrator write measurable program management objectives—"objectives that realistically describe your present and future targets for operating and improving vocational programs at your school" (*1*, p. 27). For a fuller treatment on management by objectives (MBO), refer to chapter 6.

MEDIA TECHNOLOGY AND INNOVATIVE APPROACHES

The vocational and technical education administrator should encourage the fuller use of instructional technology. Television, for example, can be used very effectively to demonstrate certain occupational processes, and to give learners the opportunity to observe themselves in the performance of an occupational skill. Audio-visual equipment, such as projectors and tape recorders, should be readily available to teachers, and budget provisions should be made for commercially produced films, film strips, tapes, transparencies, and charts. Perhaps more important, teachers should be encouraged and helped to develop their own teaching aids and to program instruction. The administrator should make available the needed resources. Teachers can package much of their instructional content so that it is available to students when and as needed on an individual basis. But the development of programmed instruction requires considerable staff time. Although still in the developmental stage, computer-assisted instruction has tremendous potential and should be considered an instructional aid. Special sources such as Wittich and Schuller (*15*) should be consulted for specific information about the instructional technology.

Vocational and technical programs generally require larger blocks of time, especially when shop and laboratory experiences and outside work experiences are a part of the program. The administrator of vocational programs must see that time modules appropriate to the particular program are provided. In the past this has presented problems for some scheduling officers, but the use of the computer for scheduling purposes has helped solve this difficulty.

There should be a high degree of horizontal articulation between instruction provided in the specific competencies of the occupation (usually taught in a shop or laboratory) and related instruction (usually taught in a classroom). Communication skills, scientific concepts, and the mathematical competencies needed by the worker in a particular occupation are often taught in separate and so-called "related" courses. Unfortunately, in some schools, there is very little relatedness between the shop or laboratory courses and the related courses. To overcome this weakness the administrator might encourage more team planning among those teachers of the shop, laboratory, and related courses which go to make up a particular specialized program. Arrangements might also be made for team teaching by two or more teachers who might jointly provide both the practical and the related instruction. The related instruction might also be completely integrated with the shop or laboratory instruction where both are taught by the same person, a practice sometimes rejected because it ties up expensive facilities for extended periods.

Vocational and technical instruction, especially that which occurs in shops and laboratories, can be both improved and operated more efficiently through the use of differentiated staffing. A skilled worker in the occupation can be employed as a paraprofessional and serve as an assistant to the professional teacher, thereby increasing the number of students served and the quality of instruction.

INSTRUCTION IN SHOPS AND LABORATORIES SHOULD IMITATE REAL WORLD

The learning environment for the practical and applied aspects of vocational and technical programs should be as nearly like the work environment as possible. This suggests the need for shops and laboratories which are organized and equipped like the comparable workplaces in the community. To make the learning experiences in school facilities realistic, it is also necessary to have problems or projects which are "real" in that someone will use the product or the service produced. Too frequently students in vocational programs are required to learn through contrived experiences or exercises only. This is not to say that there is no place for well-planned exercises in the shop or laboratory, but as soon as practicable the learner should be given the opportunity to work on "live" projects. For example, students in automotive repair should learn their trade by working on cars which have a malfunction, students in a cosmetology class should work on "clients' " hair, and youth in a commercial foods program should prepare and serve food to paying customers. That this practice is desirable may appear self-evident, but one need only to visit a number of schools to find students who are working on meaningless exercises which will become waste, when they could just as well be working on something with some economic, aesthetic, or social value.

A caution, however, needs to be expressed. Occasionally, the economic value of the product of a school shop or laboratory is allowed to dominate the activity. Graphic arts laboratories which produce school newspapers, student handbooks, programs for social and other school events, forms for the principal's and superintendent's offices, and miscellaneous other items can become so over-burdened with these "real" problems and projects that instruction takes second place to production. This, of course, should not be tolerated and requires operational procedures through which the teacher can control the amount and type of work to be accepted. Production should be subservient to and enhance instruction, not the reverse.

THE CLUSTER CONCEPT

The fact that the Dictionary of Occupational Titles (DOT) describes 21,741 separate occupations in the labor force in the United States is sometimes used as an excuse to do nothing about specialized education to prepare people for these occupations; the problem, it is said, is too complex to tackle. But when we consider that 95 percent of the workers in the labor force are employed in only 409 of the total number of occupations, the problem becomes more manageable. Furthermore, not all of these occupations are found in every community.

The Bureau of Adult, Vocational and Technical Education in the United States Office of Education has identified and codified fifteen occupational clusters. Their categories are: Agri-Business and Natural Resources, Business and Office, Communication and Media, Construction, Consumer and Homemaking, Environment, Fine Arts and Humanities, Health, Hospitality and Recreation, Manufacturing, Marine Science, Marketing and Distribution, Personal Services, Public Services, and Transportation. These clusters are groupings of occupations which are related because they require similar teachable skills and knowledge.

The clusters-of-occupations concept, or what we have called families of occupations, is not a new idea. Educators interested in developing general education exploratory programs in the practical arts areas have used this concept in curriculum development. Through a project known as the Industrial Arts Curriculum Project, instructional techniques and materials have been developed for "The World of Manufacturing" and "The World of Construction." While these programs are designed for use on the junior high school level, the cluster concept is now being applied to the senior high school where the emphasis is on preparation for employment within a cluster of occupations, rather than in a specific occupation. Oregon embarked on a state-wide program several years ago in which students select a career cluster (they have eighteen) at the beginning of their high school experience and then tie a majority of their high school experiences into this generalized career goal. That is, the knowledge and skills common to the occupations which comprise a cluster or family form the basis of most of the students' learning experiences and, perhaps most important, provide the motivation for learning. Proponents of *The Oregon Way,* including the

Oregon State Superintendent of Public Instruction, (Parnell, *13*) see this arrangement not only as having a motivational impact, but also as a method of preparing youth for entry into a broad family of occupations rather than a specific one.

While we believe the cluster approach makes good sense for many students, some high school youth are ready for more specialized preparation for a particular occupation. In fact, the Oregon plan makes provision for these students.

Improving Instruction for Persons with Special Needs

The administrator who is serving the needs of the disadvantaged and handicapped must make special arrangements for them. Disadvantaged persons are defined as those who have academic, socioeconomic, cultural, or other handicaps which prevent them from succeeding in regular vocational programs without special assistance or service. Handicapped persons include the educable mentally handicapped, the emotionally disturbed, and the physically handicapped who cannot succeed in regular vocational programs and who require special assistance or a modified vocational program.

Each state has provisions in its state plan for persons with special needs. The needs of disadvantaged and handicapped may be served through special classes or in regular vocational classes with supplemental assistance. A practice which has worked quite well is scheduling several handicapped or disadvantaged students in regular shop or laboratory classes and providing the instructor with an assistant who can give whatever additional help the special students need. In addition to special assistance in the shop or classroom, the disadvantaged and handicapped may need special counseling and guidance services, financial aid, health services, and special help in finding employment and making satisfactory adjustment on the job. Boss (*2*) discusses *What School Administrators Should Know About Vocational Education for Disadvantaged Youth in Urban Areas,* but he believes the disadvantaged should have separate facilities, faculty, and curriculum. *We believe the disadvantaged and handicapped should be a part of the regular school or college programs to the maximum extent possible, but with supplemental assistance and services.*

Lockette and Davenport (*8*) give a list of nineteen important considerations in developing and operating vocational education programs for the disadvantaged, most of which would improve vocational and technical programs for those who are not disadvantaged as well as for those who are.

Teacher Education and Improvement of Instruction

The professional development of the faculty will be considered in chapter 11, but it is appropriate here to call attention to the relationship of in-service teacher education and the improvement of instruction. To structure the work situation to make it conducive for teachers to be meaningfully engaged in course and program development activity is an excellent form of in-service teacher education. Professional development through experiences which are related to and grow out of the daily work of the teacher can be more valuable than many other structured professional growth experiences.

REFERENCES

1. Borgen, Joseph A. and Dwight E. Davis. *An Illinois Occupational Curriculum Project (I.O.C.P.) Planning Manual.* Springfield, Illinois: Division of Vocational and Technical Education, Illinois State Board of Vocational Education and Rehabilitation, 1972.

2. Boss, Richard. *What School Administrators Should Know About Vocational Education for Disadvantaged Youth in Urban Areas.* Columbus, Ohio: The Center for Vocational and Technical Education, 1971.

3. Butler, Roy L. and Edwin G. York. *What School Administrators Should Know About Cooperative Vocational Education.* Columbus, Ohio: The Center for Vocational and Technical Education, 1971.

4. Impellitteri, Joseph T. and Curtis R. Finch. *Review and Synthesis of Research on Individualizing Instruction in Vocational and Technical Education.* Columbus, Ohio: The Center for Vocational and Technical Education, 1971.

5. Larson, Milton E. *Teaching Related Subjects in Trade and Industrial and Technical Education.* Columbus, Ohio: Charles E. Merrill, 1972.

6. Likert, Rensis. "Diagnose Your Teaching Role." *The Instructor,* August/September 1968, pp. 50–51.

7. Little, J. Kenneth. *Review and Synthesis of Research on the Placement and Follow-up of Vocational Education Students.* Columbus, Ohio: The Center for Vocational and Technical Education, 1970.

8. Lockette, Rutherford E. and Lawrence F. Davenport. *Review and Synthesis of Research on Vocational Education for the Urban Disadvantaged.* Columbus, Ohio: The Center for Vocational and Technical Education, 1971.

9. Mager, Robert F. *Preparing Instructional Objectives.* Belmont, California: Fearon, 1962.

10. Mager, Robert F. and Kenneth M. Beach. *Developing Vocational Instruction.* Belmont, California: Fearon, 1967.

11. McMahon, Gordon G. *Curriculum Development in Trade and Industrial and Technical Education.* Columbus, Ohio: Charles E. Merrill, 1972.

12. McPartland, James, et al. *Student Participation in High School Decisions: Summary and Excerpts.* Baltimore, Md.: Johns Hopkins University, not dated.

13. Parnell, Dale. "The Oregon Way." *American Vocational Journal* 46, No. 12 (December 1969).

14. Wilhelms, Fred T. "The Curriculum and Individual Differences." *Individualizing Instruction.* Sixty-first Yearbook of The National Society for the Study of Education, Part I. Chicago: NSSE, 1962.

15. Wittich, Walter A. and Charles F. Schuller. *Instructional Technology: Its Nature and Use.* 5th ed. New York: Harper and Row, 1973.

Chapter 10 STUDENT DEVELOPMENT SERVICES

Student development services in vocational-technical education include a wide variety of career-related, nonclassroom developmental activities which are concerned with the well-being of the whole student. The purpose of this chapter is to review the student development services which are critical for the success of vocational-technical education institutions and to provide the reader with an understanding of some of the major issues related to these services.

The purposes of this chapter are to help the reader:

1 to understand and explain the variety of nonclassroom educational services which a vocational education institution might offer;
2. to develop his own philosophy about which services should be provided at institutions of different levels;
3. to understand and explain the unique problems in student development services for vocational-technical education;
4. to develop the student services which are common to and critical for all vocational education.

In the two decades following World War II student personnel services blossomed as a distinct professional field. Educators in general became more concerned about programming a host of nonclassroom developmental activities which supplemented the students' academic experience. The student personnel services profession developed experts in such diverse areas as counseling, placement, discipline, cultural activities, housing, and a variety of other functions. What had originally been primarily the domain of the principal, or a dean of men, became a burgeoning bureaucracy. Educational institutions increasingly involved themselves in every aspect of their clients' lives.

Student personnel workers at all institutional levels laid claim to a major stake in the educational enterprise.

> *The Primary Purpose* of a program of pupil personnel services is to *facilitate* the maximum development of the individual through education. (*9*, p. 2)

> Student personnel service, therefore, being concerned with the whole student in his total environment, recognizes that what the student learns and experiences in his out-of-class life has a direct bearing upon his aspirations, motives and achievements in class. (*12*, p. 1)

> The student personnel program should be the pivot, the hub, the core around which the whole enterprise moves. It provides the structure and creates the pervasive atmosphere which prompts the junior college to label itself as student centered. (*3*, p. 13)

Definitions of student personnel services vary, but usually include counseling and guidance; testing; discipline; admissions, registration, and records; health services; placement; remedial programs; cultural and athletic activities; and student government. At the secondary level, additional pupil personnel services may include speech and hearing therapy, special education, and school social work. At the post-secondary level, student personnel officers often have responsibility for campus security, financial aids, fraternities and sororities, residence halls, religious activities, veterans' affairs, and special development programs for ethnic minority groups. One U.S. Office of Education study (*1*) identified twenty distinct services prevalent in higher education and grouped them in four basic categories: (1) welfare functions, (2) control functions, (3) activities functions, and (4) teaching functions.

There have been some problems in relating student personnel services to the specific needs of vocational and technical students. Personnel functions are generally centralized and personnel officers seldom have vocational education backgrounds.

> Most junior college student personnel workers have a strong academic orientation; their egos were nourished in the university and their knowledge of occupations other than their own limited largely to summer jobs and occupational monographs. (*8*, p. 217)

As a result, in many cases student services and activities are administered without significant input from vocational educators. Typically, for example, athletic and cultural events are scheduled without much concern for the vocational student whose laboratory, shop assignment, or cooperative education job then precludes his participation.

The student services emphasis has been healthy for vocational and technical education, forcing the recognition that occupational education involves more than the acquisition of skills and concomitant career attitudes; that it involves the whole person. For this reason, it is important for vocational educators to become actively involved in the programming and delivery of such services.

Recently, the whole student personnel services field has come under question. Post-secondary education has finally accepted the demise of the *en loco parentis* posture where colleges acted as parental surrogates. Secondary education is recognizing increasingly the legal and personal rights of students. As a result, student personnel services professionals are now questioning what student services should legitimately be performed for students. For example, discipline has come under attack at both the secondary and post-secondary levels. Students, parents, and ultimately the courts question the extent to which schools have the right to dictate and enforce dress and grooming codes, or to dictate hours or living rules in residence halls. Changes have not come at the instigation of educators but through social initiatives permeating our society. The right to vote for eighteen-year-olds, and concomitant changes in residency laws, contract rights, liquor legislation, and other associated societal norms have dramatically affected the student personnel services functions in education. No longer do many schools or colleges control who can drive a car, whether their students can consume alcohol or tobacco, or whether females can wear shorts or slacks.

While the control functions in student personnel services have changed, most of the others have continued, albeit in an altered form. In general, these functions are more frequently being referred to as student development services. In the broadest sense, they are career-related and justified on the basis of their contribution to the development of the whole student. The importance of career-related student development services can be seen in the emphasis placed on them by the Vocational Education Amendments of 1968.

The variety of student development services provided by a vocational-technical education institution will vary according to the level, type, and size of the institution. It is our contention, however, that certain student development services are requisite to the success of any vocational education program, whether it be in a comprehensive high school, an area vocational center, a comprehensive community college, or a four-year technical college. Each of these levels and types will of course need to emphasize different aspects. Some will offer a great many additional student services, depending on the resources available to them and the aggregate needs of their defined student clientele. Our analysis is intended to review those developmental services which are basic for any vocational-technical education institution. At a minimum, those student developmental services include: (1) admissions and induction, (2) testing, (3) counseling, (4) registration and records, (5) financial assistance, and (6) placement.

Admissions and Induction

The admissions function has traditionally been associated with selective entrance into elite four-year post-secondary institutions. However, admissions is a crucial aspect of every vocational program at every level, secondary or post-secondary.

A basic foundation of the admissions function is the institution's educational philosophy about who should be educated. Open admission to vocational programs has not been a significant problem in secondary education. Too often, rather, administrators and counselors in comprehensive high schools have attempted to keep students out of occupational programs which interested them because the counselors felt the students were "capable of more." Most comprehensive community colleges and many technical four-year colleges adhere to an open door policy. The open door policy holds that any student, regardless of his previous academic success or failure, should be admitted and allowed to try a program which interests him. Increasingly, the open-door policy is being accepted by most post-secondary institutions. However, the problem for vocational-technical education has now changed. Declining enrollments in higher education in general have been associated with a growing interest on the part of students and society in occupational programs.

Unlike liberal arts programs, where another all-purpose classroom and an additional instructor will enable a school or college to schedule more classes, vocational institutions often cannot easily expand their enrollment quotas. Thus, with a fixed number of shop, laboratory, or cooperative education work stations to fill, the admissions function in vocational-technical education assumes critical importance. For example, in the fall of 1972 one college had 700 applicants for 80 openings in dental hygiene and over 1000 applicants for 125 openings in automotive programs. The problem for the admissions office is to determine who should be admitted to a limited program quota and on what basis. Should there be admissions requirements? If so, should they be related to past academic achievements, to evaluated abilities, proven interest or experience, or merely to evidence of interest as demonstrated by early application? The answers to these questions must be determined by policy makers and the chief administrator in light of the defined purposes of the institution. It is our contention, however, that admission at any level, secondary or post-secondary, to vocational and technical programs should be based on interest, and schools should respond on an open door, first-come-first-served basis. After admissions quotas are filled, a waiting list based on date of application should be developed to allow the institution to compensate for no-shows and early attrition. There is a fallacy, however, in establishing a waiting list for more than one year in the future. Applicants assigned to program quotas two years hence are likely to become "ghosts," and enroll in other programs in other institutions. Thus, the application process should be renewed each year and prospective students should reapply at a given date for a new year.

Conversely, a related admissions problem has to do with recruiting students for new or unfilled quota programs where demonstrated employment opportunities exist. Particularly with respect to emerging new occupations or new careers, there is often a public communications gap. Students may not have become aware of the nature of the program or the job openings that exist in the field. As a result, the admission office has to play an active recruiting and proselyting role. For example, many parents and prospective students are still not aware of the role and the employment possibilities for legal assistants, social service technicians, plastics technologists, or inhalation therapy technicians. The admissions office must assume a public relations and external education posture with respect to these programs.

Given the contemporary interest in vocational and technical programs at all levels, the problem of articulation between levels becomes increasingly crucial. Where does the admissions office place a student in a community college automotive program if the student has completed a two-year automotive service curriculum in a comprehensive high school? How does a student transfer in a technical program from a comprehensive community college to a four-year technical college? Faculty maintain almost a religious jealousy about the integrity of their programs and are often loath to matriculate anybody anywhere except at the entry point. The problem of the admissions office is to guarantee fair treatment to students, rewarding due recognition for earlier education without compromising the curricular integrity of their programs. There is a need for virtually continual interaction between administrators of vocational programs at all levels to insure adequate understanding of their curricula. Another tool in managing this problem is the development of nationally or regionally normed behavioral competency tests in occupational areas which will allow meaningful assessment of the students' progress to date.

Closely related to the admissions function is the problem of induction-orientation. It includes dissemination of pre-admission information to the prospective student, dissemination of information to the enrolling student about institutional policies, procedures and services, and assistance to the student in getting acclimated to the school or college. Induction-orientation activities can be carried out in a number of ways, including individual and peer counseling, group orientation seminars, distribution of handbooks and related literature, informal discussions, or formal orientation courses for credit. "The specific content and activities of an orientation program are not as important as the degree to which the resources of the total institution are mobilized to effectively communicate the essential nature and demands of the college" (*12,* p. 26).

Induction-orientation essentially is a socialization process which helps the student understand the expectations and norms of the institution. Effective orientation, which provides the student with a positive image of the school and his role in it, is a primary requisite for educational success. One of the most important aspects is the communication, both direct and indirect, that vocational programs and students are particularly worthwhile and important.

In any event, it is abundantly clear that vocational administrators must pay more attention to admissions and induction functions. A bad admissions decision, inadequate admissions counseling, or poor orientation can result in student frustration and attrition, lowered educational and economic efficiency, and a generally bad image for the school or college. In a sense, admissions is a year-round function which must involve all staff members. Recruitment, entrance counseling and induction, institutional articulation, and program publicity are major administrative responsibilities.

Testing

Directly related to admissions is the testing service. The admissions philosophy will determine what, if any, entrance requirements are appropriate to a given program. Once a value judgment has been made about the need for aptitude testing, the institution must be able to administer such tests. Many occupational programs require certain levels of mechanical, analytical, mathematical, verbal, or manual dexterity aptitude. A variety of aptitude tests are used to measure these propensities as well as the general intellectual ability of the prospective student. While the authors question the predictive value of general ability instruments, they may be used to provide some indication of a student's strong points. The literature is replete with studies of general abilities tests (intelligence measurements) and their relative lack of both validity and reliability. Even veteran test developers such as Educational Testing Service will admit that the predictive validity (in forecasting success in college) of their tests is not much better than the student's high school grade-point average.

Minority scholars and others have long criticized these tests for their cultural bias, which in effect leads to poorer showing by nonwhite and non-middle-class students. While this is particularly true of tests measuring verbal skills, the critique can be extended to most ability tests. An additional flaw in ability testing is use of imperfect and invalid instruments to develop expectations about a student's performance. Too often these expectations become self-fulfilling prophecies. One comprehensive community college used to put orange dots on the record folders of students who scored in the lowest ten percent of a given aptitude test. Counselors, instructors, clerical staff, and even other students came to call these students "orange dotters," and everyone had a failure expectation of them. Later, when the error of the policy was recognized and rectified, the rate of failure and attrition among this group of students declined substantially.

Perhaps a more relevant testing service in vocational and technical education is provided by instruments which seek to measure a student's interest. Tests such as the Strong Vocational Preference Test, Kuder, or Minnesota Vocational Interest Inventory apply logical quantitive analysis to the expressed interest indications of students. While relying heavily on the honesty of the student and his willingness to express his real interests, they contribute to successful program selection. All institutions involved in occupational education should offer such testing opportunities and have someone on the staff experienced in the administration and interpretation of them. These kinds of tests are particulary important as educational placement tools and can assist in customizing courses to meet individual student needs.

A third testing function which has a growing relevance for vocational education is competency testing—the measurement of acquired behavioral skills required for a given occupation. Liberal arts institutions have led the way in developing advanced placement policies based on competency examination. More recently, the problem of articulation, mentioned earlier, between various levels of vocational-technical education has fostered significant growth in the development of behavioral measurement of achievement in vocational skill areas. Standardized occupational skills are being categorized, defined, and measured to develop national and/or regional norms. Thus, a student who achieves a certain level of competence in drafting in an area vocational center can be tested and placed at an appropriate program level in a community college or technical institute. Rutgers University is currently coordinating a national effort at developing such tests for a wide variety of occupations. In response to its students and the need for improved institutional articulation, every post-secondary vocational-technical institution should secure competency test batteries as soon as they are available for all the occupational programs it offers.

The testing function can also be a form of public service which the institution offers to nonstudent clientele in its service area: returning military veterans, middle-aged housewives seeking a second career, unemployed youth, or displaced workers seeking new employment avenues. Offered as a community benefit, perhaps at a minimal fee to cover costs, this service soon becomes an effective student recruiting device and helps the institution develop a positive public image in the community.

Counseling

The counseling program in any vocational institution uses testing as one of its basic tools; but it also relies on a personal one-to-one face contact with students to help them in their career development. In a vocational institution, counseling faces a basic philosophical issue: should it be limited to career information and choice or should counselors attempt to deal with the wide variety of personal problems that may have an effect on the students' performance? Psychologists and guidance personnel have long recognized that individuals do not effectively separate or discriminate between their problems. Thus, a career choice decision may be intimately related to a personal crisis of finance, family relationships, peer acceptance, broken romance, etc.

The authors recognize the fact that counseling must deal with the "whole person," with all the interrelated problems which affect career planning and career decisions and education. This does not mean, however, that counselors must resolve these problems or take primary responsibility for therapeutic assistance. Counselors must be able to recognize which problems are essentially information-seeking and general self-discovery versus those which require substantial professional therapeutic care. Where information and empathetic rational discussion will help the student, the counselor should handle the problem. Where specialized assistance related to mental health, drug abuse, alcohol, sex, family breakdowns, or other personal problems is required, the counselor must be prepared to make consultation referrals. A real problem in educational counseling occurs when counselors fail to recognize the limit of their responsibilities and capabilities.

Many vocational institutions serve clientele with special counseling needs: unemployed veterans, displaced migrant workers, disadvantaged students, foreign students, older persons in need of job retraining, handicapped and rehabilitation students, and special students studying under programs financed by federal and state agencies. In these cases, special counselors are frequently required because they understand the unique problems of their clientele. Similarly, an open door institution is responsible for providing special counseling and remedial education for students with deficient educational experience. Without additional counseling and support services, the open door policy quickly becomes the revolving door policy.

Many studies have been written about the organization of the counseling function in education. There are essentially three options, with variations of each, for organizing counseling services in vocational education. The first is a centralized counseling office with full-time counselors; the second is the provision of released time to selected faculty to allow them to counsel for a fraction of their contract; the third is to insist that all faculty counsel and advise a small number of students as part of their regular job responsibility.

Full-time counselors will usually be trained in guidance and counseling. They will be available to students at all hours, and will keep abreast of new information in the field, articulation problems, degree and transfer requirements, problem referral assistance, and basic institutional policies. However, they may not be well-versed in vocational curriculum problems or employment opportunities in specialized fields. Furthermore, full-time counselors often tend to assume therapeutic counseling responsibility beyond their training and capability.

The second counseling alternative is to recruit, select, and train a small group of regular faculty who will counsel on a released-time basis. These people will be familiar with curriculum, faculty, field placement opportunites, and the general skills needed in the occupation. They may or may not have guidance and counseling training, but they can be given in-service education as part of the prerequisite for the job. One of the problems in this arrangement is that faculty may pay disproportionate attention to either teaching or counseling, to the detriment of the other. Further, such persons are not as available to students as are full-time counselors. Finally, released time for counseling may become a plan reserved for faculty with seniority or as a reward for other forms of service, instead of utilizing those persons most qualified.

Another counseling option is to insist that all faculty perform this function for a limited number of students. Thus, every teaching faculty member counsels twenty to thirty students in his discipline. In this instance, counseling relates most closely to educational or occupational questions, although it may be hard for the faculty member to develop a broad perspective about the students' problems. Faculty counselors tend to know their own vocational area but may be relatively ignorant about related occupations. Also, faculty counselors may be biased in favor of their own occupational area and may not be most helpful to a student interested in shifting to another field. Few enter teaching with the expectation of having to provide a wide range of counseling services to students. Their office hour availability may also present a serious problem. It is difficult, if not impossible, for these professionals to keep abreast of their own occupational discipline and also maintain contemporary knowledge about course requirements, placement and career information, counseling techniques, and other information necessary for successful counseling.

Counseling is as important as formal education itself. Successful counseling requires maximum information about the client-student, the education system, occupational opportunities, and local referral services for personal problems. While the organization of such services will depend on the general orientation and needs of the institution and its students, the authors favor a structure which combines full-time counselors with some released-time faculty counseling. The critical factor in counseling is an attitude of *helpfulness* which supercedes any experience or knowledge requisites. At the same time, it is imperative that all faculty view informal counseling as part of their job responsibility. Full-time faculty are those most likely to be related to and conversant with the demands of their occupational field. In occupational education they therefore remain as the critical reality contact points for students.

Records and Registration

An often overlooked aspect of critical importance in student development services is the records and registration function. For most students and faculty, registration is a problem only during the first week of the academic term. Students, particularly, tend to forget that their transcript, the record of their educational performance, usually follows them throughout their careers, and at least their educational career.

One of the critical issues in registration and records has to do with accounting for vocational curricula. In secondary schools all credits are expressed in terms of Carnegie Units. In some comprehensive community colleges and technical four-year colleges, less than degree level vocational programs are measured in terms of contact or "clock" hours instead of conventional credit hours. Many programs are awarded "certificates" instead of "degrees," and hours or courses spent in pursuing this certificate are not always transferrable to degree programs. Fortunately, more and more training for entry level skills in an occupation at the "certificate" level can be applied to further education for an associate or baccalaureate degree in the "ladder" or "lattice" concept.

Registration involves scheduling of classes and placing students in them. In larger secondary and post-secondary institutions this process can be time-consuming and frustrating for all concerned. Recent developments in data processing have reduced some of this difficulty by introducing registration through direct computer access by cathode ray tubes (CRTs). Direct access registration, like making airline reservations, is being adopted in many large institutions, allowing maximum student choice and administrative flexibility.

The question of administrative record keeping has become more complex in this age of automated data processing. The ability of government agencies and others to assemble and disseminate information on individuals has significantly reduced the privacy of the individual. Major issues arise regarding an institution's right or responsibility to release information to inquiring agencies. Many institutions now refuse to release information to the FBI, Selective Service Boards, or others, unless requested by the student. This issue becomes particularly difficult when a group like a Joint Apprenticeship Training Committee asks for information about a former student applying for apprenticeship in a given trade. Questions about confidentiality and release of records cannot be answered easily, but they deserve the attention of administrators.

The problem of articulation affects records and registration, as it does admissions and counseling. Course equivalencies at different institutions is always an issue, particularly if one institution is secondary and the other post-secondary. An ultimate goal for vocational education is the establishment of records systems which have equivalent meanings across institutions in a state or region.

The vocational or technical education administrator ignores the records and registration function at his own peril. Many operational problems can be avoided at the outset by establishing clear and consistent records and registration policies which permit maximum institutional flexibility and responsiveness to students.

Financial Aids

Ordinarily, secondary occupational programs in comprehensive high schools or area vocational centers are provided to area students free of cost as part of the basic public education system. The cost issue becomes more complex in higher education. Some states, such as California, have held that higher education, particularly at the lower division level, should be free to resident citizens. Other states take the position that the primary financial burden should rest on the student.

In those institutions charging tuition and in those requiring student residence, the question of student financial aid becomes critical. The federal government has taken an active position in providing the financial resources to allow an economically disadvantaged student to attend the institution of his choice. For this reason, particularly at the post-secondary level, the vocational-technical administrator should be conversant with federal legislation and programs.

Federal legislation, including the Education Amendments of 1972, has structured financial aid to students in higher education through three distinct programs: Educational Opportunity Grants, National Direct Student Loans, and Work-Study Assistance. The financial aid requirements of students are analyzed through an application and a Parents' Confidential Statement (PCS) about income and resources. Based on the ability of the student and his parents to pay for his education, a financial need level is established according to the costs of the institution which the student intends to enter. The financial aids office of the institution then establishes the amount and kind of aid that the institution can offer. This "financial aid package" is generally a combination of the three basic kinds of aid: grants, loans, and employment.

GRANTS

In colleges, Supplemental Educational Opportunity Grant funds are administered by the institution but provided by the federal government. They are not awarded on the basis of academic proficiency or scholarship, but rather on the basis of the need of any student who meets minimal qualifications. Awards are usually on a first-come-first-served basis until funds are exhausted. The only criteria for the recipient, beyond need, are that he be at least a half-time student and that he maintain acceptable academic standing. Individual institutions may offer their own funds in the form of scholarships based on academic proficiency.

LOANS

The second kind of financial aid consists of institutional loans to students which are funded by the National Direct Student Loan Program. Like EOG, the NDSL program is supported by the federal government and is available to students on a first-come basis. Loan funds are appropriated to colleges for disbursement to student recipients. A similar program is Guaranteed Student Loans where the federal government guarantees to local banks the repayment of educational loans to students. Education institutions do not administer these loans, but financial aids officers must make a determination of need in accordance with federal regulations.

WORK-STUDY

The third major form of financial aid to students, the work-study program, is particularly relevant for vocational education. The federal government funds eighty percent of the monies for work-study programs, and colleges or high schools which administer the program must provide the matching twenty percent. Students who apply for aid and qualify for work-study assistance are allotted a certain maximum amount they can earn during the year. Ordinarily, they are then placed in part-time job slots in the institution or on the campus and paid at prevailing job rates for the kind of work they perform.

Usually, financial aids offices in higher education attempt to combine the three forms of aid to give roughly equal proportions of grants, loans, and work-study assistance. In many instances, work-study job stations are used primarily to supplement institutional part-time employment budgets. Students perform secretarial, janitorial, groundskeeping, library clerk, food service, mail service, or other relatively low level services. Unfortunately, such jobs are often make-work and may not contribute substantially to the career development of students.

Cooperative occupational training has long been the main form of financial assistance to vocational-technical students. In comprehensive high schools and vocational centers across the country, career-related job experience in cooperative education work stations has provided more than good education; it has provided the economic basis for economically disadvantaged students to complete high school rather than dropping out at age sixteen. The problem with cooperative education in terms of student financial assistance is that it requires strong support from cooperating employers who pay the wages. In a tight economy, employers are often less able to hire cooperative education students. Furthermore, many public agencies and philanthropic or social service organizations do not have the funds to permit hiring students under these circumstances.

The federal government has taken the position that work-study monies may be used to provide job slots in any nonprofit institution. Thus, innovative high schools, community colleges, and four-year institutions are combining their work-study and cooperative education programs to place students in a wide variety of public service occupational areas. Students are gaining meaningful educational experiences working for human relations commissions, police departments, mental health agencies, poverty agencies, family service agencies, agricultural extensions, city planning commissions, and a wide range of other agencies. The advantage to a cooperating nonprofit institution, in addition to its important role in educating young citizens, is that it can augment its staff paying only one-fifth of the cost. In some instances, educational institutions administering the work-study program may even carry the matching twenty percent if the cooperative job slot is particularly meaningful. Combined work-study and cooperative education programs help to reduce attrition at all levels by providing work experience and needed income to economically disadvantaged youth.

The Educational Amendments of 1972 (PL92–318) have significant effects on vocational-technical education, but particularly on the financial aids structure in higher education. They reinforce the current concepts of tripartite aid: grants, loans, and work-study assistance, and in addition provide for a Basic Opportunity Grant level of $1,400 for each student, less the amount which the student or his parents can contribute to his education. If the program is not fully funded the Basic Opportunity Grant level will be reduced according to a schedule provided in the legislation. The Amendments require that the first three categories of aid receive appropriations before the Basic Opportunity Grant program is funded.

Given the continuing national commitment to provide individual financial aid in order to equalize educational opportunities, it is particularly important that vocational institutions make adequate provisions to assist their students in obtaining financial support. Shaffer and Martinson argue that

> Regardless of the size of the institution, student aid should be a centralized function. Experience has clearly demonstrated that institutional responsibilities and the needs of the individual cannot be met when a variety of personnel and other offices act independently of each other under inconsistent and contradictory policies. (*12,* p. 28)

While the administration of financial aid is a specialized function, every vocational administrator should be familiar with basic policies and types of programs at his institution.

Placement

The most important student development function in vocational-technical education is placement of students in jobs. Placement is both a service and a critical evaluation criterion regarding the success of vocational programs. If employment preparation is the major goal of vocational-technical education, then placement and retention of students in jobs is the paramount measure of program effectiveness.

As we indicated earlier, placement in part-time jobs prior to graduation is vitally related to financial aid, either through work-study, cooperative education, or a combination of the two. It is important that the part-time, work-study, and cooperative education placement effort be integrated with the graduate placement function. The employer contacts are likely to be the same and the involvement in the development of an integrated series of educational job experiences leads directly to graduate employment placement.

While there seems to be general agreement on the fundamental aspects of job placement operations, one major issue has not been satisfactorily resolved. This has to do with whether the placement function should be centralized under a placement director or diffused throughout the institution and assigned to the various department heads, counselors, and faculty who are most closely related to the occupational fields for which their students are being educated. In most colleges, and many area vocational centers, the tendency has been to create a distinct placement office with a director and staff even though there may be many informal placement operations functioning in individual schools and departments of the institution. In comprehensive high school vocational programs, the placement function may be carried out by the cooperative education coordinator, vocational guidance counselors, individual faculty, or formally not at all. The advantages of a centralized placement officer are his specialized knowledge about the function, his continuing files and records, his broad and continuing relationship with employers, and the fact that he is the publicly recognized point of contact for both students and employers. Presumably, however, he is less informed about specific occupational requirements, about changing employment patterns in a given field, and about specific needs of employers in that occupation. Probably the best organizational arrangement is to create a centralized office, but assign partial placement responsibility to a given faculty member in each major occupational department or division. This responsibility should be in lieu of some of his other teaching and counseling duties. The department heads and all the faculty must be made cognizant that placement is everybody's responsibility and that, indeed, the continuing stability and progress of their department depends on successful placement.

In its operations, the placement function must relate closely to the guidance and career information service. Whether this service is provided by counselors, the library, or the placement office is not as important as that it be provided. Students are often unaware of the wide variety of job alternatives, even within a given occupational skill area. A comprehensive vocational information resource library should be available somewhere in the school or school system, or on the campus. The more closely it is integrated with both counseling and placement, the better both of these functions will be performed.

Additional Student Services

While the foregoing student development services constitute a nucleus requisite for any vocational-technical institution, other services should be considered. In area vocational centers and community colleges where students continue to reside at home but may attend a school thirty miles away, a critical service may be transportation. Particularly at the secondary level, busing is virtually the only practical solution. In community colleges it may be the only way to open the door to economically disadvantaged students who lack personal means of transportation. Related to the question of transportation is the choice of location for new facilities. In some community colleges and technical institutes, a critical issue may be how much, if any, college-owned housing should be developed. As student life styles have changed and the control function in education has decreased, there has been a severe decline in student and parent interest in dormitory living. As a result, many colleges find themselves with highly mortgaged housing facilities with unfilled beds. Student housing will likely tend toward privately owned student apartment or boarding/apartment complexes run by business for profit. While residence halls offer opportunities for out-of-class educational programming, the amount of administrative time devoted to the management of residence halls, and the social and disciplinary problems associated with them, is probably disproportionate to the benefits, except in areas where alternative housing is simply unavailable.

Other student services are indirectly related to the successful function of vocational programs; health services (which may be obtained by referral to a community agency), discipline, cultural and athletic activities, etc. In general, the trend in post-secondary technical education is away from those services. At all levels, however, the vocational technical administrator should attempt to keep abreast of how these services function and the impact they have on his students.

Student development services force occupational educators to remember that the purpose and focus of all their efforts is the student and his career development. Accordingly, all faculty and staff must be concerned about the delivery of the critical career-related student services. In higher education particularly, student personnel services have become so specialized and separate that staff often fail to interact with one another, much less with faculty. Worse yet, separate student personnel services divorce the teaching faculty member from his raison d'etre. Student development services are inextricably related to each other and to the teaching-learning process. It is imperative that all educational personnel be involved in the delivery of those services, no matter who has primary responsibility for them.

REFERENCES

1. Ayers, Archie R., Philip A. Tripp, and John H. Russel. *Student Services Administration in Higher Education.* Washington, D.C.: U.S. Government Printing Office, 1966.
2. Blocker, Clyde E. "Student Personnel Services for Occupational Education." In *Emphasis: Occupational Education in the Two-Year College.* Washington, D.C.: American Association of Junior Colleges, 1966.

3. Collins, Charles C. *Junior College Student Personnel Programs: What They Are and What They Should Be.* Washington, D.C.: American Association of Junior Colleges, 1967.

4. Ferguson, Donald G. *Pupil Personnel Services.* Washington: Center for Applied Research in Education, 1963.

5. Frederick, Robert W. *Student Activities in American Education.* New York: Center for Applied Research in Education, 1965.

6. Hummel, Dean L. and S. J. Bonham, Jr. *Pupil Personnel Services in Schools: Organization and Coordination.* Chicago: Rand McNally, 1968.

7. London, H. H. *Principles and Techniques of Vocational Guidance.* Columbus, Ohio: Charles E. Merrill, 1973.

8. O'Banion, Terry and Alice Thurston. *Student Development Programs in the Community Junior Colleges.* Englewood Cliffs, N.J.: Prentice-Hall, 1972.

9. *Pupil Personnel Services.* Washington, D.C.: Council of Chief State School Officers, 1960.

10. Raines, Max R. (Principal investigator). *Junior College Student Personnel Programs: Appraisal and Development.* A Report to the Carnegie Corporation, November 1965.

11. Roeber, Edward C., Garry R. Walz, and Glenn E. Smith. *A Strategy for Guidance.* Toronto, Ontario: Macmillan, 1969.

12. Shaffer, Robert H. and William D. Martinson. *Student Personnel Services in Higher Education.* New York: Center for Applied Research in Education, 1966.

13. Warnath, Charles F. *New Myths and Old Realities.* San Francisco: Jossey-Bass, 1971.

14. Williamson, E. G. *Vocational Counseling: Some Historical, Philosophical, and Theoretical Perspectives.* New York: McGraw-Hill, 1965.

15. Zeran, Franklin R. and Anthony C. Riccio. *Organization and Administration of Guidance Services.* Chicago: Rand McNally, 1962.

Chapter 11 PERSONNEL ADMINISTRATION

Schools and colleges are human systems; their primary resources, as well as their products, are people. In the broadest sense, every educational administrator is therefore a personnel administrator. One chief administrator confided that he felt all he needed to do to succeed was select capable subordinates, plan with them how to achieve the institution's objectives, and provide a meaningful reward system. Perhaps this is an oversimplification, but it illustrates the paramount importance of personnel administration in vocational education.

The purposes of this chapter are to help the reader:

1. to analyze the personnel structure and policies of existent vocational-technical institutions, or to design a general personnel administration system for a new institution;
2. to understand and explain the critical aspects of personnel recruitment, selection, orientation, and development functions for vocational education;
3. to develop his own philosophy about personnel performance evaluation and reward;
4. to understand certain basic human relations aspects of personnel management;

5. to identify personnel problems unique to the administration and supervision of vocational and technical education.

Schools and colleges are comprised of fascinatingly complex sets of inter-relationships of human beings. The quality of any vocational-technical department, school, or college depends more on the character of these interrelationships than on the specific capabilities of its individual staff. Personnel administration has to do with the structuring of these relationships and therefore is the very essence of successful educational administration.

Besides comprising the basic fabric of the educational system, people represent the most expensive financial decisions that an administrator makes. While in some elite universities the proportion of the operational budget allocated for personnel costs may be as low as sixty percent, in most technical and vocational colleges or schools, personnel costs will represent seventy-five to eighty percent, or more, of the annual operational expenditures.

In the past, faculty have been reasonably mobile, moving with relative ease between institutions because of a scarcity of supply. At all educational levels the supply and demand function has changed. Millett pointed out that

> For the past 30 years an individual university has not been considered as a career choice; the academic profession has been the career rather than a particular institution. With the changing conditions of the academic market place, I believe we have now entered a new era in which a particular university will become a career service for faculty, administrative staff, and others. (*1,* p. 12)

While this reduction in job mobility will not be as apparent for vocational-technical faculty, it is likely that staff appointments in a given institution will increasingly become more permanent. Thus, a decision to employ a new faculty member at an entering annual salary of $10,000 really represents $250,000 to $300,000 over the next 20 to 30 years, given inflation, promotions, and built-in salary increases. Viewing each professional staff member as a quarter of a million dollar decision helps put personnel administration in perspective. On this basis, there can be little disagreement that the primary objective of personnel administration in education must be the selection and retention of competent staff.

The personnel of any educational organization can be categorized in various ways. Commonly, they are divided into three categories: (1) instructional services staff—faculty, librarians, and counselors, (2) supporting services staff—clerical, maintenance, food services, groundskeeping, (3) professional administrative support services—chief administrators, deans, principals, business officers, department heads, etc. While the primary focus of educational personnel management tends to be on instructional service staff, administrators must be vitally concerned with personnel throughout the system. For example, supporting service staff often serve as the primary point of contact in the institution for students and the general community. The principal's secretary in fact *represents* the school when she interacts with anyone desiring to see him. Most administrators readily acknowledge that the supporting staff is what provides institutional continuity.

Because of the distinct categories of personnel and the differences between secondary and post-secondary staffing patterns, personnel organization for vocational and technical education varies widely. The one fact, almost universally true, is that there is seldom a personnel office or officer which deals solely with vocational-technical personnel. In secondary level institutions, individual high schools or area vocation centers are seldom large enough to warrant their own personnel function. Personnel offices tend to be located at the district level for purposes of economy and efficiency. The personnel office may have distinct components which deal with the different categories of personnel, but it is usually headed by an assistant superintendent who reports directly to the chief administrator. Thus, at the secondary level, the personnel officer is usually a staff, as opposed to line, officer who has the entire personnel function and nothing else.

In community colleges and technical colleges the responsibility for the personnel function is often divided. Personnel administration for supporting service staff may be through a personnel office reporting to the business vice president. This officer may also administer fringe benefits and some other personnel functions for instructional services staff as well. The tasks of recruitment, selection, orientation, development, and appraisal of faculty tend to fall to the academic line officers, often with active involvement of faculty peer groups. Driven by the impetus of faculty collective bargaining, which will be discussed later, many post-secondary institutions are now developing a more centralized, unified, personnel administration structure, whose responsibility includes academic staff.

It must be emphasized, however, that in any educational institution every administrative officer has some personnel responsibilities; by definition a supervisor deals with people. This in no way negates the need for a separate personnel office. We agree with Davis and Nickerson that "The creation of a separate personnel department, headed by an educational administrator trained in employee relations and *directly responsible to the superintendent* is mandatory in every school system" (*5*, p. 106). A real concern for vocational educators, however, is to make sure that the personnel officer understands some of the unique problems related to technical-vocational staff, and that the institution's personnel policies respond adequately to the unique needs of these people.

There is an abundance of good literature which deals with general personnel administration in educational institutions. Our analysis, therefore, will deal primarily with personnel functions as they relate to the special problems of the instructional staff in vocational-technical schools and colleges.

Personnel Philosophy, Policy, and Regulations

In every human organization there is a philosophy about personnel management, although this philosophy may be implicit rather than explicit. How people are treated in the organization is often a reflection of the philosophy of the central administration. This philosophic posture involves such issues as whether decisions are made autocratically or participatively; whether administration is viewed as an art or a science—intuitive or based on empirical data; for whom the institution exists and to whom it is responsive. We assume that vocational institutions exist solely to serve the needs of students in developing occupational skills which will make them employable. Personnel management philosophy and other major administrative decisions should always reflect this singular goal. A corollary is that the teacher is the most important single resource in achieving this goal.

While personnel administration is partly a staff function, delineation of the institutional philosophy and basic personnel policies is a function of the chief administrator and the major line officers. Personnel administration should involve the active participation of the various staff elements of the school or college and reflect its basic educational goals. Davis and Nickerson suggest that "The policy statement must encompass all matters relating to the provision of professional personnel services, be developed through open involvement of all personnel, be written in language which reduces misinterpretation to a minimum, be provided to all personnel in complete form and have built-in provisions for constant evaluation and revision" (*5*, p. 11).

In addition to a generally stated personnel policy, there should be a specifically formulated set of procedures and regulations which provide basic guidelines for personnel functions. These procedures and regulations should never be taken as static or as truly encompassing the total personnel system. Any set of procedures is subject to change and modification. Many schools and colleges find it beneficial to establish a personnel policy and procedures committee to provide continuous review and revision input. Involvement of technical faculty on this type of committee is imperative, especially in comprehensive educational systems which are only partially devoted to vocational education. Personnel administrators tend not to have vocational education backgrounds and need to be made aware of differing needs and problems of technical-vocational faculty. The following discussion relates some of these problems to the essential personnel administration functions.

Basic Personnel Functions Related to Vocational-Technical Education

The basic personnel functions can be categorized according to critical tasks: (1) recruitment, selection, and employment; (2) orientation and continuing development; (3) provision of incentives, rewards, and a classification system; (4) appraisal and evaluation; (5) personnel system management; and (6) collective bargaining.

RECRUITMENT, SELECTION, AND EMPLOYMENT

Until recently, recruitment of faculty for all levels and types of education has been a major problem because of inadequate supply. Within the past few years educators and the public have become aware of the apparent surplus of available faculty in some areas. Thus, education in part at least has become an employer's market and the problem of locating qualified personnel is no longer universally critical. However, in vocational-technical education, demand is increasing due to the new public awareness of career preparation needs. The correspondent accelerated growth of vocational and technical programs at the secondary and post-secondary levels maintains the continuing shortage of qualified personnel.

One problem in recruitment is the determination of what skills the prospective staff member must possess. In vocational education, the faculty member obviously must have practiced the occupational skills which he is to teach. In addition, he is usually expected to have the necessary academic preparation in pedagogy—related to course development, class preparation, learning psychology, evaluation, instructional media, etc. Across the country, state certification is the official recognition that a person possesses these skills and experience, at least for secondary level teaching. The problem with certification, however, is that there are too many kinds of certificates and no common meaning or connotation for a given certificate, especially across states. Except in a few states such as California, teacher certification is not required in post-secondary technical institutions. This allows colleges more flexibility in the recruitment of technical faculty since they can go directly to personnel functioning in the occupation. Employment of these people engenders other problems in staff development related to the acquisition of pedagogical skills.

Recruiting from business, industry, and occupations directly is hindered by the problem of salary differentials; frequently, a prospective staff member takes a significant cut in pay to teach. Often, graduates of vocational-technical teacher-training programs elect not to enter education because salaries are not competitive with those their skills bring in occupational practice. Thus, while personnel officers in many educational institutions are finding it less necessary to run an active recruiting program to attract faculty, there is still a need to do so for vocational and technical programs. If the acute shortage persists, it may be necessary to revise secondary certification requirements to permit freer entrance of skilled tradesmen on a provisional or probationary basis, pending the acquisition of necessary pedagogical training. The relative flexibility of community colleges and some area vocational centers in this regard may presage change in general secondary systems.

The selection process essentially involves the acquisition of sufficient information on a prospective candidate to permit a decision regarding his qualifications and attractiveness to the institution. As Castetter has pointed out: "the major selection devices employed to compile information are the application blank, selection tests, interviews, medical examination, academic transcripts, and background investigation" (4, p. 204). Even with these various means, the selection process is still an inexact science. Application blanks and background resumés tend to point out essentially what the candidate wants to emphasize. Recommendations on file are seldom anything but flattering and seldom should be relied on. Woodburne noted:

> In examining hundreds of dossiers of qualifications one will seldom find more than the unsupported statement—"he is a good teacher." There is no evidence adduced, but we are left with a statement of opinion which is no better than the writer's ability and opportunity to judge a teaching operation. When one considers how personal the teaching relationship is with students, the value of someone else's subjective judgments, based at times on campus gossip, is very low indeed. It would be quite justifiable to conclude that no reliable information is available at all. (12, p. 50)

If the application form, references, and resumés leave something to be desired, the interview process is probably worse still. Many administrators believe they have a knack for identifying good people quickly through a face-to-face meeting. While it is true that first impressions in interviews tend to be lasting ones, it is equally true that interviews are affected by the time and place, the emotional state of the candidate, the prejudices and predispositions of the interviewers, the ability of the candidate to pick up clue words and respond accordingly, and the existence of a halo effect where interviewers ascribe a series of good or bad traits to a candidate based on one identified trait. Candidates tend to be selected on the basis of their verbal facility, which may or may not indicate teaching ability, especially in vocational-technical areas.

Schools and colleges are often reluctant to ask a candidate to demonstrate his technical skills, yet these skills are probably correlates to the research and publication skills demanded by the "academic" community in higher education. While neither technical skills nor research publications guarantee teaching effectiveness, they do demonstrate competence in a field or discipline. Vocational personnel selection procedures should emphasize skill review.

The other device commonly used by businesses and government, but often neglected by educators, is a comprehensive reference and background check. Once the selection process has narrowed to one or two candidates for a position, direct contact should be made with his former supervisors, peers, subordinates, and students, assuming candidate permission. If he does not give his permission, there is ground for some suspicion. These background checks can be made by telephone or by direct visitation. If the expense seems inordinate, remember that the cost of the selection decision may be a quarter of a million dollars.

Selection is probably the key personnel task since all else follows it. Because of the inexact nature of the devices available, a number of people should be involved in the selection process to guarantee a variety of perspectives. Higher education commonly uses a peer group selection process which sometimes includes students. Involvement of staff in the selection of future colleagues fosters institutional cohesiveness and should be supported in all levels of vocational and technical education. However, the final decision or selection is an admininistrative one and no professional staff member should ever be appointed without the direct involvement and recommendation of the chief administrator.

No matter what the labor supply market looks like, really good people are always at a premium. It is a wise administrative policy to keep a comprehensive file on exceptional individuals, even if they are not currently seeking to change jobs. It is common practice in some school systems to create a pool of qualified and available applicants. The trouble is that this pool is never static, since available applicants may take other open positions. A good administrator is always seeking outstanding personnel even if he has no current openings.

The employment decision is critical because it is so much harder to fire people in education than to hire them. In making the decision to hire, one should always remember the problems associated with dismissal, especially given tenure, collective bargaining, and a notorious soft-heartedness among educational supervisors.

Once the decision to hire has been made, the question of contract arises. Most academic appointments are seen as nine- or ten-month appointments. In vocational-technical education programs often operate year-round to make optimum use of equipment and facilities. Technical faculty usually have less difficulty in securing outside summer employment than do other faculty members. Thus it may be necessary to provide twelve-month appointments for vocational staff members if they are to be available for summer teaching.

ORIENTATION AND CONTINUING DEVELOPMENT

The orientation or induction program may be the first significant involvement the new staff member has with the institution. It deals with his adaptation to his position, the institution, his peers, and the community. It is both a socialization process and an information dissemination effort.

> The induction process, in its broadest sense, is an extension of the recruitment and selection processes in which administrative efforts are designed to match the man and the position, to enable the man to achieve position satisfaction, and to utilize fully the satisfactions and the abilities of the man in attaining the goals of the educational program. (4, p. 215)

The induction effort is particularly important for technical faculty coming into the education system from the business world, since they are generally not familiar with pedagogic jargon, norms, and mores of educational institutions, work routine in schools and colleges, and the expectations held by peers and students.

For most staff, continuing professional development is directly related to job satisfaction. The need for individuals to grow in capability and knowledge is important for the institution as well, since the technological revolution and knowledge explosion can make programs as well as people obsolete if professional development is not a continual process. Continuing professional development can take place individually or in a group, inside or outside the institution. Personnel policies must be structured to provide released instruction time to develop new media or curricula, or to do applied research. Vocational-technical institutions do not have research expectations of faculty but should encourage those who wish to experiment. Sometimes outside professional development is an issue since academic courses and conferences at other institutions are often inappropriate. Industrial experience or company training courses (as in data processing) may be the major developmental option. Vocational and technical teachers should be given leaves of absence and sabbaticals for appropriate work experience to upgrade technical competencies.

Continuing development activities should be programmed for individuals and groups within the institution. Staff seminars or workshops on new developments in education, technology, administrative policy, or didactic approaches are all appropriate. In-service training for technical faculty is especially needed in three major areas: (1) relating their occupational area to manpower and career education problems in general; (2) upgrading specific technical skills to keep all faculty current; and (3) teaching skills involved in evaluation, media technology, curriculum development, and student counseling. The chief administrator and line officials should be involved in planning and budgeting for a professional staff development program. While both morale and staff competency can be enhanced in this fashion, personnel and organizational development funds are often the first to be reduced or eliminated in periods of austerity. This is short-sighted administrative policy.

INCENTIVES, REWARDS, AND CLASSIFICATION

Every social system operates on the basis of incentives and rewards, both implicit and explicit, intrinsic and extrinsic. The implicit, intrinsic rewards of teaching are relatively obvious, but vary in intensity for different individuals. They include the satisfaction of helping others grow, growing yourself, determining your own use of time, having a large amount of social interaction and intellectual stimulation, etc. While these incentives and rewards are partially affected by personnel administration policy, they are affected much less than the extrinsic variables.

The definition of the extrinsic incentive and reward system for vocational schools and colleges is the total compensation package. The total compensation package involves salaries, extra income opportunities, insurance, sick leave, retirement benefits, and other financially related variables. The compensation process and package must continually be reviewed and re-evaluated since they affect everyone directly and immediately. The most important element in the compensation package is salaries. Salary determination and distribution of funds can be the source of more institution-wide conflict than any other single decision. "Because the size of a man's paycheck is related to the satisfaction of both his economic and non-economic needs, the process by which remuneration in a school system is determined is a crucial significance to its ability to implement an effective manpower plan" (*4,* p. 168).

In secondary systems, salaries are most frequently based on a published salary schedule. An individual salary level is determined essentially on the basis of two factors: training (in terms of degrees, hours of credit, or years in school) and experience. While the salary schedule is the easiest administrative approach to salary determination, it can discriminate against vocational faculty since their training may not have come in a traditional academic setting and they may not have degrees and credits to show for it. Further, "experience" in teaching is often given more weight than industrial or occupational experience.

The development of a salary schedule is a complicated problem involving decisions about how many steps within a given category from minimum to maximum salary, what ratio factors should be used to weigh experience and training, and finally whether there should be any provision for merit increases. The whole merit increase issue is sticky. Merit pay attempts to differentially reward people in similar positions with similar responsibilities on the basis of quality of performance. The issue of merit pay evolves around whether or not we can really measure quality of performance adequately. Traditionally, four-year colleges have not had fixed salary schedules, but most community colleges now follow a salary schedule. Whether individually negotiated or based on a published schedule, there is still a question about whether a specific individual's salary level should be made public. It is the authors' opinion that the salaries of all staff in public, tax-supported institutions should be a matter of public record. In fact, perhaps total compensation level should be published, including summer payments, evening courses, and other supplemental forms of remuneration.

The problem with fixed salary schedules, particularly those with no merit pay options, is that it is hard for technical faculty to move up, i.e. be promoted, into a higher category. Experience increments are given on the basis of years of experience, but training is usually calculated in terms of B.A., B.A. plus so many hours, M.A., M.A. plus so many hours, and Ph.D. For an instructor in welding, cosmetology, printing, or a host of other occupational fields, there may be no appropriate substantive baccalaureate or master's degree program, much less a doctorate. As a result, his progress in salary is largely determined by his willingness to take education courses at the nearest university or teachers college. A workable salary schedule for vocational-technical faculty must include promotional categories based on achievements in the instructor's occupational field.

Historically, moonlighting has been relatively common, if not a veritable economic necessity, for secondary school staff. At the post-secondary level, this supplementary employment has taken the form of teaching extension or evening courses, working as a consultant, or writing professionally. Most post-secondary institutions have adopted policies concerning consulting time or external employment. The problem of supplemental employment for vocational-technical faculty is more complex than for "academic" staff. First of all, they are usually more employable, more in demand. Second, they have a professional and psychological need to keep themselves up-to-date and employable. Institutional policy should be flexible enough to allow outside employment in a variety of ways, as long as there are no conflicts of interest and no negative effects on ability to fulfill their teaching commitments.

The incentive and reward structure of personnel administration must necessarily take into consideration the issue of work load. In fairness to the

school or college and to the faculty member, there should be a clearly
defined statement of institutional expectations of the staff, involving the
number of credit or contact hours to be taught, office hours to be reserved
for student consultation, committee assignments, public service commitments, administrative tasks, or whatever. The determination of teaching
load, i.e. type and number of hours taught each academic term, is a line
responsibility of principals, deans, department heads, etc. Since teaching
load, in terms of classes assigned and student credit or contact hours, is
usually used as a measure of productivity, it is in a sense the reciprocal of
the pay scale. It is, therefore, of major concern to all academic administrators. The problem, particularly at the post-secondary level, is the number
of contact hours per week usually required in occupational programs versus
the lesser hours taught in nonoccupational programs. It is difficult to get
an acceptable agreement about the ratio equivalency of occupational contact hours to academic lecture hours.

Fringe benefits assume increasingly larger proportions of the total compensation package in education, as in business and industry. The value of
fringe benefits as a percentage of total compensation ranges from ten percent to over thirty percent across institutions and levels. The typical fringe
package includes a retirement plan (either a state or local employee, state
teachers retirement, or Teachers Insurance Annuity Association), medical
insurance, some level of life insurance (usually term), and a sick-leave
policy. Some schools and colleges extend their fringe benefits program to
include family medical insurance, dental insurance, disability insurance,
and personal leave days. Since fringe benefits are tax-free, there are advantages for employees to seek more of them in the total compensation package.
Increases in fringe benefits are usually most advantageous to faculty with
families since they are usually the major beneficiaries of such benefits. One
problem for the school or college is that once a fringe benefit is awarded,
it is viewed by staff as a given, even though the cost of that benefit may
increase substantially in the future (when insurance or medical plan premi-
ums rise).

Retirement management may become a major personnel administration
tool during the potentially lean years ahead in education. For example, a
senior teacher, eligible to retire at age 60 but not forced to retire until age
65, could receive $2,500 per year extra retirement pay for the period be-
tween 60 and 65 if he retires at age 60. If he is at the maximum of $12,500
per year for his bracket and the institution could replace him for $8,000 per
year, this would be an economically advantageous situation for all parties
involved. This is particularly true where the program or occupational area
of the retiring employee is declining and he could be replaced by someone
in a new program area. As collective bargaining develops in both secondary

and post-secondary education, more attention will be given to the fringe benefit package.

APPRAISAL-EVALUATION

Appraisal and evaluation are inherent in every human system. We are always evaluating other people by a variety of measures, many of which are invalid. In education, the purpose of evaluation is not to determine pay raise levels but to help improve teaching. The problem is that in evaluation we too frequently apply the wrong measures for the wrong reasons. In the ever-present evaluation of others, the questions we must always ask are: (1) How reliable and consistent are our instruments and measurements? (2) Are they valid in that they really measure what we want them to measure? (3) Are the means formalized so that others know how we made the appraisal? (4) Are the measurements as objective as possible, reflecting a minimum of our bias? (5) Does the person being evaluated understand what is being measured and how, and is he able to use the information to help himself? There are only five categories of people who can evaluate vocational teaching effectiveness: (1) supervisors, (2) peers, (3) students, (4) the teacher himself, and (5) the general public who employ the students or evaluate their learning. Measures by any of these categories alone are likely to be inadequate; an eclectic approach is required, blending these elements in some rational fashion. Whatever combination is used, it should be accepted ahead of time by the people being evaluated, and results should always be viewed with some skepticism because of inherent limitations. As Castetter has pointed out: "The real problem is to develop and improve valid appraisal procedures and to create greater understanding of the purposes and limitations of performance appraisal so that results derived from its application will not be misused" (4, p. 273). Above all, appraisal must be used as a continuing feedback mechanism, not a once-a-year tool.

A variation of a performance contracting evaluation model is being tried by some vocational institutions. In these cases the instructor is evaluated on how successful his graduates are in finding a job, and how successful they are on the job, as viewed by their employer. The model uses this performance measurement as a direct input on determining salary levels of faculty. The approach has merit, but the primary purpose of the appraisal should not be to determine salary increments but to help improve teaching performance.

PERSONNEL SYSTEM MANAGEMENT

There are a number of ongoing personnel management and maintenance activities which have implications for vocational and technical education:

grievance procedures, the affirmative action program, substitute faculty policy, tenure and academic freedom policies, safety and health programs, and system feedback.

Unfortunately, most large human organizations require a formalized grievance system, a procedure which guarantees due process and equity in institutional policy application. In collective bargaining, grievance refers to an alleged violation of the specific contract. As used here, grievance is an alleged inequity or misapplication of any institutional policy which adversely affects the grievant in a substantial manner. A grievance procedure should be initiated only when the grievant has exhausted all administrative channels of appeal. The specific procedure should be formulated by the faculty and staff of each individual institution in order to reflect its specific needs. A grievance procedure and the way it is structured can be especially important for vocational and technical faculty in a comprehensive high school or community college where there are perceived differences between general education instructors and occupational education staff. Since a grievance committee or hearing body is composed of peers, it can serve as an integrating force.

The major problem with a grievance procedure is that in guaranteeing full investigation and due process to all concerned, it can become a cumbersome, time-consuming process. To alleviate this problem, many larger institutions have instituted an ombudsman system. The ombudsman is a faculty member who has no official power, but operates on the basis of his own referent power and the prestige of the office in attempting to ameliorate administrative capriciousness and minor grievances. He attempts to cut red tape and resolve problems and conflict through reason, discussion, and peer pressure. The ombudsman approach has not been widely evaluated and the long-run benefits and costs remain to be seen. The concept is most practicable in large colleges or schools, and even there it may be psychologically threatening to administrative staff. However, an ombudsman can resolve some problems which may otherwise result in formal grievances.

Increasingly, federal and state governments are taking steps to regulate personnel policies and operations of educational institutions with respect to the treatment of minority group members and women. Institutions receiving federal funds (which includes most vocational schools and colleges) must show evidence that they are equal opportunity employers and that they have a specific Affirmative Action program to rectify previous inbalances and inequities based on race and sex. The Affirmative Action program is particularly concerned with the areas of recruitment-selection and compensation. In many cases, vocational-technical institutions will be particularly hard hit in the Affirmative Action effort since they are often largely staffed by white males. Often, there are few available minority or female instructors in certain occupational areas. Because of union and trade entry restrictions, perceived lower prestige and income in some vocations, bad programming and teaching in some comprehensive secondary systems, and poor counseling, many minority group people have not wanted to enter occupational programs. Few program matriculants means even fewer potential faculty. Similarly, because of existent norms and social expectations there have been relatively few women in certain vocational programs, particularly in the trade and industrial area. Corrective steps and Affirmative Action programs will be a growing concern of personnel administration in vocational-technical education.

Another area of federal concern and legislative involvement relates to the 1970 Occupational Safety and Health Act (OSHA). While educational institutions are currently exempt from OSHA, business and industry are being required to take a more active concern in improving their health and safety standards, particularly in shops and laboratories. Because of its impact on industry and the likelihood that it will be extended to educational institutions sometime in the future, vocational schools and colleges should attempt to meet the general provisions of OSHA. For the sake of its students and staff, every vocational institution should form a safety and health committee and assign coordinating responsibility to one person. The committee must be concerned with such things as exhaust and ventilation systems, waste chemical disposal, radioactivity safety precautions, safety equipment and regulations in shops, and a variety of other problems related to specific occupational programs.

Policies dealing with part-time and substitute faculty are of particular concern in vocational education. Most secondary systems and some community colleges maintain a roster of qualified substitutes in the event of illness or other absence of regular faculty. The difficulty is in locating qualified substitutes in occupational areas. In most colleges the substitute system is handled in a collegial fashion where one professional fills in for another, except in cases of extended absence. In larger vocational-technical schools and colleges, the collegial responsibility pattern can work if specific occupational programs are big enough to have multiple faculty staffs. In small programs where one instructor handles all the occupationally related course work, there usually is no one on the staff qualified to replace him. One approach to amelioration of this problem is to use noncertified, local practitioners in the occupation for short-term substitution. This is easier to do in metropolitan areas (where the supply is greater) and in post-secondary institions which are not restricted by the teaching certification problem.

There is growing public concern about the questions of academic freedom and tenure at all levels of education. Tenure is commonly awarded, presumably to protect academic freedom, after a given number of years of satisfactory performance. Many critics of education argue that academic freedom in this country is now adequately protected in the courts and through many pieces of legislation and is no longer a justification for tenure. In many ways, tenure has become the academic equivalent of economic or job security. "The current concern about tenure is twofold; whether or not the practice of tenure is hampering the development and enforcement of standards of individual job performance, and whether or not the practice of tenure is hampering the adjustment of personnel to the changing economic circumstances of individual colleges and universities. When does protection of academic freedom become, instead, protection of professional incompetence?" (*1*, p. 18). Academic freedom is seldom a major issue among technical and vocational faculty at any level. If not administered carefully, a tenure policy can result in isolating faculty from the need to keep technologically current. Nevertheless, the tenure policy must be uniformly administered across the institution.

One other major concern in personnel system management is that of obtaining negative feedback. Many staff members are reluctant to bring constructive criticism into the open, even though it is the major substance of coffee lounge interaction. One important mechanism for eliciting this feedback is the exit interview for resigning, retiring, or terminated staff. Although sometimes tempered with bitterness, their analysis of the system is usually forthright and frank, and can provide new insights for the administrator.

COLLECTIVE BARGAINING

The academic union movement has had a most dramatic impact on education during the past decade. Teachers unions are now widely accepted in secondary institutions and are beginning to make significant inroads into post-secondary education. From 1970 to 1972, the number of colleges operating under collectively bargained contracts doubled (*6*). "Collective negotiations may be defined as a process in which representatives of school personnel meet with representatives of the school system to negotiate jointly an agreement covering a specific period of time and defining the terms and conditions of employment" (*4*, p. 329).

Since in education the "conditions of employment" can cover virtually anything that goes on in the school or college, collective bargaining can have a substantial impact on almost all the personnel administration issues discussed in this chapter. The issues remain, as do the various alternative solutions, but the major difference under collective bargaining is the *process* of arriving at the resolution. The pros and cons of collective bargaining in the professions can be argued *ad nauseam,* but for many vocational administrators it is simply a fact of life. A real problem in comprehensive high schools and community colleges, where vocational-technical staff are a minority, is to insure that the collective bargaining process represents their interests adequately. To achieve ratification of a negotiated contract, union leadership seeks to meet the needs of the majority of members, sometimes at the expense of members whose interests, backgrounds, and working schedules are at variance with the majority.

Primary administrative responsibility for collective bargaining is usually centralized and given to a specialist in labor relations. However, the administrative bargaining team should provide expertise on all aspects of institutional operation, and it is incumbent on the vocational administrator to make sure that vocational-technical education is adequately represented, at least on the management side. Typically, the collective bargaining specialist will not have come from the ranks of vocational-technical education, and may not even be particularly sympathetic to the needs of occupational programs. Key vocational education administrators in every school or college system should become familiar with the collective bargaining process and get involved in actual negotiations whenever possible.

Human Relations—A Matter of Attitude and Perception

Almost twenty years ago Katz (9) made some incisive observations about administrative skills. He said that an administrator needs three kinds of skills: technical, human, and conceptual. A high degree of technical skill is required of lower level administrators who are directly involved in the management of production. Middle level administrators require a heavier emphasis on human skills, and chief administrators need more emphasis on conceptual skills. Human skills are necessary, however, at all levels of management. The concluding portion of this chapter deals with the matter of human skills and relations.

It is our contention that attitudes and perceptions, more than techniques, determine good human relations in an organization, although techniques are necessarily involved. "Good human relations in a school system are built on a feeling of good will and mutual respect and faith in the dignity and worth of human beings as individual personalities" (8, p. 19). Good human relations are based on an attitude which focuses on administration as a supportive-catalytic-expediting function in addition to its controlling function.

The matter of perception has to do with how the administrator looks at people. People are the major resource of the educational institution, the major product and its raison d'etre. Social scientists and accountants have recently been collaborating in developing models for *Human Resource Accounting (3)*. These models attempt to put dollar values on the human organization—on the acquisition and replacement costs of human resources, and on their economic worth to the organization. The important point is the perception of people as economic resources which the institution must conserve and help develop.

Perception as it relates to human relations has two other important aspects for administrative behavior. The first is that administrators should recognize that perceptions of problems, personalities, and even physical environments are at best incomplete, may be erroneous, and will differ significantly from one individual to another. This essentially means that all problem areas are complex and that people involved are usually acting rationally in terms of *their perceptions* of problems. A second element of perception is the generally recognized psychological phenomenon of self-fulfilling expectations. What you reasonably expect people to do, if they are aware of your expectations, frequently is what they do. Thus, when people know they are expected to be professional, responsible, honest, etc., they usually are. While the question of self-fulfilling expectation can be regarded as more a matter of faith than absolute fact, it is generally a good operating principle.

Given the attitudinal and perceptual requirements for good human relations, there are also some practices which should be observed. First of all, all administrative decisions and actions should be characterized by consistency, equity, and integrity. In making a response to any question or problem the administrator should ask himself whether the decision is consistent with earlier decisions and general policy, whether it affords equitable treatment to all people currently involved or potentially to be involved, and whether it maintains both institutional and individual integrity.

Frequent face-to-face encounters are critical for continuing good human relations. People need to feel that they can relate to those administering the organization. The larger the school or college, the more difficult it is to arrange face-to-face meetings with key administrative personnel on a frequent basis; but this does not lessen the need. Implicit in these encounters is the need for *two-way communication.* All staff must be aware of major institutional policies and issues which affect them, and should be able to communicate their ideas and concerns in response. A significant concern for all administrators should be how to achieve such a two-way flow of communication, particularly the continuing staff feedback.

Key administrative staff must become part-time social scientists, attempting to become aware of the individual needs of their faculty and staff. They must be concerned with helping them fulfill these needs wherever possible, when such fulfillment can also help achieve the goals of the institution. Even when it is not practicable to take a given action, the mere evidence of concern and awareness will make a major positive contribution to staff relations.

Much has been written about participation in educational administration and the construction of an organizational democracy which is consistent with the ideals of political democracy. Castetter defined organizational democracy as "a system in which provisions are made to make possible for each of its members fair treatment, strong leadership, decision participation, recognition of individual rights and responsibilities, individualism, and opportunities for self-realization" (*4*, p. 352).

The basic premise of organizational democracy is that people have a right to participate in decisions which affect their lives. In schools and colleges, this must include students, staff, and the supporting community. Students and faculty should be involved in operational committees wherever legally and fiscally feasible and have the opportunity to provide their input on major organizational policy decisions. Since personnel policies are those which most directly affect faculty and other staff members, they particularly should have a voice in their formulation, irrespective of whether or not there is a formalized collective bargaining relationship established under law. It is important to remember, however, that schools are also part of the political democratic system. They are governed by boards who are elected by the constituents of the system, or who are appointed by the elected representatives. Ultimate responsibility for vocational and technical institutions rests with the community, through the governing board and the chief administrator it appoints. Accordingly, the right of faculty and staff to participate in personnel policy determination does not mean that they have the final voice. The chief administrator must ultimately be held accountable for personnel administration.

REFERENCES

1. Academy for Educational Development. *Personnel Management in Higher Education.* Washington: Management Division. Academy for Educational Development, October 1972.

2. Berman, Louise M. *Supervision, Staff Development and Leadership.* Columbus: Charles E. Merrill, 1971.

3. Brummet, R. Lee, Eric G. Flamholtz, and William C. Pyle. *Human Resource Accounting.* Ann Arbor: Foundation for Research on Human Behavior, 1969.

4. Castetter, William B. *The Personnel Function in Educational Administration.* New York: Macmillian, 1971.

5. Davis, Donald E. and Neal C. Nickerson, Jr. *Critical Issues in School Personnel Administration.* Chicago: Rand McNally, 1968.

6. Garbarino, Joseph W. "Faculty Unionism: From Theory to Practice." *Industrial Relations,* February 1972.

7. Gibson, R. Oliver, and Herold C. Hunt. *The School Personnel Administrator.* Boston: Houghton Mifflin, 1965.

8. Griffith, Daniel E. *Human Relations in School Administration.* New York: Appleton-Century-Crofts, 1956.

9. Katz, Robert L. "Skills of an Effective Administrator." *Harvard Business Review* 33, No. 1 (January-February 1955): 33–42.

10. Moore, Harold E. *The Administration of Public School Personnel.* New York: The Center for Applied Research in Education, 1966.

11. VanZwoll, James A. *School Personnel Administration.* New York: Appleton-Century-Crofts, 1964.

12. Woodburne, Lloyd S. *Principles of College and University Administration.* Stanford: Stanford University Press, 1958.

Chapter 12 FISCAL AND PHYSICAL PLANNING AND MANAGEMENT

As taxes are an expression of political philosophy in dollar terms, so budgets in vocational-technical institutions are expressions of their educational philosophy in dollar terms for a fixed period of time. School facilities, like budgets, also reflect the educational philosophy of the institution and provide the physical setting for its implementation. The purpose of this chapter is to review perspectives and problems related to fiscal and physical planning and management, particularly as they relate uniquely to vocational and technical education.

The purposes of this chapter are to help the reader:

1. to understand and articulate the need for effective fiscal and physical planning and management in vocational and technical education;

2. to express his own philosophy about how a budget should optimally be developed, and to illustrate various approaches to budget planning;

3. to analyze the operational, control, and evaluation aspects of a budget system in a given vocational-technical institution;

4. to explain what he considers to be an optimum method to plan for physical facility development;

5. to explain alternative approaches for analyzing building and equipment utilization and to plan for their replacement.

Financial planning and facilities planning in school systems have traditionally been favorite topics of education authors. The literature is replete with innumerable books and articles on both subjects. Fifteen years ago, one leading facilities textbook (*11*) estimated that a complete school plant bibliography at that time would contain over 10,000 entries. Until recently, the research and writing on financial and facilities planning and management in vocational and technical education were not nearly so prolific. Within the past few years there have been several studies of comparative costs of occupational and general education programs, as well as the specific problems in developing vocational-technical facilities. This chapter will focus primarily on financial and physical planning and management as they relate to vocational and technical education. Because of the complexity of these functions, the reader will be referred to other texts in relation to specific problems.

In education as in architecture, form should follow function; determination of an educational philosophy and objectives for the institution is a necessary prerequisite to establishing a financial system and physical facilities. "The most elementary rule about the budgeting process is that educational planning precedes financial planning. Nonetheless, it is the rule that is most frequently broken" (*7,* p. 240). However, since both educational planning and budgeting are continuing processes, they must be accomplished concurrently. As in the case of curriculum and personnel policy formulation, financial and physical planning and management require the direct involvement of the chief administrator. The implementation of these policies can be left to subordinates, but not the basic policy. The structure of the budgetary process and the physical plant either facilitate or inhibit the effective functioning of any human organization; they are unlikely to be nonaffective elements. An inflexible budgeting process restricts innovation and new program development. A building which is unsuitable or not adaptable for new programs extends programs which may no longer be occupationally relevant.

Factors in the Budgetary Process

The budgeting process is essentially the planning, management, and evaluation of the use of available resources, particularly financial resources, to achieve the objectives of the organization. "By whatever adjective, the budget is a kind of specification of a program for a given period of time to achieve particular purposes which features an estimate of expenditures and the proposed sources of financial support" (7, p. 209). While the budgetary process enables the system to allocate resources to meet priority objectives, the primary purpose of a budget is to keep expenditures within income. This is particularly true for educational institutions, since they ordinarily do not have the legislative mandate permitting deficit financing.

In the long run, resource availability is presumably an elastic variable; that is, local people can be persuaded to pass additional millage issues, state legislatures can increase appropriations for education, federal or philanthropic sources can provide grant support for specific programs. In the short run, however, the budgetary process operates on the premise that expenditures must be kept within available income. As a result, the internal budgeting process at an educational institution for the short-run (one-year) period resembles a zero-sum game. In a zero-sum game, the various demands exceed resource supply, and what is allocated to one purpose cannot be allocated to another. Treating the budget as a zero-sum game is like viewing it as a pie of a certain size; if someone gets a bigger piece, someone else must necessarily get a smaller piece. In a school system, the revenue for a given budget period is at a fixed level, and institutional elements compete with one another for the limited resources. Through the budget process, the allocation of resources is often determined on an advocacy basis.

In an optimally rational system, presumably those programs which demonstrate the highest socioeconomic benefits for their cost would receive highest funding priority. However, the advocacy budget process is often hindered by a relative lack of reliable empirical data on both the specific costs and benefits of occupational or general education programs. Frequently, budget decisions are based on political factors, responding to specific pressures both within and outside the institution. In a comprehensive high school or community college offering both occupational and nonoccupational programs it is the responsibility of the chief vocational education administrator to serve as the advocate for adequate budgeting of resources for occupational programs. It is for this reason, particularly, that vocational administrators must understand the operation of the budgetary process, even though they will probably not have primary institutional responsibility for its total development and administration.

Recent studies (6, 20) which have attempted to cost out vocational programs in relation to general academic programs have found most occupational offerings to be more expensive. In both secondary systems and in community colleges, programs in health-related occupations, trade and industrial, and engineering technologies generally range from 1.5 to 2.0 times as expensive as the standard academic program in the same institution. The only major area where occupational programs are not consistently more costly per student or student credit hour is business and distributive education.

The primary reasons for these higher costs patterns are: lower student-faculty ratios, sometimes required by accrediting agencies (particularly in allied health occupations); greater requirements for capital expenditures in equipment and specialized facilities; limited student training stations (in shops and laboratories); greater consumption of expendable supplies; and higher salaries often required to attract qualified technologists into teaching. As a result, if credit hour production or number of graduates produced for the resources allocated are used as determinant budgeting criteria, occupational programs may not have the highest priority. If, however, other output or benefit variables, such as job placement success or income earned by graduates, are used, the occupational program moves up on the priority list.

During the past decade the resources and funding available for occupational programs have changed substantially due to federal inputs. The Vocational Education Act of 1963 (PL88–210), the Vocational Education Amendments of 1968 (PL90–576), and the Education Amendments of 1972 (PL92–369) have all enabled significant additional federal resources to be applied to vocational and technical education. Under the VEA of 1963 and 1968, some states have begun to provide support for occupational programs on the basis of *added cost.* "The *added costs* of a vocational program are measured by calculating the difference between the average cost (or marginal cost) of the vocational program and the average (or marginal) cost of the *alternative* secondary academic program" (*6,* p. 18). In some instances, added cost monies are merely federal funds channelled through the state coordinating agency; in other cases, they are funds appropriated by the state legislature. The point is that vocational-technical educators can often now use the availability of these funds to gain leverage in the budget advocacy process.

Budget Planning

The budgeting process is typically divided into at least two and sometimes three phases: budget planning, budget control, and budget (or financial) evaluation. In this three-fold sense, budgeting is a continuous process. Because of differing requirements for planning, control, and evaluation, there may in fact be three distinct budgeting formats, although each must be interrelated to the others.

It is difficult to overstate the importance of the budgeting process, especially if it is deliberately charted and intelligently conducted. At any

dynamic college or university planning is a continuous process, and perhaps the most regular and precise form of planning is through the preparation of the institutional budget. Planning and budgeting are inseparable,
and they represent essential and ongoing activities of the academy. (*3*, p.
13)

A major critique of the budgeting process in education is that historically
it has been structured to assist fiscal accounting rather than to facilitate
institutional planning and program development. The majority of budgets
in educational institutions are what have been called function-object budgets (*10*, p. 129). Operations are broken out by major function (e.g. instruction, central administration, student services, business operations, etc.) and
by object within those functions (e.g. salaries, wages, and other personnel
associated costs; supplies and operational costs including communication
and travel; and equipment). This process is not tied tightly to planning or
goal achievement. Usually, the function-object budgeting system assumes
a current operating level as given in planning the following year budget. It
permits minimal comparison between functions when the institution is
attempting to lay out priorities.

PROGRAM BUDGETING

During the past decade, beginning at the federal level and extending
through all kinds of government entities, the planning, programming, budgeting system (PPBS) has won wide acceptance. As the major component
of this approach, program budgeting differs sharply from function-object
budgeting insofar as budget planning is concerned.

> Program budgeting relates the output-oriented programs, or activities, of
> an organization to specific resources that are then stated in terms of budget
> dollars. Both programs and resources are projected for at least several
> years into the future. Emphasis is upon outputs, cost-effectiveness meth-
> ods, rational planning techniques, long range objectives and analytical
> tools for decision-making. (*10*, p. 76)

Program budgeting operates on the premise that both the cost of individual
programs and the output can be quantifiably measured. It begins by delineating the specific institutional objectives and by conceiving alternative program possibilities to accomplish those objectives. Each of these program
alternatives is then evaluated in terms of the resources required and the
estimated benefits to be gained. The most optimal alternative, in terms of
a benefit cost ratio, is then selected for implementation. Program budgeting
is usually based on a five-year projection, although the budget is admittedly
more sketchy the further it is projected into the future.

Program budgeting has major implications for institutional change, not only within educational organizations but also across state-wide systems. If one accepts the premise that costs and outputs of individual programs can be measured and compared, the subsequent logic of program budgeting is inescapable. In fact, most educational administrators give some kind of verbal homage to PPBS, and program budgeting in particular, although less is practiced than preached. Educational administrators are in general agreement that, given enough time and effort, specific costs of educational programs can be broken out with reasonable precision in a given institution. Given computerized data-processing assistance, even institution-wide costs (like insurance, debt service, etc.) can be item-analyzed and factored out to programs. There is much less agreement that the costs of similar programs (cosmetology, automotive body, etc.) can be compared across institutions, due to "unique" institutional factors.

The real issue of program budgeting hinges on the ability to make reliable and valid measures of program output. Output must be defined more broadly than simply student credit hours generated in a program or graduates produced. Academic or general education programs are at a loss when some further index is required to measure the effect of the educational program. How do you measure the value of a liberal arts education to an individual? For occupational education, however, program budgeting may be an ideal tool. Extended output, or "impact," measures are indeed available. There are quantifiable, behavioral measures to test whether a vocational-technical program graduate actually has acquired the skills needed for a specific occupation. There are certification and licensing examinations which must be passed in many occupational areas prior to full professional or paraprofessional employment. Another measure is, of course, employment within the vocation for which the graduate was trained. Related to this is the salary level at which he can enter the job market after his specific training. Program budgeting, particularly as it relates specific program costs to impact or extended output variables, provides the vocational educator with a meaningful weapon in the budget advocacy process. It provides vocational education an opportunity to prove what it has been asserting for so long.

From an adminstrator's viewpoint, PPBS offers at least four important advantages over traditional practices: 1) information on total system costs is output, or program, oriented; 2) analysis of possible alternative program objectives is more extensive; 3) the planning process is continuous and includes multiyear plans so that future year implications of present decisions are explicit identified; 4) policy is an ordered process in a well defined organization which directs major lines of action toward perceptible program goals." (*10*, p. 86)

In short, in the budget planning phase a program budget approach is one important means to relate educational planning to specific fiscal decisions in a rational decision-making process. The authors view program budgeting as particularly appropriate for vocational and technical education.

PARTICIPATION IN BUDGET PLANNING

The budget planning phase is the aspect of the budgeting process which should involve the widest participation of the organization. The ideas and proposals of faculty, students, and staff should be given maximum consideration at this stage. While general fiscal parameters, based on knowledge of expected revenues, must be set by the chief administrator and the governing board, proposals for allocation of these resources across programs and objectives should emanate from the broadest spectrum possible. Faculty, staff, and students should have access to basic financial data and to the critical assumptions or premises upon which ultimate budgeting decisions are made. While one person must be responsible for the preparation of the planning budget, many schools and colleges use a budget-planning committee to help coordinate this effort. Such a committee usually includes the budget officer, administrative representatives from major organizational elements (e.g. the vocational division, the general academic division, support services), faculty, and sometimes students. The committee can review preliminary budget requests by program or organizational elements (departments or other basic administrative units), and suggest new allocation approaches or ways to effect savings. Assuming its meetings are open, any staff member or student can use the committee as a means through which to propose ideas. Ultimately, the chief administrator must decide how the final planning budget is to be structured and must recommend a single, comprehensive, and integrated budget to his governing board for review and approval.

Budget Control and Operation

The planned or requested budget may or may not be that budget which actually becomes operational. Financial resource availability may change because of changes in the economy, changes in state appropriation levels approved by legislatures, or political budget limitations placed on the institution by its governing board.

Once available resources for the operating period (usually one fiscal year) are definitively ascertained and the operating budget level is formally approved by the governing board, there is the problem of allocating revenue surpluses or deficits from the proposed or planned budget. This allocation process should follow the original planning process and focus on institutional priorities. After final allocations have been made, the execution of the approved budget becomes a more centralized administrative function. While budget operation and control must be flexible, this phase does not and cannot involve faculty and staff as widely as the planning phase.

> The act of budget execution involves performances and implementation, and budget control and reporting are important parts of performance and implementation. Strictly from a financial standpoint, budget control is the most critical facet of the operating budget. Control, as used here, means the constant review of budget allocations against expenditures and encumbrances to determine that operating units have not overspent or over encumbered their funds as originally approved in the operating budget. (*9*, p. 85)

For purposes of operation and control, budgets are almost universally broken down into object categories of (1) personnel (salaries, wages, fringe benefits); (2) operating supplies and expenses; and (3) equipment.

PERSONNEL

The personnel component is the major one in education; as indicated earlier, salaries, wages, and fringe benefits of all faculty and staff commonly account for seventy-five to eighty percent of the entire operating budget. In most secondary systems and community colleges, *instructional* personnel costs will equal at least fifty percent of the total operating budget. In California, by law fifty percent or more must be allocated to instructional personnel costs. Budgeting control of personnel costs is usually handled on the basis of (1) approval to hire personnel to fill new or existent but vacant positions, and (2) decisions related to promotion and across-the-board compensation increases, including fringe benefits. In all but the very largest systems, approval of new positions and the authority to fill them should rest with the chief administrator, subject to final review by the governing board. Particularly in time of austerity and/or budget decreases, the personnel segment of the budget is critical for any cost savings. Approved positions vacant for just short periods can result in significant savings. The same is true with early retirement incentives, careful use of part-time or temporary assistance instead of permanently contracted professional positions, planned personnel allocations across departments to avoid seasonal unemployment compensation claims, and judicious development of student and paraprofessional positions.

OPERATING SUPPLIES AND EXPENSES

Control of supplies and operational expenses like communications, travel, and equipment repair can usually be handled on a more decentralized basis. What a department or program plans to spend is decided before the budget is approved; the manner of spending it need not be centrally controlled. However, many school systems and colleges use a perfunctory pre-audit check of requisitions to insure that the program account does indeed have sufficient funds to cover encumbrances or expenditures. Usually, department chairmen or program heads may transfer funds between subcategories within the overall supplies and expenses account category without higher approval.

EQUIPMENT

Equipment budgeting is a perennial problem for vocational and technical institutions. Equipment is usually expensive, and equipment expenditures are often seen as deferrable. Thus, if there is a financial resource deficit, equipment tends to be the first category to be cut. Most occupational education administrators recognize the need to provide adequate equipment to initiate a new vocational program. In many cases, the program simply cannot begin operating until the equipment is there. The real problem comes with establishing an equipment *replacement* schedule that will be adhered to. For example, in a business program focusing on secretarial and office equipment skills, the effective working life of electric typewriters is approximately four to five years. It is not difficult to establish an inventory-based equipment replacement schedule based on data about the expected working life of each piece of equipment, and its acquisition and expected replacement cost. Such a system can be developed through the operating budget, with equipment life estimates from faculty and technicians, so that each year an appropriate amount of funds will be available by program for replacement needs. Too often equipment budgets are reduced and shortcuts are sought. Educators look for surplus government equipment or industrial donations. In many cases, the education system is merely serving as a depository for what government and industry know is no longer really usable. Even donations of new equipment by industry may not fit the educational program needs. It is much wiser for an institution to budget adequately for equipment and save funds subsequently if what it really needs is available on a loan, discount, or donation basis from government or industry.

It is the position of the authors that operational budget controls should be as flexible as possible so as to best meet instructional needs. While transfers of budgeted allocations between the three major account categories (personnel, supplies, and equipment) should require central administrative approval, pre-audit review of expenditures within categories should largely be advisory. Within categories, budget control operates best on a management-by-exception basis. Thus, the chief administrator or major business officer need only be involved if monthly or quarterly budget summaries indicate that expenditure and encumbrance rates are significantly above or below the pro-rated allocation. That is, if a monthly budget summary indicates a program or department is expending monies from its supplies account at a rate which, if continued at that level, will result in a significant percent over-run for the year, then an inquiry is necessary. Other than review of exceptions at a given percentage level, evaluation of budget performance should be handled on a post-audit basis.

Budget Evaluation

Both the planning budget and the operational budget officially go out of existence once the period for which they were approved is past. The budget never serves as the official financial record of the institution. Unfortunately, too frequently neither does it serve as any sort of postoperations evaluation measurement.

The official financial record of any school system or college is its audited fiscal statement. It is important that program heads and faculty have the opportunity to review the formal report of the financial audit. It is even more important that the past year's approved budget be used as an evaluation device in budget planning. Administrators must be held accountable for budget overruns and for mistakes in expenditures. The first question in reviewing budget planning requests is, "What did you do with the money budgeted for last year?" If expenditures exceeded allocations or if account transfers were not made, or funds not expended in some categories, the responsible staff member must be held accountable. The evaluation function of the operational budget obviously must be carried out conjointly with the evaluation of program results. The program which lives within its allocated budget but fails to achieve its objectives has hardly been a success.

In larger organizations, an integral part of budgeting control and evaluation is the role of the internal auditor. The function of the internal auditor is to review and analyze institutional operations, particularly financial aspects, to insure that its procedures are lawful and adequate, and *are being followed.* Internal audits of procedures and financial operations should ordinarily be coordinated in advance with responsible supervisors, although in areas involving cash transactions, securities, and large inventories, surprise internal audits should be undertaken periodically. In smaller school systems or colleges, the business officer or one of his accountants may be able to perform this function on a part-time basis.

Correctly related to the educational philosophy and objectives, the planning, control, and evaluation phases of the budget process reflect virtually every operational aspect of an educational institution. It is essential that the chief administrator be continually involved with the operational budget and that all personnel be aware of how it is constructed and implemented.

Facilities Planning

The previous discussion focused on the operational budget, about ten percent of which is devoted to physical plant maintenance and operation in a typical institution. The question of plant operation deserves further consideration. In addition, a second major area of administrative concern is the capital outlay budget, and facilities planning and construction. Educational facilities development is a complicated process which requires a good deal of specialized knowledge. It is not our purpose, nor is it possible in this book, to provide that kind of information. Our interest is mainly to indicate some general principles related to facilities development which the vocational administrator should understand.

Planning and management of physical facilities is an integral part of responsible fiscal administration. As Greene has pointed out: "Lack of planning for physical facilities can cause overbuilding or poorly utilized facilities either of which is disastrous financially" (*9*, p. 52). On the other hand, lack of adequate physical facilities can limit enrollment, impede educational programming, and create unsafe conditions.

LONG-RANGE FACILITIES PLAN

The first step of a meaningful facilities planning process is the establishment of a long-range facilities master plan which projects tentative needs for a future period of ten to twenty years. The development of a facilities master plan presumes the existence of an educational academic long-range plan projecting enrollment and curriculum patterns. Planning is always tentative, and both facilities and educational master plans are subjects for continuous review, revision, and updating. Part of the problem is simply getting faculty, administrators, the governing board, and the public at-large to take a comprehensive, futuristic view of the organization.

Meckley suggests that educational facilities planning should be consistent with four guiding principles:

1. The educational program is the basis for planning space and facilities.
2. Significant changes in occupational education programs are likely to occur over short periods of time. . . . This condition calls for adaptability and flexibility in building design.
3. The occupational education program should serve the needs of a variety of groups in the community.

4. Expanded programs are needed to reach not only average and above-average occupational students, but also the unusually gifted, the mentally retarded and the culturally deprived. The programs are encouraged by the 1968 Amendments to the Vocational Education Act of 1963. (*16*, p. 70)

It is particularly important to plan for the problem of technological change and the development of new vocational programs. To construct a facility which responds to the demands of an occupational program meeting current needs may be dysfunctional in the long run. Any building proposed for construction should be architectually designed to provide a maximum amount of program flexibility.

Unfortunately, expectations of both the general public and professional educators tie excellence of educational programs to the existence of architectural monuments. As a result, a cardinal rule in facilities planning is often ignored: seek existent facilities before constructing new ones. Particularly in vocational and technical education, it may actually be educationally more appropriate *not to construct* facilities, but to use existent buildings in the community: local shops, plants, service buildings, bowling alleys, or whatever may be easily converted to educational purposes, are available at relatively low costs, meet basic pedagogical requirements, and are most accessible to students. One unfortunate development in some comprehensive community college districts is the construction of new campuses on the periphery of a metropolitan area. Leaving less esthetically attractive premises, they also leave the integral community relationship and easy accessibility for economically disadvantaged students. Every occupational education institution should give serious consideration to beginning or continuing physical decentralization of its programs within the community.

One method for developing program-related facilities plans is to involve the program-curriculum citizens advisory committees. Their involvement can expedite the review of existent community facilities, as will the development of a program statement and the educational specifications for either new construction or remodeling to meet program needs. It is especially important to involve faculty in the formulation of the program statement and educational specifications for any new facility. The faculty and students will be most affected by the adequacy or inadequacy of the facility, and the instructional staff is best equipped to review its educational specifications.

Educational facility planning culminates in *educational specifications*. Educational specifications are a written description of the educational program and the resultant facility requirements; they are equally necessary for a new building or the modification of existing educational facilities, as they normally contain descriptive information about the community programs to be housed, general building design, a list of facilities to be provided, and

detailed room descriptions. Although written educational specifications
are the responsibility of educators, they are used by the architect for
guidance in facility design. (*16,* p. 1)

In the development of new schools or new buildings of a multi-unit institution, a faculty-citizen building program committee can also be helpful in site
selection. Site selection involves several considerations, but student and
community accessibility is probably the most important.

Facilities planning and development in occupational education has
become somewhat more complex procedurally during the last decade, concomitantly with greater availability of funds. The Vocational Education Act
of 1963 and the Vocational Education Amendments of 1968 represented a
change in the historical posture of the federal government by making a
commitment for substantial support for construction of vocational education buildings. Under the 1963 Act, the federal government would provide
only fifty percent of required funding. The 1968 amendments removed this
limitation. Combining various other federal and state sources with VEA
monies, it is now possible for local school districts to construct vocational
education facilities with only ten to twenty percent of the total investment
needed from local millage or bonding sources. At the same time it has
increased the number and kind of proposal forms and studies, as well as the
need for political *savoir faire* on the part of the chief administrator. The
stipulation of the VEA legislation that there be a state plan for vocational
education has, however, resulted in the development of uniform state-wide
formats for analysis and review of the educational specifications for any
building for which state and federal funding support is sought.

While uniform state standards and formulas for the review of educational
specifications for new facilities have helped insure at least a minimum of
community-based educational planning, state formula or standard designs
cannot substitute for direct planning and unique specifications for each
community. As in the case of curriculum development, there is no simple
formula for facilities which can or should be dictated to local constituencies;
educational and esthetic specifications are peculiar to each locale. Educational needs must be defined locally, and as Meckley points out: "No matter
how beautiful or structurally sound the building, *if it fails to provide the
environment needed to facilitate instruction and learning,* it is educationally
inadequate" (*16,* p. 29).

Facilities Management

To the seeming surprise of some educators,
instructional facilities do not manage themselves. Someone must be dele-

gated the responsibility for daily custodial care, periodic repairs and maintenance, inventory update and replacement, and minor remodelling and
repairs. In a multiple-building system this is a particularly difficult problem.
The custodial staff and the chief business officer can be held responsible for
daily care and cleaning, but who is responsible for equipment inventories?
As space requirements of programs change, how are space allocation assignments to be determined? For responsibility to be meaningful in regard to
facilities, it must be assigned to people who work in the buildings. Thus,
it is our position that responsibility for specific buildings in multi-facility
institutions should be delegated to the senior administrator in the building
—whether he is a principal, department head, dean, assistant superintendent, or whatever. He should be concerned about daily care, general maintenance, building security, equipment inventories, and general utilization.

The problem of developing a comprehensive maintenance, replacement,
and repair schedule belongs to the chief business officer no matter how
many buildings the institution has. It is also his responsibility to develop
an inventory and equipment replacement schedule for budgeting purposes,
as described earlier.

Someone has said that there is nothing more sacrosanct to staff members
than their offices and their parking spaces. By the same token, the assignment of class schedule times seems to have significant symbolic meaning.
Nevertheless, it is a fact that, next to churches, schools are probably the
least efficiently used buildings in any community. The importance of space
analysis and facilities scheduling in occupational education cannot be overemphasized. Because of the high cost of laboratory and shop space, as well
as equipment, it is particularly important that they be maximally utilized.
For some public school educators it is virtual blasphemy to suggest that 16
to 18 year-olds could attend occupational education programs from 4:00
P.M. to midnight, yet many of them work that shift, or part of it, at the local
hamburger or dairy haven. Less than one percent of occupational education
facilities are operated on a third shift (from midnight until 8:00 A.M.) but
how many industries run such a shift? Surveys indicate that employed
adults seeking further education often prefer intensive weekend experiences,
yet how many continuing education programs in vocational institutions are
offered on Saturdays and Sundays? Classroom, shop, and laboratory utilization anlaysis in virtually every community college in the country will indicate that considerably less than fifty percent of available student stations are
utilized on any given Friday afternoon.

The point is that as we build needed new facilities for occupational
education, we also have to devise delivery systems which will permit better
utilization of existent facilities, including those empty in the community.
Any educational specifications statement for large-scale occupational facilities will increasingly have to justify the use of currently occupied facilities.

Any way it is measured, available unused space is a financial loss, bad programming, and even worse budgeting. A skeptical public will no longer tolerate this, even from career-relevant programs.

REFERENCES

1. Baker, Joseph J. and Jan S. Peters. *School Maintenance and Operation.* Danville: Interstate, 1963.

2. Boles, Harold W. *Step By Step to Better School Facilities.* New York: Holt, Rinehart and Winston, 1965.

3. Budig, Gene A., ed. *Dollars and Sense; Budgeting for Today's Campus.* Chicago: McGraw-Hill, 1972.

4. Castaldi, Basil. *Creative Planning of Educational Facilities.* Chicago: Rand McNally, 1969.

5. Chase, William W., Johnny W. Browne, and Michael Russo. *Basic Planning Guide for Vocational and Technical Education Facilities.* Washington, D.C.: U.S. Government Printing Office, 1966.

6. Cohn, Elchanan, Jacob J. Kaufman, and Teh-wei Hu. *The Costs of Vocational and Nonvocational Programs. A Study of Michigan Secondary Schools.* University Park, Pennsylvania: The Pennsylvania State University, Institute for Research on Human Resources, 1972.

7. Gauerke, Warren E. and Jack R. Childress, eds. *Theory and Practice of School Finance.* Chicago: Rand McNally, 1967.

8. Gerwin, Donald. *Budgeting Public Funds.* Madison: University of Wisconsin Press, 1969.

9. Greene, John L., Jr. *Budgeting in Higher Education.* Athens: University of Georgia, 1971.

10. Hartley, Harry J. *Educational Planning-Programming-Budgeting.* Englewood Cliffs: Prentice-Hall, 1968.

11. Herrick, John H., Ralph D. McLeary, Wilfred F. Clapp, and Walter F. Bogner. *From School Program to School Plant.* New York: Holt, Rinehart and Winston, 1956.

12. Jellema, William W., ed. *Efficient College Management.* San Francisco: Jossey-Bass, 1972.

13. Leu, Donald J. *Planning Educational Facilities.* New York: The Center for Applied Research in Education, 1965.

14. McGivney, Joseph H. "Accountability: Promise and Problems of PPBS." In *Contemporary Concepts in Vocational Education,* Gordon F. Law, ed. Washington, D.C.: American Vocational Association, 1971.

15. McGivney, Joseph H. and William C. Nelson. *Program, Planning, Budgeting System for Educators, Volume I: An Instructional Outline.* Leadership Series No. 18. Columbus: The Center for Vocational and Technical Education, The Ohio State University, August 1969.

16. Meckley, Richard F. *Planning Facilities for Occupational Education Programs.* Columbus: Charles E. Merrill, 1972.

17. Meckley, Richard F., Ivan E. Valentine, and M. J. Conrad. *A General Guide for Planning Facilities for Occupational Preparation Programs.* Columbus: The Center for Vocational and Technical Education, The Ohio State University, August 1970.

18. Meckley, Richard F., Ivan E. Valentine, and Zane McCoy. *A Guide to Systematic Planning for Vocational and Technical Schools.* Columbus: The Center for Vocational and Technical Education, The Ohio State University, August 1970.

19. Stromsdorfer, Ernst W. *Review and Synthesis of Cost-Effectiveness Studies of Vocational Education.* Columbus: The Ohio State University, Center for Vocational and Technical Education, 1972.

20. Tomlinson, Robert M. and Chester S. Rzonca. *An Exploratory Analysis of Differential Program Costs of Selected Occupational Curricula in Selected Illinois Junior Colleges.* Springfield: Illinois Board of Vocational Education and Rehabilitation, January 1971.

21. Van Dyke, George E. *College and University Business Administration.* Washington: American Council on Education, 1968.

Chapter 13 BUILDING A CONSTITUENCY

Some experts hold that public education in the United States is in trouble because it has developed a crisis of credibility with its constituency. In recent years, local millage and bonding issues for education have failed much more frequently than in the score of golden years following World War II. At the state level, legislative bodies are increasingly reluctant to raise tax revenue to support higher budgets for secondary and post-secondary occupational or liberal education. The American public no longer sees public education as the panacea for its social ills. As a result, more than ever before, the vocational-technical educator must understand the dynamics of his constituency, maintain a two-way flow of communication with that constituency, and build its understanding and confidence in exactly what his programs can and cannot do.

The purposes of this chapter are to help the reader:

1. to analyze the dynamics of his community and understand where to begin building his constituency;
2. to understand and use the basic techniques of involving his community constituency;
3. to understand and use the basic channels for disseminating and gathering information from his constituency;
4. to develop a constituency which views his institution as its own.

Given our premise that educational institutions are open systems related to larger systems of which they are a part, it is important for the vocational educator to be aware of the interrelation with and the impact of outside groups on his institution. The school or college affects these other systems and is affected by them.

Two terms are central to this chapter: community and constituency. By community we mean both those people residing in a given locality who share certain norms, customs, history, and governance; and social groups who share certain interests, backgrounds, or goals. With respect to an educational institution, one important community obviously is the geographical one in which it is located. Other important communities for it include: organized labor, industry, the education establishment (both professional organizations, and state and federal bureaucracies), students, and the legislative community. A successful vocational-technical educational administrator must understand the dynamics of all of these communities. Constituency is simply defined as a body of people who support a given institution or person. The problem for the vocational educator is how to build constituencies from the various communities mentioned above.

For the comprehensive high school, area vocational center, or community college, the geographical community is the most important one, since most of its students come from that community, a substantial portion of its finances are derived from that community, and its operations fall under the general laws and regulations in effect there.

Analyzing the Local Community

To administer effectively any institution which relies upon and interacts closely with a geographic community requires that the administrator understand that community, its historical perspective as well as its contemporary social milieu. This involves careful, systematic study of individuals, informal groups, and formal organizations—the positions they have taken on major issues and the alliances they have formed. One approach to community study is social psychological force field analysis. Force field analysis was originally used by psychologist Kurt Lewin and his colleagues as a psychological approach to understand individual decision making processes. Thus, in any given situation or instance, the individual consciously or subconsciously perceives a variety of forces potentially supporting or opposing his alternative actions. At the community level, social force field analysis is an effort to determine what pressures are on what groups or individuals to encourage or dissuade them from taking a given action. Relative to occupational education, analysis at the community level is necessary to determine which groups and institutions will be supportive, what local channels of communication are most effective in reaching them, where major sources of resistance to vocational-technical programs are likely to be found, and what critical leverage points can be used initially to move individuals, groups, and the entire community to provide active support for the vocational-technical institution. The most critical point of analysis may well be how to minimize opposing forces. Force field analysis is important initially because some subsequent decisions should be based on it. The vocational education administrator must be aware of both psychological forces operative at the individual level and social forces operative at the larger system or community level. Social force field analysis involves ascertaining which groups have supported actions in the community related to occupational education and which groups have resisted such actions; on which side various groups and individuals have aligned themselves in significant community battles; what positions various representatives of the mass media have taken on such issues; and which groups or organizations seem to have exercised the most influence both in deciding major community battles and in keeping other issues from becoming major battles. Social force field analysis requires that the administrator develop a continuing sensitivity to sociopolitical forces. In part, this means acquiring a new perspective in viewing events and decisions.

Related both to social force field analysis and to building a constituency in the local geographical community is the identification and involvement of three classes of people in the community: formal leaders of institutions or agencies who interact with occupational education; community influentials; and opinion leaders.

POSITIONAL AUTHORITIES

Many formal leaders holding positions of authority in the local community must be effectively drawn into the vocational-technical education picture. The administrator must first of all establish good working relations with other educational leaders in the area: superintendents, principals, community college president and deans, board members, etc. Community residents often derive their opinions about vocational institutions from other educational authorities. Managers of local industry, local financial institutions, and local government are also important for occupational programming, as are employers of graduates. The support of the local labor council and the mass media are critical. In the case of each of these groups there are specifically designated leaders who by virtue of their positions speak for the organizations, and who can have a positive effect upon vocational programs. It is the administrator's responsibility to be aware of who these people are and to become acquainted with them as quickly as he can.

COMMUNITY INFLUENTIALS

Community influentials, a second group of individuals the vocational educator must learn to identify, are often considerably more important than the formal local authorities, although many of the latter may also be real influentials. For nearly a score of years social scientists have studied actions by local leaders trying to ascertain who, in fact, are the people who really make the decisions about key issues in given communities. In addition to observing people in formal positions of authority, they have attempted to find out who has the *reputation* for being influential by asking local people which individuals they think influence, persuade, or advise the positional authorities. Another approach analyzes important past decisions in the community to ascertain which individuals played crucial roles. The presumption in this case is that these same people will be involved in subsequent key issues. Some influential people may be involved in many types of decisions in varying subject areas, particularly in smaller and more stratified local communities. In larger, more urban and cosmopolitan areas, community influentials are likely to exercise their influence only in particular spheres; that is, one set of influentials may be involved in educational decisions, another in political affairs, another in commercial decisions, and so on. This is likely simply because influence is in part based on knowledge and it is virtually impossible for one person to be well-informed on all major public issues in a complex technical society.

Whether the community power structure is dispersed across issue areas or more concentrated, in any community the key influential people can provide substantial support and legitimation for vocational education. Researchers may quibble about sophisticated methods for identifying such people, but there are some "quick-and-easy" ways through which the educational administrator can do almost as well with a lot less effort. These include talking with people whose jobs depend in part upon their knowledge of where influence lies: newspapermen and representatives of other mass media, various kinds of change agents (agricultural extension agents, community development workers, political organizers, labor organizers, etc.), urban and regional planners, and operational managers of large organizations in the area. Community influentials may be people whose names appear frequently on boards of directors, as honorary sponsors of programs, or who are members of elite clubs. In comparing these lists, some indication of the community power structure is often apparent.

In identifying people who may be influential with respect to vocational-technical education in a given local community, it is often worth a trip to the local newspaper to review its file on articles related to education over the past five to ten years. This review will clarify which people have been publicly active with respect to educational problems in the area, but it will not necessarily indicate the extent of their influence. Understanding local power structure and the role of community influentials requires that the educator make a conscious effort to develop a sense of sociopolitical acuity. A good place to begin is a discussion of the question of community power and influence with sympathetic members of the school or college's board of trustees. The fact of their election to the board is proof that they have developed some level of sophistication in this area.

OPINION LEADERS

Opinion leaders are also important at the local community level to the vocational educator. "Opinion leader" is the term first used by Lazarsfeld, Berelson, and Caudet (9) to describe individuals who were instrumental in influencing their peers' voting behavior in national elections. The term has since been generalized to refer to those people to whom others turn for information and advice. Whereas community influentials are people who have the demonstrated or perceived ability to make or influence critical decisions which affect one or more aspects of the total community life, opinion leaders are informally influential in a smaller group of peers with whom they interact frequently. They exercise influence on the attitudes and behavior of their associates, frequently serving as important communications linkages about a variety of public questions and issues, including those related to vocational education. The opinion leader is the person who can help legitimize new ideas and new practices. When broad-based local support is needed for increased funding, acceptance of new occupational curricula, or development of a new facility, the opinion leader is critical. Katz and Lazarsfeld (7) have demonstrated that sociopolitical information is likely to flow through a two-step channel—from the originator to opinion leaders who take the time to become informed, then to the people for whom they serve as opinion leaders. Varying kinds of pragmatic sociometric tools are available to help identify such individuals, but the most important point is that the educator recognize that opinion leaders exist and that he should make special efforts to keep track of who these people are as he encounters them in his area.

Other Communities

Besides having a thorough knowledge of the local geographical community in which his institution is located, the vocational education administrator must understand the dynamics of a variety of other communities and their leadership. Among the more important are his own students and staff (which form a subsystem of his geographical community), organized labor in his region, state and regional educational bureaucracies, industry in the region, and the state legislature.

STUDENTS, STAFF, AND BOARD OF TRUSTEES

Understanding the socioeconomic, political, and attitudinal backgrounds of students and staff is paramount. The attitudes that these people have about the school or college will be those most rapidly transmitted to the local community. If they are proud of it and find their association with it satisfying, the general feeling will be widely shared in the community. The opposite is also true. To be informed about his students and staff, the administrator must be able to answer such questions as: (1) what is their family income and occupational background? (2) what are their reasons for enrolling or teaching at this institution? (3) what are their aspiration levels? (4) what social and economic problems most concern them? (5) with what groups do they identify? Educators should remember that if the institution's faculty and students are not supportive it is unlikely that any other community or group will become a constituency for that institution.

The primary objective for staff members at all levels in the institution must be interpretation of the technical program. Of all those groups to whom it must be interpreted, none is more important than the board of trustees. The board is an immediate and key group of lay officials who must be thoroughly educated to the role of occupational education. The board not only controls the purse strings essential to the further development of occupational education but its members are invariably active in economic, civic and political relationships; their understanding and belief in the programs, once attained, provide one of the most effective communication avenues to community-wide groups and leaders. (*15*, p. 33)

The importance of the support of the board of trustees for vocational programs cannot be overemphasized. Board members can provide entree to community influentials, positional authorities, and opinion leaders in many fields.

ORGANIZED LABOR

A second interest community which is important to any vocational institution is organized labor. Organized labor may be one of vocational education's closest allies or its severest critic, depending on labor's conception of what the institution is attempting to do. The vocational administrator should meet periodically with local and regional labor councils and with the key people in the major trade unions in his region. It should be made clear that the school or college is willing to supplement and collaborate with apprenticeship efforts in joint apprenticeship-training programs and that its students will not be competitors for jobs which the union seeks to control. In the political arena at both the state and local level, organized labor's support of an educational institution can make a crucial difference.

INDUSTRY

Major industrial employers in the area form a critical community which the vocational administrator must identify and with which he must establish communication and working relationships. Industry, if it perceives the educational programs to be of high quality, can channel many resources to the institution, including the use of its own plant facilities for some educational programs. If, on the other hand, industry feels that the institution is not responding to its manpower training needs, it may become increasingly resistive to paying more taxes for vocational education, to employing the institution's graduates, or to providing equipment or other forms of support to the educational program. Among other representative organizations, the Chamber of Commerce, the local manufacturers association, and the industrial development corporation are all usually worth cultivating. In many instances, it is worthwhile to join these organizations and work with their administrative staffs and elected officers. As the major consumer of his institutional product, industry is one of the most important external communities with which the vocational administrator must maintain close communication.

THE EDUCATION ESTABLISHMENT

Another community which must be considered and cultivated is the "education establishment." By this we mean the state bureaucracy in the department of education, various regional and intermediate school district personnel, and the representatives of the various educational-professional groups who will frequently review programs for accreditation. Depending on the organization of vocational-technical education in the state, the officials in the department of education may have responsibility for program approval for the institution, recommendations for basic level budget support, or for the actual distribution of special vocational education funds either from the federal government or from special state appropriations. Thus, it is imperative that the administrator establish a face-to-face familiarity with key members of the administrative staff of the state department of education.

They should feel that his institution is a show place where they can run conferences or bring visitors who have come to see examples of vocational programs in that state. Acceptance by professional educators at the state and regional levels may mean the award of special project funds, the opportunity to provide personnel for state-wide committees or study groups which will have subsequent direct impact on the institution, or merely a good word to legislative or other funding bodies about the institution.

The various professional associations and the administrative personnel who staff them are important to the vocational-technical institution. These groups also can provide political support, special funding for developmental projects, or the opportunity to provide substantive input about studies and task forces in the political arena. Most importantly, however, the professional groups are likely to be involved directly in those programs which require certification of graduates. Their perception of the institution will have a direct effect on the continuing accreditation of the institution's programs and subsequently the certification and licensure of its graduates.

THE LEGISLATURE

A final important community for the vocational education administrator is the state legislature and other legislative-political bodies in the region. While the state legislature is not involved directly in the administration of vocational education, its impact is significant because of the budget appropriation process. This is particularly true for technical colleges whose budget appropriations may come directly from the legislature. Most monetary support for vocational institutions will come from the legislature, through some fixed formula, via the state department of education or the bureau of budget. However, the legislature can be made aware of the special needs of vocational institutions, and direct contact with key legislators is well worth the time spent in developing them. Bureaucrats in the state and local offices tend to be most responsive when a legislator inquires about a program of interest to him in a given institution. A close and familiar working relationship with the state legislators who represent its district can pay real dividends for a vocational institution.

In short, no matter whether the educator is dealing with a geographic community or a community of interest, he is dealing with people and organizations who have their own goals and objectives which may or may not coincide with those of his institution. It is imperative that he become a serious student of these communities, of the sociopsychological forces operative on them, and the influentials and opinion leaders who in large measure lead them. The success of his vocational programs may in part rest upon the socio-political-psychological acuity of the administrator in analyzing these communities and gaining their support.

Means for Building a
Constituency from a Community

Developing the support of the institutional community—students, staff, and governing board—is slightly different from building a constituency from external communities. The key element in internal constituency development is a continual two-way flow of communication and a positive open-door administrative philosophy. Students, staff, and the governing board should be constantly informed about policies, programs, and institutional priorities. Similarly, wherever possible, they should be given an opportunity to provide input about their ideas, problems, and preferences. Continuing face-to-face communication between students, staff, and top administration is time-consuming but imperative. The governing board, of course, has a structured opportunity for such communication, but it is important that the chief administrator communicate informally with the board between formal meetings.

Based on a careful analysis of the varied other communities and systems with which his institution interacts and on which it depends, the administrator must then use a variety of mechanisms to involve those communities and mold them into his constituency. These mechanisms include but are not limited to periodic surveys, advisory committees, cooperative education programs, job placement services, the community school approach, and public service functions.

PERIODIC SURVEYS

Local manpower surveys are commonly used to help determine curriculum needs. Formal and informal surveys can also be used effectively to get feedback from various communities about perceptions of the school or college and how it is fulfilling its mission. This kind of survey may be highly structured and seek a large sample response from the grass-roots public; or, it may be a series of informal chats and telephone calls with community influentials and opinion leaders. The information received may not be as important as the public awareness that the institution actively seeks feedback. As part of his own evaluation process, the administrator must carefully analyze which publics and communities his institution is serving and where it is falling short. At the college level, and perhaps at the secondary as well, classes in social science and/or English may carry out various kinds of public surveys about local perceptions of the institutional mission, community knowledge of the institution, and community preferences for future developmental direction. In specific questions of major public interest, local newspapers may be willing to poll readers through their "action" column. In some communities, local banks and supermarkets run weekly surveys on community issues and their customers give their opinions whenever they do business there. Community feedback may be sought in many ways, and the administrator must be open continually to new channels.

ADVISORY COMMITTEES

It has become almost axiomatic that citizen advisory committees are a requisite for curriculum development and review in vocational-technical programs. They are also important in building a constituency. In addition to lay advisory committees for occupational programs, the administration may want to develop a large overall institutional advisory committee, a committee on minority affairs, a committee on college community services, or any other area of importance to the institution. As one community college president noted:

> Community college advisory committees are of inestimable value. They contribute effectively to maintaining acceptable standards, to employment of the graduates, and to interpreting the colleges to the various publics. Extensive utilization of advisory committees should be encouraged and their relationships expanded at all colleges if more leadership in our communities is to become involved with our colleges. (15, p. 29)

Irrespective of which or how many committees are established, they must be actively consulted. Too frequently, curriculum advisory committees are nominal committees which meet once a year for a cursory review of the educational program. In the constituency-building process, lay committees must be given meaningful tasks and then the administrator must be willing to respond to their recommendations. Selection of committee membership is clearly the critical step in the process. People appointed should be willing to participate and should be made fully aware of the expectations of the administrator. While the chief administrator should meet with the committee initially and at subsequent periodic intervals, he need not do so regularly. There should be, however, a liaison person from the school or college who can provide staff administrative services for the committee. It is his job to make sure that the committee has adequate institutional inputs.

A sign on the lawn of a Midwest Protestant Church reflected that "God so loved the world that he did not send a committee to save it." Committees are not a panacea, particularly if they are not well used. In building a constituency, however, advisory committees comprised of community influentials and opinion leaders who are actively involved in the mission of vocational-technical education are a most important mechanism for linking the school or college to its communities.

COOPERATIVE EDUCATION

Cooperative education programs are an important curriculum function in the students' vocational-technical learning process. However, they also serve as a key linking mechanism to the community. Every employer who provides a cooperative education job slot has already begun to become involved in the institution. He should not be viewed merely as a job or learning environment provider, but rather as an important constituent to be cultivated. Providing him opportunity for interaction with the chief administrator or with personnel other than the cooperative education coordinator demonstrates institutional concern. He should be on the general mailing list of the school or college and be invited to social functions where appropriate. An annual employer's banquet or picnic can effectively bring together employers, students, and parents. As the administrator develops his own list of community influentials and opinion leaders, he should encourage the coordinator of cooperative education to seek out these people, where appropriate, as possible cooperative education employers. Active involvement in the educational process with students is one of the quickest, most effective ways to build a constituency.

Using local people as occasional teachers is also a most effective way of involving them in the institution. Local tradesmen, businessmen, labor, and government leaders are usually flattered if they are asked, not too frequently, to teach a class or serve as resource persons. Besides making the class more interesting, local people provide an important world-of-work relationship to what is being learned.

PLACEMENT AND CAREER INFORMATION

As we indicated earlier, placement and career information is the most important student developmental activity in vocational-technical education. It is also a major element in developing a community constituency. Employer satisfaction with graduates of the vocational-technical institution will largely determine their attitudes about its program and effectiveness. Good placement services means meeting the needs of both graduates and employers. The placement officer should be made aware of key influentials and opinion leaders, so that he can contact them to inquire about their manpower needs.

In addition to the placement of graduates, effective part-time and summer student placement can be a helpful tool in building a constituency. Public attitudes about students and the institution are often shaped through individual contact. A qualified student meeting the felt need of an employer is the best possible advertisement for a vocational-technical school or college.

VOCATIONAL-TECHNICAL INSTITUTIONS AS COMMUNITY SCHOOLS

For the past two decades or more, a growing concept in American education has been that of the community school. The community school is an attitude or philosophy as much as it is a program. It holds that the school is a facility which should be used by all the community, not just youth, for as many hours each day as possible, and that educators must build adult education and recreation into the school's operating program. Originated in Flint, Michigan, with active support from the Mott Foundation, the community school concept focuses primarily on the local elementary and general secondary schools in order to reach neighborhoods directly. However, the concept is equally valid for vocational-technical institutions serving a wider area. It involves an open-door approach and a willingness to respond to new ideas of service to the entire age range of citizens. It means that the facilities of the institution should be available, free of charge, to any legitimate community group wishing to use them for a nonprofit, educational purpose. Most importantly, it means that all faculty and staff must develop an attitude of open responsiveness to widespread public involvement in the affairs of the school. A community becomes a constituency when it refers to an educational institution as *our* school.

PUBLIC SERVICE

Closely related to the community school philosophy is the public service function of vocational-technical institutions. Public service includes activities commonly classified as extension, community service, continuing education, and adult education. It includes evening adult classes (credit and noncredit); special workshops, institutes and seminars; laboratory or shop services available to the community at cost; and provision of special services in response to community need.

Adult evening classes are commonly provided by comprehensive high schools, comprehensive community colleges, and university extension services. At the secondary level, these courses often are remedial or structured to allow adults to complete a high school degree, although many are also intended for leisure time enrichment. At the post-secondary level, college credit programs as well as a variety of noncredit general education and enrichment courses are offered to adults.

The need for continuing education programs to provide technical courses for job upgrading, career exploration, and avocational development is acute. Adult educators talk glibly about life-long learning, a decreasing half-life of knowledge, the problem of adaptation or coping with future shock, and the need to provide vocational retraining three or four times for most workers in the next generation. They are largely referring to vocational-technical education. Vocational and technical institutions can and must deal with part of this continuing education need. They must provide opportunities for people to change vocations, upgrade their skills to improve their economic level, develop alternative avocational skills, or merely find out more about new facets of the world of work.

Part of this function may be fulfilled by short-term intensive learning experiences in institutes, conferences, workshops, or seminars as opposed to long-term continuing classes. For example, this might be a one-day workshop on new developments in emission control for automobile mechanics, or a three-day seminar on new office practices for secretaries, or a week-long institute on new hair styles for cosmetologists.

Many regular vocational-technical programs can provide services to the community while improving their own curricula. For example, an automotive service or automotive body repair program in a comprehensive high school or comprehensive community college functions best when advanced students work on real problems under faculty supervision. Thus the school or college can provide automobile repair service to community constituents for the price of parts. A radio-television repair program can do the same thing. Cosmetology and dental hygiene students need clients and patients on which to practice under close faculty supervision. These kinds of services can be most effective in building community support as long as there is rigorous quality control on services rendered. A bad job can have serious repercussions.

The institution can provide other services, such as giving technical advice to local industry and government. Students can often fill volunteer positions in crises. Faculty expertise can be made available as needed. Each time that these resources are effectively utilized, another block in the constituency foundation is put in place.

One final aspect of public service has to do with the location of evening courses and continuing education activities. Vocational courses that are offered in easily accessible community facilities can build good relations with the community agencies or industries who operate those facilities, as well as make vocational education more available for the public in a given area.

In sum, public service-continuing education is a key facet in building a constituency as well as being worthwhile in its own right. Every vocational educator, at any level, should be concerned about how his institution can provide relevant services to the community and meet the continuing technical education needs of his constituents.

TWO-WAY COMMUNICATIONS: PUBLIC RELATIONS

Building a constituency requires continuing two-way communications between the school or college and the communities on whom it depends. There must be a constant dissemination of the institution's goals, problems, successes, and critical decisions to its constituency; and there must be adequate means to obtain valid and reliable feedback about the community's responses to these goals, problems, successes, and decisions.

Communicating information about the school and its programs, as well as administering other functions which deal with the external contacts of the institution, are commonly delegated to a public relations officer. The public relations operation gets larger and more complex in post-secondary institutions. While comprehensive high schools usually leave public relations and news services to the office of the district superintendent, most comprehensive community colleges have a public relations officer, even if he is a journalism instructor released part-time to handle public relations. In addition to preparing press releases, program description brochures, catalogues, and alumni bulletins, he may also prepare some kind of special newsletter which is mailed to friends of the college, particularly community influentials and opinion leaders.

At every level, however, public relations is everyone's business. As noted earlier, the administrator should make special attempts to know key people in the newspapers, radio, and television stations in his area. The chief administrator should make periodic informal calls on these people. When possible, the mass media should be notified in advance of significant impending events, either through telephone calls or a special press conference. All major reports available to the public should routinely be circulated to the mass media. Whether the public relations function is assigned specifically to a given administrator, or handled generally through the chief administrator's office, the most important element is a general attitude of openness and cooperation throughout the institution. "Far more interest, activity, and concern on the part of the faculty is needed in cooperation with administrators to help inform community publics of the vital role of occupational education and the varied services of the institution" (15, p. 34).

In addition to formal communication of information through the mass media, another dissemination channel is through students. Particularly at the secondary level, students serve as linking mechanisms between the school and parents. Obviously, parent-teacher associations are other potential dissemination channels at that level. At the post-secondary level, college open houses one or more times a year are common. As part of the recruiting and articulation function, most high schools host college admissions officers on "college night" to inform their students about post-graduation opportunities. These and other articulation efforts offer important dissemination channels to colleges.

Both dissemination and feedback can be achieved through a variety of public forums and workships sponsored by the school or college. One recent popular method is the "charrette," in which a diverse representative assembly from the community is sought out (although anyone may participate) to review the goals and functions of the institution in an intense two- or three-day workshop. Other kinds of workshops or forums may be sponsored by the school or college to explore various special problems. For example, one college has formed what it calls a campus-community communications council which is designed as a general discussion and problem-solving mechanism. Students, staff, and community members share ideas and concerns about college-community relations in monthly meetings. This particular mechanism has been most successful in resolving potential "town-gown" conflicts.

In the process of building the various communities into his constituency, the vocational administrator must essentially become a social scientist, actively seeking feedback information about people and their attitudes and perceptions about his institution. The information dissemination function can be administered by someone assigned that specific duty, but seeking feedback is also the responsibility of the chief administrator. The requirements for building a constituency are that the community should be informed about what is going on, that it should be able to have input on crucial decisions of the institution, that it should feel that the resources and facilities of the institution are open to the people, and that the administration should actively seek its opinions and preferences about the directions the institution should take.

REFERENCES

1. Bice, Gary R. *Working With Opinion Leaders to Accelerate Change in Vocational-Technical Education.* Information Series No. 26 Columbus, Ohio: Center for Vocational and Technical Education, November 1970.

2. Burt, Samuel M. *Industry and Vocational-Technical Education.* New York: McGraw-Hill, 1967.

3. Burt, Samuel M. "Involving Industry and Business in Education." In *Contemporary Concepts in Vocational Education,* Gordon F. Law, ed. Washington, D.C.: American Vocational Association, 1971.

4. Dahl, Robert A. *Who Governs?* New Haven, Conn.: Yale University Press, 1961.

5. Hunter, Floyd. *Community Power Structure.* Chapel Hill, N.C.: University of North Carolina Press, 1953.

6. Jennings, Kent M. *Community Influentials.* New York: Free Press, 1964.

7. Katz, Elihu and Paul F. Lazarsfeld. *Personal Influence.* New York: Free Press, 1955.

8. Kimbrough, Ralph B. *Political Power and Educational Decision-Making.* Chicago: Rand McNally, 1964.

9. Lazarsfeld, P. F., B. Berelson, and H. Caudet. *The People's Choice.* New York: Columbia University Press, 1948.

10. Little, J. Kenneth. *Review and Synthesis of Research on the Placement and Follow-up of Vocational Education Students.* Columbus, Ohio: Center for Vocational and Technical Education, February 1970.

11. Masters, Nicholas A., Robert H. Salisbury, and Thomas H. Eliot. *State Politics and the Public Schools.* New York: Alfred A. Knopf, 1964.

12. Parsens, Cynthia. "Community Involvement: An Essential Element." In *Contemporary Concepts in Vocational Education.* Gordon F. Law, ed. Washington, D.C.: American Vocational Association, 1971.

13. Polsby, Nelson W. *Community Power and Political Theory.* New Haven, Conn.: Yale University Press, 1963.

14. Sanders, Irwin T. "The Community Social Profile." *American Sociological Review* 25, No. 1 (February 1960): 75–77.

15. Wilbur, F. Parker. "Occupational Education and Administration." In *Emphasis: Occupational Education in the Two-Year College.* Washington, D.C.: American Association of Junior Colleges, 1966.

recent analyses of educational evaluation has defined it as "the process of delineating, obtaining, and providing useful information for judging decision alternatives" (*9*, p. 40). The major purpose of evaluation is to improve institutional performance. It must assist the decision maker in ascertaining whether or not program objectives have been achieved, and even whether or not they should be changed.

For some people, evaluation merely means empirical measurement with no inferences as to the value of the measured characteristic. In education, evaluation has frequently been viewed as the determination of the degree to which performance meets the stated objectives of the program. Too often, there is insufficient evaluation of the objectives themselves. Another definition, perhaps most common in education, equates evaluation and professional review or judgment. Based on experience, professionals are asked to make value judgments about the quality of an institution or a program. Typically, this has been the approach of assorted educational accrediting agencies.

In another sense, there are at least four categories or objects of evaluation in education: context, input, process, and output (*9*, p. 218). Context evaluation has to do with the determination and revision of institutional goals and objectives, and is evaluation for overall educational planning. Input evaluation has to do with such things as resource allocation (equipment, materials, salary levels), program structure, and course content. Process evaluation relates to educational operations: classroom functioning, services to students, educational interaction, and most of all, teacher performance. Product or output evaluation has to do with the result of the process, the student who has completed the program and presumably is employable in a given occupation. A frequent critique of educational evaluation is that it has too often focused primarily on process and input, and only secondarily on context and product. As a result, educational goals and objectives are frequently not revised to reflect society's priorities, and institutional operations are not modified in response to the career needs of students and graduates.

Another definitional problem is the determination of what segment of the educational system is to be evaluated. Evaluation may be concerned, in ascending order, with: individuals, programs, a specific school or college, school systems, state educational systems, multi-state regional efforts, or even the entire national scene. In this chapter we are concerned primarily with the evaluation of local vocational institutions or systems and their programs. We define evaluation as a continuing systematic review of institutional objectives and performance which will provide organized information on which to base educational decisions. While our primary focus is on the evaluation of programs and schools, this in no way denies the importance of faculty and staff performance evaluation (see chapter 10) or of the evaluation of individual student academic achievement.

Accreditation—One Form of Evaluation

Historically, accreditation has been the major form of institutional evaluation in education. Accrediting procedures were developed originally by colleges and secondary schools in a given region to facilitate admission of students from high school to college—the process we now refer to as articulation (*11*, p. 418). Institutional accreditation by regional accrediting agencies has now developed into a highly structured process. In addition, during the last half century, many professional and occupational disciplines have adopted their own accreditation procedures, carried out through professional associations. This is particularly true in health-related vocations. Beyond this voluntary accreditation, there are some instances of government accreditation by state or federal agencies, such as in avionics by the Federal Aeronautic Administration. Accreditation has become recognized as the standard by which an institution, or an academic program, is judged to have met certain acceptable minimal standards. It protects the public and the educational institutions themselves from shoddy and unquestionably unacceptable educational programs, without direct control by state or national government. As accepted as the process has become in education, it is not without its critics, especially with regard to vocational and technical education:

> Accreditation, as it relates to public occupational education, is deceptive in appearance in that it claims to be voluntary and extra legal in nature; it is a false idea in that it claims to be democratic in precept; it is erroneous of character in that it claims to improve the quality of education through effective measurement and enforcement of minimum standards; and as a process it fails to satisfy the conditions of valid or correct inference in that it is based largely upon the false assumption that quality (whatever that is) in the process of education assures quality of the product of education. (*14*, p. 407)

Much of this criticism may be valid. It is hardly voluntary when institutional accreditation is a requisite condition prior to applying for and receiving federal and state monies. The regional accrediting agency boards are certainly not chosen in a democratic fashion: few noneducators are on the boards, or even on the visitation teams. More unfortunate for occupational education, there is usually inadequate representation of vocational educators on boards and visitation teams. And as noted earlier, accreditation essentially equates evaluation with professional judgment of process.

The amount of effort required for accreditation by regional agencies, professional associations, and in some cases by government can be a special problem for vocational education. A given institution may have to prepare for several accreditation visits during one academic year, especially if it offers a wide variety of allied health programs.

The problem of accreditation, particularly as it relates to occupational education, has at least been recognized, if not resolved. Operations of regional agencies are increasingly reviewed by the Accreditation and Institutional Eligibility Staff of the U. S. Office of Education and the National Commission on Accrediting. In the allied health professions, a major study has been undertaken in conjunction with the Association of Schools of Allied Health.

NATIONAL STUDY FOR ACCREDITATION OF VOCATIONAL-TECHNICAL EDUCATION

The American Vocational Association, supported by the U. S. Office of Education, through its National Study for Accreditation of Vocational-Technical Education, has developed instruments and procedures for evaluation and accreditation of both vocational *institutions* and *programs* (*1*). While these procedures and instruments have been disseminated only on a pilot test basis, they are clearly the most comprehensive materials available which are specifically geared to occupational education.

The AVA National Study proposed a three-step evaluation process which focuses both on process (i.e. the institutional setting) and on outcomes or product (i.e. the changes that have occurred in students). The process begins with an intensive self-evaluation by the institution itself, with assistance from the instruments developed by the National Study. The self-study is followed by an on-site audit by a visitation team of experts from outside the school or college. Finally, there is review by an independent third group to insure rational, comparable, and equitable interpretation by both earlier groups of data and instruments. This process assumes that the burden and responsibility for evaluation falls on the local institution and not on an outside party. It further assumes that the vocational school or college can only be judged in the light of its own objectives and the degree to which they are appropriate for their particular constituency.

Justification and explanation for each of the three steps of the process is as follows:

> The self-evaluation study should provide staff members with a systematic means of analyzing institutional and program operation and should help them gain new perspective and insights into the various institutional operations and resources open to them. It provides an opportunity for a kind of in-depth study that is otherwise often not possible in the ordinary course of work.
>
> Visiting Team members verify the accuracy of data reported by the institution; they check the extent to which reported data give a full and true picture of actual conditions and operations; they verify the extent to which outcomes coincide with stated objectives and with need; and they check

the adequacy of the institution's systems for producing data needed for decision-making, evaluation, and quality service.

Review by a third group helps to bring about comparability in the application and interpretation of instruments, inasmuch as the same reviewing group will normally be reviewing materials from many institutions. By drawing on its broader experience, the review group is also in a position to improve the evaluative instruments and procedures and to resolve any differences of opinion between institutional personnel and on-site visitors. (*1*, p. 14)

It appears that this procedure will bridge the process-product dichotomy, as well as take into account the unique aspects and judgment criteria relevant to vocational education. Clearly there is a continuing need for some sort of external accreditation process, whether by a voluntary agency or by government, because it forces each local institution to take a comprehensive look at its complete operation.

ACCOUNTABILITY: EVALUATION AT THE LOCAL LEVEL

Well-structured evaluation focused on measuring the achievement of specific program objectives in local institutions is the essence of educational accountability. Lessinger sums it up: "In short, accountability requires that the school take three steps, each of them a novelty in most school districts: 1) frame performance criteria for each program, 2) obtain an independent educational accomplishment audit to measure the actual performance against these criteria, and 3) provide for the auditor to make a public report of his findings" (*5*, p. 32).

The first step in evaluation and accountability is the delineation of the major goals of the school or college, and of each occupational program. Goals reflect the basic purposes of the institution and its programs—the broad, overall, long-range targets. In the context of these goals, specific, performance-related, measurable objectives can be formulated. Evaluation, like curriculum planning, requires first a clear statement of both goals and objectives. Only then can meaningful performance criteria be determined which will permit optimal program or institutional evaluation to insure educational accountability.

We assume that in occupational education a principal goal will be to provide every matriculated student the necessary knowledge, attitudes, and behavioral skills to be successfully employed in the occupation for which he is being trained. The specific knowledge, attitudes, and skills required must be defined in light of the particular needs of the local community and its employment market. In each case, the institution should be able to define what the student must know in his discipline, what occupationally related attitudes are required, and what job skills he must be able to demonstrate.

Most educators will not disagree with the statement on knowledge and skills, but might question the definition of requisite attitudes. Yet the student's attitude toward work and the specific occupation may be the most important characteristic in his successful employment.

If the single most important performance criterion for a vocational institution is the rate of successful, education-related employment of its graduates, then evaluation should focus more on the product than the process. In a sense vocational-technical education should operate on a sort of modified performance contract with its community-constituency. "Essentially, a performance contract is an agreement by a firm or individual to produce specified results by a certain date, using acceptable methods, for a set fee" (5, p. 18).

The constituency has a right to know what educational outcomes it can expect for the money it is putting up. While the primary purpose of evaluation is to improve institutional performance, the public should be aware of the quality of this performance and the extent to which educational goals and objectives have been achieved.

Measuring Performance in Occupational Education

Performance criteria for educational institutions essentially can be divided into two categories: outputs and impacts. Outputs refer to program completion (versus attrition) rates, student competencies, program costs per unit production, etc. Educational impacts refer to such things as placement and advancement of graduates in education-related employment, and student and employer satisfaction. Educational outputs can generally be measured through use of data continually generated by the institution itself. Impact measurement requires special studies of graduates and employers.

The literature of vocational education is replete with examples of graduate follow-up studies (6). The type of study ranges from highly structured interview surveys of an entire graduate population to informal conversations with selected graduates or employers. The problem with most evaluations of outcomes is that they measure only the graduates of the institution, not its dropouts or people who are employed in comparable positions but who never attended the school or college. In effect, there is no control group for the measurement process. Similarly, the selection of employers to be surveyed in follow-up studies is usually based on firms who are known to employ program graduates, and the studies do not query the opinions of other employers relative to the skills and education of their employees.

The evaluation and performance measurement process at the local level requires several essential elements. Byram and his colleagues list the following:

1. A commitment to the evaluation effort by the local administration.
2. A strategically placed local leadership team.
3. An active staff steering committee.
4. A functioning citizen's committee, advisory to the staff.
5. An allocation of time to the leadership team.
6. Training in research and evaluation procedures.
7. Communication and visibility.
8. Qualified consultant services. (2, p. I:5)

Byran correctly emphasizes that evaluation requires a central administration commitment of time, money, and staff resources. However, it should also be emphasized that this must be a continuing commitment, since evaluation is a constant process. Some outcome measurements may be repeated only on a yearly or bi-yearly basis, such as an employer survey. Output evaluation, however, goes on all the time.

Evaluation Criteria

Critical evaluation criteria in occupational education, depending on institutional and program goals, may include: program completion, student competency, cost-efficiency, employment-placement, and employer-student satisfaction.

PROGRAM COMPLETION

Student completion of occupational programs is readily available information, as is attrition. The reasons attrited students dropped out need to be evaluated. It may be that the educational program is too extensive for the occupational skills required on the job and that students who drop out can find employment in the occupational field. It may be that the dropout finds the program too difficult or inappropriate for him, which gives some indication that student counseling and guidance services should be reviewed. Another question related to student program completion has to do with whether students are completing their studies on the expected schedule or not. If students are unable to complete an occupational program within the number of academic terms projected, it may be that the number of credits required per term is unrealistic for the type of student clientele.

COMPETENCY

Student competency is a second performance or evaluation criterion on which it is relatively easy to obtain meaningful data. Unfortunately, student competency is too often judged on the basis of course grades received. Broader-based competency examinations are needed to provide comparative information on competency across institutions. Professional certification examinations fill this need in some cases. Thus, in dental hygiene, the student competency criterion can be evaluated with relative ease by the institution in terms of the percentage of its students who pass the board examination. In occupations where no professional competency examinations exist, local employers and practicing members of the vocation can be used to help set up acceptable levels of competency for local graduates. In many occupations, there are national or regional standardized competency examinations being developed. One example noted previously is the set of four automotive service examinations initiated in 1972 by the National Institute for Automotive Service Excellence and the Educational Testing Service.

COST-EFFICIENCY

The cost and efficiency criterion requires more effort to develop acceptable and reliable data, unless the institution has already accepted program budgeting. The real problem is developing means for distributing costs, not only to individual programs but to the individual acquisition of skills and to the production of an employable graduate. Lessinger pointed out that:

> Many of the available indexes measure our competence as financial managers; but how many of them evaluate our effectiveness as educational managers? It would make much more sense if we moved from the concept of per-pupil cost to the concept of *learning-unit cost,* and focussed on the cost of skill acquisition rather than on the cost of maintaining children in school. (*5*, p. 11)

Related to the question of cost and of student competency is that of efficiency. The institution must ascertain whether it is teaching students superfluous information and skills beyond what they need to be successfully employed in the occupation of their choice. For example, a data processing program teaching student programmers how to key-punch programs when most firms in the area are using direct access terminals is not demonstrating educational efficiency.

EMPLOYMENT PLACEMENT

Probably the most important criterion for evaluating vocational-technical programs is the successful employment placement of its students. If students are competent but still unable to find employment, the school or college needs to restructure its efforts. Having qualified graduates with job skills who are unable to be placed in the occupation for which they were trained indicates that the institution must review its program goals and resurvey the job market. Similarly, if students can find jobs in the vocation for which they were trained, *but choose not to,* the school must take a serious look at its guidance and counseling program. The data on employment placement are harder to obtain than on the other criteria we have discussed. Employment data require follow-up studies of graduates, many of whom will not leave easily identified forwarding addresses. Except in unusual circumstances, follow-up surveys will never elicit a complete response from all graduates. In larger systems it may be necessary to undertake a stratified (by program) random sample survey of graduates. Employment surveys undertaken immediately after the student graduates may not be valid indicators for program evaluation, since graduates frequently elect to delay their full-time occupational employment to take a summer vacation, a holiday trip, a honeymoon, or merely to move to a new location. Follow-up studies made at graduation or immediately thereafter will usually indicate an unusually high rate of nonvoluntary unemployment. Follow-up studies of occupational graduates should be made not only following program completion but at selected intervals (three to five years) thereafter. The repetitive follow-up study can provide information on job advancement and satisfaction of graduates, as well as provide some indication of the continuing job market. This survey can also help the institution structure continuing education programs to meet the graduates' needs for new skills.

EMPLOYEE-EMPLOYER SATISFACTION

Employee satisfaction and advancement, and employer satisfaction constitute another important evaluation criterion. If employers find the knowledge, attitudes, and skills of the institution's graduates inadequate or unsatisfactory, program revisions are probably required. Similarly, if graduates indicate that certain facets of the educational program did not meet their on-the-job needs, careful review is merited. One good indicator of educational program adequacy is the extent to which employers have to undertake induction training prior to putting graduates in productive positions. If induction training is limited to the specific, unique requirements of employers, occupational education is meeting local needs. But if employers are providing basic instruction in the vocational area, the educational institution may not be performing adequately.

As indicated earlier, the criteria of employment and satisfaction must be measured against some control group to give a valid indication of successful institutional performance. The school or college should make an effort to follow its own dropouts as well as a sample of people who are employed in the area but who never matriculated in their institution.

Who Should Evaluate?

There is some disagreement among theorists about who should implement the evaluation process. On the one hand, Lessinger (*5*, p. 32) argues for an independent educational audit to measure institutional performance; on the other, Byram and Robertson argue that, "One of the principles of evaluation receiving increasing acceptance is that those who are to be affected by an evaluation effort and who will be the beneficiaries of changes which may result from it should be involved in the process of evaluation" (*2*, p. I:2). Ash (*1*, p. 14) argues that the evaluation process is a responsibility of the local institution itself. It is our position that the basic responsibility rests with the local institution but that the process will be enhanced and legitimated if there is broad-scale community involvement. Like curriculum and program development, evaluation should involve local lay people. They can add insights and keep the institution "honest." An audit by an outside party of "experts" is useful on a sporadic basis, but is not necessary on a continual basis.

Who within the institution should conduct the evaluation? Evaluation should be as participatory as possible, involving faculty, students, staff, and administration. Since evaluation is related to program quality and improvement of institutional performance, it should be everyone's concern. In larger institutions, coordinating responsibility may rest with a specific office of research or evaluation. If not, the coordinating staff member must be released from some of his other duties to implement evaluation.

INSTITUTIONAL RESEARCH

Large secondary school districts, some community colleges, and most four-year post-secondary institutions have developed institutional research functions which, among other things, are usually involved in evaluation. In addition, these offices are responsible for developing and disseminating other kinds of information which can improve management decision making. In fact, institutional research and system evaluation are part and parcel of the same function. As Dressel has pointed out, "The subjects of institutional research can be divided into three major topics: the institutional environment, the processes and operations carried on in that environment, and the ultimate outcomes achieved" (*4*, p. 31).

The creation and maintenance of an institutional research function and a system of management information involve virtually all aspects of the institution: administrative decision making, curriculum development, personnel, fiscal, and physical policies and planning, and most of all, evaluation of the entire organization's performance.

Institutional research has been viewed with suspicion by many educational administrators who often relegate to it tasks of simple data collection, filling out the myriad of required and voluntary questionnaires which barrage an institution, and coordination of various institutional reports. By the same token, it is often downgraded by academicians in that it does not follow faculty research guidelines.

> Institutional research is different from the research of faculty members in a number of ways. It does not share the mantle of academic freedom; it is primarily utilitarian and therefore has a distinctive set of values; and its ultimate success depends less on the research findings than on the promotion of action to alleviate functional weakness and to increase the effectiveness of the institution. (4, p. 38)

The most important role of the institutional research office is to stimulate and initiate valid evaluation research which can serve as a model for repetition by other staff members in the institution and which will be used by the chief administrator to make decisions to improve performance.

A major problem with many institutional research reports, evaluations, audits, and follow-up studies is that they are immediately shelved, to collect dust. Part of the administrator's responsibility in any institution is to insure that evaluation and research are used as inputs for decision making, that planned change is based on empirical data derived from evaluation.

There is an abundance of literature on planned change in education. A recent review and synthesis of it concluded:

> In actuality, the process can be entered into at almost any step. However, the consensus among most persons seems to be that the *Evaluation* step should be the point of entry into the cycle. This is the step where planners, and others desiring to effect change, take a look at "what is." (13, p. 31)

The first important step in the use of evaluation is making sure that reports are widely disseminated, that results are communicated to faculty, staff, students, and the public constituency. Evaluation essentially indicates whether or not the institution has a problem; and if it does, how significant it is. Developing alternative change strategies and selecting one to rectify a problem is the responsibility of the decision maker. The evaluator's role is to point out the need for change and to provide sufficient information to help the decision maker make his choice. The important point in vocational and technical institutions, as in any other system, is that the rationality of decision making is directly related to the reliability and validity of the information which prompts the decision.

Key administrators in any school system must recognize that adequate evaluation and institutional research requires a commitment of time, staff, money, and moral support. Evaluation should be the business of every person on the staff, but effectiveness of the evaluation function is largely dependent on the attitude of the chief administrator.

REFERENCES

1. Ash, Lane C., Helen Kempfer, and Margaret McNeil. *Instruments and Procedures for the Evaluation of Vocational/Technical Education Institutions and Programs.* Washington, D.C.: American Vocational Association, National Study for Accreditation of Vocational/Technical Education, December 1971.

2. Byram, Harold M. and Marvin Robertson. *Locally Directed Evaluation of Local Vocational Education Programs.* Danville, Illinois: Interstate, 1970.

3. Dressel, Paul L., ed. *Evaluation in Higher Education.* Boston: Houghton Mifflin, 1961.

4. Dressel, Paul L. and associates. *Institutional Research in the University.* San Francisco: Jossey-Bass, 1971.

5. Lessinger, Leon M. *Every Kid a Winner: Accountability in Education.* New York: Simon and Schuster, 1970.

6. Little, J. Kenneth. *Review and Synthesis of Research on the Placement and Follow-Up of Vocational Education Students.* Columbus: ERIC Clearinghouse on Vocational and Technical Education, The Center for Vocational and Technical Education, The Ohio State University, February 1970.

7. Messersmith, Lloyd E. and Leland L. Medsker. *Accreditation of Vocational Technical Curricula in Postsecondary Institutions.* Berkeley: Center for Research and Development in Higher Education, 1969.

8. Nerden, Joseph. "Statewide Evaluation of Vocational Education." In Gordon F. Law, ed. *Contemporary Concepts in Vocational Education.* Washington, D. C.: American Vocational Association, 1971.

9. Phi Delta Kappa National Study Committee on Evaluation. *Educational Evaluation and Decision Making.* Bloomington: Phi Delta Kappa, 1971.

10. Schure, Alexander. "An Accountability and Evaluation Design for Occupational Education." *Educational Technology* 11, No. 3 (March 1971): 26–37.

11. Seldon, William K. "Accreditation of Postsecondary Occupational Education." In Gordon F. Law, ed. *Contemporary Concepts in Vocational Education.* Washington, D. C.: American Vocational Association, 1971.

12. Starr, Harold. *A System for State Evaluation of Vocational Education.* Research Series No. 45. Columbus: The Center for Vocational and Technical Education, The Ohio State University, August 1969.

13. Wall, James E. *Review and Synthesis of Strategies for Effecting Change in Vocational and Technical Education.* Columbus: ERIC Clearinghouse for Vocational and Technical Education, The Center for Vocational and Technical Education, The Ohio State University, April 1972.

14. Ward, Charles F. "Some Fallacies in Accreditation." In Gordon F. Law, ed. *Contemporary Concepts in Vocational Education.* Washington, D. C.: American Vocational Association, 1971.

Part IV FUTURE DIRECTIONS

Chapter 15 WHERE TO FROM HERE?

The emergence of the career education thrust and the increasing interest of students and the general public in vocational-technical programs have generated a need for rapid expansion of employment-related education. The career education process is obviously incomplete if students lack opportunities to complete the final phase—specialized vocational preparation. The growth of interest and need has raised many questions related to the administration of vocational and technical education. If vocational educators fail to provide leadership in their resolution, someone else will provide the answers. This chapter poses some of the questions and discusses their implications and our responses.

Questions for the Future

Is Preparing Youth for Employment through Specialized Education an Acceptable Goal of Public Education? As financial resources available for education have become more scarce, the public increasingly questions the value of many programs and educational functions. One question is whether job-related education should legitimately be performed in the public sector, or whether employers should accept this responsibility directly.

Society has long accepted preparation for employment in the professions as a valid goal of publicly supported colleges and universities. Professional schools and colleges have for many years prepared youth and adults for careers in such fields as medicine, dentistry, law, engineering, architecture, public health, and education at public expense. More recently, community colleges have accepted the preparation of youth for careers in technical and paraprofessional occupations as a major goal, in addition to their transfer function. Specialized vocational and technical schools on the secondary level have had preparation for employment as a primary purpose. The stated purposes of comprehensive high schools includes both preparation for college and preparation for employment. One might then ask, what is the issue?

The issue is whether preparation for employment *really* has been accepted as a legitimate function of secondary education. We believe that society—particularly taxpayers and parents—expects schools and colleges to provide opportunities for youth to become employable, but we are not so sure that the education "establishment" has fully accepted career preparation as a valid function. Quite naturally, there is great variation in the degree of acceptance of this goal from community to community or even from school to school within the same community, depending on the community and the educational leadership. One need only to examine the statement of philosophy and goals of a school or school district to detect the strength of the commitment to vocational education.

It is likely that both secondary and post-secondary institutions will make an even stronger commitment to vocational and technical education in the future, not only in their published statements of philosophy and goals, but, more significantly, in the allocation of resources available to them. They will take this posture because more youth are demanding education which prepares them for jobs and because society is more willing to support education which has career preparation as its purpose. While the high schools of the future may not be "turned around" as some people think they should be, they will be reoriented to the extent that the needs of employment-bound youth will be given higher priority. Community colleges will also shift their emphasis even more toward occupationally oriented programs because of student demand.

At What Level Should the Specialized Aspects of Occupational Education Be Provided?

Some secondary school administrators would postpone *all* specialized education for employment until after high school, even though the majority of youth will not continue their formal education beyond high school. Others take the position that preparation for a career should be broadly based so as to give the individual greater flexibility in the labor force. Still others take the position that youth are not employable unless they have some rather specific skills for which there is a market. With the growing public awareness of the close correlation between education for employment and employability, there is a danger that vocational and technical education will be defined too narrowly and that there will be too much emphasis on specific skill training for a particular occupation and not enough on preparing the student for growth and change, both in his occupation and in his avocational interests.

For a person to be employable he must have some job competencies for which an employer is willing to pay a wage or salary. These can be built on a broad base of career development and career preparation. The designs outlined in chapter 1 for a comprehensive career education program put specialized vocational education in its proper place in the total education process. Students in early secondary grades can explore families or clusters of occupations through the practical arts and later acquire some general competencies in one or more of the clusters before beginning to build specialized skills needed in a particular occupation in that cluster. In this way youth will be helped to build a set of job skills which are based upon a broad understanding of their field.

The public schools and colleges should provide for *every* student at a time just prior to his leaving the system the specialized job competencies which he needs to be employed. For those who terminate their formal schooling upon completion of high school or before, such specialized vocational education must be a part of their high school experience. For youth who continue their education for another year or two this service can be provided in a community college or technical institute. The student who chooses to continue his formal education through a baccalaureate or higher degree, would thus already have a potential source of income and a meaningful contact with the world of work.

What Can Be Done to Change the Image of Vocational Education, Especially among Students?   Preparation for college and the professions has been urged upon children and youth by teachers, counselors and parents for so long that youth have come to believe that failing to go to college, they have missed the high road of American life. Many youth have come to see vocational and technical education as second-rate, to be undertaken only after failure in a college preparatory or college transfer program. This condition grows out of the fact that the early American high school was a college prep school and nearly all youth who graduated at the turn of the century went to college. Vocational education has been added to the curriculum but does not enjoy equal status with the original college preparatory curriculum.

One reason for the negative attitude of students toward vocational education is the attitude of teachers and counselors. In 1964 Wenrich and Crowley (7) developed a scale for the measurement of attitudes toward vocational education which has since been used in numerous studies in a variety of different situations. In those studies which included teachers in the population, the teachers generally have the *most unfavorable* attitude toward vocational education; that is, the other segments of the population such as school administrators, employers, parents, and labor leaders generally have a more favorable attitude than do teachers. These studies also show that professionals, in general, have a less favorable perception of vocational education than do other groups. Yet the professionals, whether teachers, school board members, or opinion leaders in the community, have tremendous influence in the decision-making process regarding vocational education. It is important, therefore, that the vocational education administrator study the attitudes of teachers and others and take steps to develop a more favorable image. If the professional personnel in a school have a favorable image of programs which are designed to prepare students for employment, then the youth in the school will soon acquire a similar attitude. It might help if teachers and other professionals realized that the professional preparation which they received is, in fact, vocational education, and the professional schools in which they received their education are vocational schools!

Some educators have suggested that there is a stigma attached to the term "vocational" and that other terms would be more appropriate. This may be one reason why the literature on vocational and technical education on the community college level seems to favor the term "occupational education," and on the baccalaureate degree level the term "professional education" is used. We see no objection to using terms which project more positive images, but we believe vocational education is an appropriate term to designate specialized education for employment, whether such education is provided on the high school, community college, four-year college, or university level. Since vocational education is education for work, the image of vocational education might also be a product of our attitudes toward work. Youth especially are critically examining the Protestant work ethic. There is abundant evidence that youth want to work, but it must be the kind of work which satisfies their needs, some of which are other than economic. In designing programs, the vocational education administrator must be sensitive to the economic and the *social* needs of youth which can be satisfied through work.

The image of vocational education on the secondary and post-secondary levels will be improved as the occupations for which these programs prepare youth acquire relatively more status. An occupation can be attractive to youth for many reasons including potential earnings, working conditions, personal job satisfactions, etc. As conditions and wages of workers in occupations requiring no more than a high school education or a year or two in post-secondary vocational and technical education approach or exceed those of the degreed worker, the status of the technician or paraprofessional is greatly enhanced. Professions will become less attractive as they become overcrowded and graduates are unable to find employment.

The image of vocational education will be improved as vocational education administrators offer youth *quality programs* which lead to satisfying and productive employment. Many of the so-called vocational programs in our high schools and colleges today are dysfunctional, and the students know it and reject them. Quality occupational education requires closer ties to the world of work and the community. One major advantage of a well-run cooperative education or clinical component is that the relevance of the specialized training is self-evident both to the student and the employer. Improving the image of vocational and technical education depends both on upgrading the quality of programs and on making the public aware of that quality.

What Kinds of Schools and Colleges Should Offer Vocational and Technical Education Programs?   One of the most seriously contended issues in public education has been whether vocational-technical education should be provided by specialized or comprehensive schools and colleges. The advantages of both types of institutions have been debated for the past half century. Recently, the trend has been toward operating vocational and technical programs as a part of comprehensive high schools and comprehensive community colleges, although in some states there is still strong support for the separate vocational high school or technical institute.

We favor the comprehensive approach because we believe *all* youth and adults need specialized education for work as a part of their general development. They should be able to develop their occupational interests in an educational environment which can simultaneously serve their avocational or cultural interests. Although it should be possible for a student to pursue his vocational interests to the exclusion of all other aspects of his general growth and development (even in a comprehensive institution), the typical student should be encouraged to carry a balanced program consisting of both general and specialized courses. This can only be done in a comprehensive institution.

For a school or college to be comprehensive it must have diversified programs in sufficient number to meet the needs and preferences of its student body. Obviously, the minimum number of students needed for efficient operation will depend on the variety of programs offered. Some educators take the position that to be truly comprehensive a high school should have at least 1200–1500 students; we believe even 2000 is too small, unless supplemented by area vocational centers. The Carnegie Commission recommended that comprehensive community colleges should serve 2000–5000 students to be optimally efficient (*1*, p. 31).

Small communities and areas with low student enrollments and more limited financial resources have often been unable to offer comprehensive programs with a sufficient variety to meet diverse student needs. We expect to see more development of area vocational "centers" which operate vocational programs on a shared-time basis for students from several area high schools. They function as vocational "service centers" since students come for a part of each day or week for their specialized shop or laboratory courses only. Area vocational centers require special coordination between secondary administrators in cooperating high schools in such areas as program planning and development, transportation of students to the center, synchronization of calendars and school schedules, and development of policies regarding grading, discipline, and general records.

Given the growth in size of comprehensive schools and the number of area vocational centers, there will still be a need for some specialized schools and colleges to provide training for highly technical occupations with unique equipment and personnel requirements. These may follow the example of the aeromechanics institute operated by one large city school system at a local airport.

How Can Financial Support for Vocational and Technical Education Be Structured to Allow Local School Authorities Sufficient Freedom to Assess Local Needs and Plan Programs to Meet These Needs?   Given the history of federal subventions for vocational education since 1917, local schools and colleges have tended to look to the federal and state governments for funds to finance vocational programs. While the dollar amount of federal support has increased significantly during recent years, the federal contribution in proportion to the total expenditures for vocational education has declined. It is unlikely that federal funds will ever be sufficient to *support* vocational education; they can and should provide the incentive for states and local communities to initiate such programs.

As almost all federal funds for vocational education are channelled through state agencies, the state boards of education and their staffs have tended to retain the power and authority to make decisions about local programs of vocational and technical education which might better be made locally. As local school districts become larger and better staffed with qualified vocational education administrators, many of the planning decisions now made by state boards and their staffs can and should be made by local boards and their staffs. Vocational education needs vary greatly from one community to another, and cannot be assessed accurately on the state level. Furthermore, the state cannot provide enough staff to oversee local programs and *must* of necessity place this responsibility on local personnel.

The problem lies in developing a system to distribute state and federal financial support without compromising the integrity of local program control.

We believe that there should be an administrative arrangement between the state and local school districts modelled after the federal-state partnership which has worked reasonably well for more than fifty years. Under this structure local schools and colleges would submit their local plans (similar to state plans now submitted to the federal government) which, when approved, would authorize to local schools a block grant to implement their plans and programs. In effect, this would amount to a form of state, as well as federal, revenue sharing for vocational education. Presumably, much of the federal and state funding would be on the basis of *added costs* of vocational programs. If local school planners can choose between the less expensive academic programs and more costly vocational and technical programs, with the cost differential financed from state and federal sources, the program decision can be based on educational merit and the needs of students. Whatever the model or formula adopted, the financial foundation of vocational and technical education must be expanded, and at the same time curricular decision making must be further decentralized.

For such a system to work, "local" school districts must be regional in nature so that they are large enough to deal adequately with program needs and so that they are few enough in number to allow optimal interaction with the state education agency. Essentially, this means that school district consolidation must continue, or that vocational and technical programs must be administered primarily by intermediate (county or multi-county) school districts and broadly based comprehensive community colleges.

How Can Schools and Colleges Originally Created as Single-Purpose Institutions Be Restructured to Accommodate Specialized Education for Employment as a Major Function?   Most high schools and older community (junior) colleges in the United States were originally organized as single-purpose institutions to prepare youth for college or to provide lower division academic collegiate instruction. The structures created for this purpose were appropriately based upon the academic disciplines, resulting in departments or divisions following these disciplines—mathematics, science, languages, the arts, etc. As the specialized vocational and technical education component developed, schools and colleges hesitantly accepted the functions of general education and vocational education for youth who were not interested in college preparation or college transfer work, but few made changes in their basic organizational structures. In fact, the administrative structures in most high schools and in many community colleges inhibit the development of viable vocational and technical programs.

To rectify this problem, several steps must be taken. The level of the position of the vocational-technical administrator must be upgraded so that he reports to the chief administrative officer. Similarly, more vocational educators must become chief administrators. In sum, the need for leadership by vocational education administrators within schools and colleges will continue to be acute. In addition, vocational educators must increasingly get involved in making the community aware of the need for occupational programs. They should become active participants in community organizations which can foster or support vocational and technical education efforts. Where possible, vocational leaders should seek election to governing boards of educational institutions which are not fulfilling their potential for delivery of specialized occupational education. They should actively support other lay leaders who understand the role of vocational education in our society and seek their involvement on advisory committees and on governing boards. For schools and colleges to become truly comprehensive and offer viable occupational education, pressure must be brought to bear both inside the institutions and without.

What About Vocational Teacher Qualifications and Selection?

Vocational teachers should have dual qualifications; that is, they should be qualified as workers in the occupation for which they are preparing others *and* they should be qualified to teach. Which of these two components is more important, especially if teachers who are qualified in both areas are not available?

State certification codes and most employers require that vocational teachers have a minimum number of years of work experience in the occupation to be taught. The number varies from state to state and among the different occupations. Also the amount of teacher education necessary for a teaching certificate varies widely. Although the baccalaureate degree is considered minimum for nonvocational teachers, it is not always possible to find vocational teachers with the degree and adequate work experience. Consequently, the vocational administrator is presented some difficult choices. In the comprehensive high school or community college where most teachers have baccalaureate or higher degrees, the vocational teacher without a degree is sometimes at a disadvantage. But why should he be? He has other qualifications which are more important in his role!

The vocational teacher must be competent in the occupation which he is to teach, but this competence is not necessarily determined by the number of years he has worked in that occupation. We prefer the use of competency tests to determine whether or not a teacher is indeed qualified. If a choice must be made between occupational competence and competence in teaching, we would take the former and help the teacher develop the latter skills as soon as possible.

In the recruitment of teachers the vocational administrator would naturally look at the business and industrial establishment in his community as well as the customary sources of supply.

On What Basis Should Students Be Selected for Specialized Vocational Programs?

The administrator is often faced with the problem of a limited number of training stations in a given program with more students than can be accommodated seeking admission. The students' record of performance in school subjects in general or in subjects which are considered prerequisites for the particular specialized program is often used as an entry criterion.

Any student who has a reasonable chance to succeed in the program and later in employment in that occupation should be given the opportunity to succeed. Interest is the most important single criterion and students should be given the opportunity to test their interest and to prove (to themselves as well as others) that it is genuine. Prior experience, academic success, or measured ability are much less important criteria than student interest and motivation. Vocational and technical education administrators should demonstrate continually to the various public constituencies how previously unsuccessful students can be "turned on" by specialized occupational education.

How Can We Develop a Comprehensive Delivery System for Vocational and Technical Education and Related Services?

Vocational education should start on the secondary level, but for many youth this is just the beginning of their preparation for a career. Some will go into employment where they will learn new skills, while others will continue their vocational preparation in post-secondary institutions. Whether *formal* education for employment is terminated in high school or continued for a year or more beyond high school, all youth and adults will need continuing vocational education in order to remain viable in the labor force. Some of this education will be provided by the employer. A well-coordinated delivery system is needed in which each institution or agency plays its role and relates effectively with all other organizations involved in the system.

Vocational educators must take a more active role in the continuing education lifelong learning process. Opportunities must be made available for people to learn new job skills, explore alternative occupations, or upgrade their current competencies. It is incumbent on all of us to work for the development of a comprehensive, integrated delivery system which articulates specialized secondary schools, comprehensive high schools, community colleges, and technical institutes, and which will recognize and respond to the specialized occupational education needs of students from 16 to 60. Our changing technology and societal demands will not tolerate anything less.

REFERENCES

1. American Association of Junior Colleges. *Occupations and Education in the 70's: Promises and Challenges.* Washington, D.C.: The Association, N.D.

2. Bushnell, David S. *Organizing for Change: New Priorities for Community Colleges.* New York: McGraw-Hill, 1973.

3. Carnegie Commission on Higher Education. *The Open-Door Colleges. Policies for Community Colleges.* New York: McGraw-Hill, 1970.

4. Gleaser, Edmund J., Jr. *Project Focus: A Forecast Study of Community Colleges.* New York: McGraw-Hill, 1973.

5. Leighbody, Gerald B. *Vocational Education in America's Schools—Major Issues of the 1970's.* Chicago: American Technical Society, 1972.

6. Moore, Allen B. and Sue J. King. *Problem Areas in Occupational Education for the 1970's.* Occasional Paper No. 12. Raleigh, North Carolina: Center for Occupational Education, 1972.

7. Wenrich, Ralph C. and Robert J. Crowley. *Vocational Education as Perceived by Different Segments of the Population.* Cooperative Research Project No. 1577. Ann Arbor, Michigan: University of Michigan, 1964.

INDEX

287